ASIAN FOUNDERS AT WORK

STORIES FROM THE REGION'S TOP TECHNOPRENEURS

Ezra Ferraz
Gracy Fernandez

Asian Founders at Work: Stories from the Region's Top Technopreneurs

Ezra Ferraz
Makati City, Philippines

Gracy Fernandez
Makati City, Philippines

ISBN-13 (pbk): 978-1-4842-5161-4
https://doi.org/10.1007/978-1-4842-5162-1

ISBN-13 (electronic): 978-1-4842-5162-1

Managing Director, Apress Media LLC: Welmoed Spahr
Acquisitions Editor: Shiva Ramachandran
Development Editor: Laura Berendson
Coordinating Editor: Rita Fernando

Distributed to the book trade worldwide by Springer Science+Business Media New York, 233 Spring Street, 6th Floor, New York, NY 10013. Phone 1-800-SPRINGER, fax (201) 348-4505, e-mail orders-ny@springer-sbm.com, or visit www.springeronline.com. Apress Media, LLC is a California LLC and the sole member (owner) is Springer Science + Business Media Finance Inc (SSBM Finance Inc). SSBM Finance Inc is a Delaware corporation.

For information on translations, please e-mail rights@apress.com, or visit http://www.apress.com/rights-permissions.

Apress titles may be purchased in bulk for academic, corporate, or promotional use. eBook versions and licenses are also available for most titles. For more information, reference our Print and eBook Bulk Sales web page at http://www.apress.com/bulk-sales.

Any source code or other supplementary material referenced by the author in this book is available to readers on GitHub via the book's product page, located at www.apress.com/9781484251614. For more detailed information, please visit http://www.apress.com/source-code.

Printed on acid-free paper

For Margaret

Contents

About the Authors

Ezra Ferraz is the founder and managing partner of Ambidextr, a full-service content marketing studio backed by Future Now Ventures. Ambidextr (http://ambidextr. media/) executes the content marketing for some of Asia Pacific's largest tech companies. He graduated from UC Berkeley and earned a master's degree in professional writing from the University of Southern California. He can be reached directly at ezraferraz@berkeley.edu.

Gracy Fernandez is a frequent contributor to *Entrepreneur Asia Pacific*—the mother brand of *Entrepreneur* in the region—and the founder of a venture-backed tech startup, Graventure. She is a professional marketer by trade.

About the Contributors

Frances Roberto is a management honors student at the Ateneo de Manila University. A former intern at social news network Rappler, she has seen up close the far-reaching influence that technology has over all realms of life and how it could be utilized for justice and truth. She strongly advocates for a brand of entrepreneurship that would harness technology in much the same way—that is, for the good of the people.

Elyssa Lopez earned a BA in journalism from the University of Santo Tomas. She previously worked as a writer at Summit Media, including stints at both *Entrepreneur* and *Esquire Philippines*. She is a content marketer at Ambidextr.

She is also one of the authors of *Ready or Not 2020*, the forthcoming sequel to the bestselling book by serial tech entrepreneur Winston Damarillo released in 2016. *Ready or Not 2020* previews how bleeding edge technologies will continue to change the way Filipino enterprises do business.

Martina Ferrer is an AB Communication student taking the advertising and public relations track at the Ateneo de Manila University. She is a former collegiate athlete who participated in the prestigious University Athletic Association of the Philippines (UAAP). She is now a content marketer and media relations associate at Ambidextr.

Jezy Fernandez is currently taking Media Arts with the dream of becoming a film producer and copywriter. She is a former member of a swimming team in Baguio City and she has also participated in theatrical plays as an actor. She is now an Art department intern for various television commercials in the Philippines.

Gia Soliven is a sophomore studying Information Design at the Ateneo de Manila University and ranks in the top ten percent of her class. As a marketing associate of Ambidextr, she is a creative individual driven to initiate sustainable social impact through writing and business. She is also a campaign deputy of Kythe-Ateneo and a marketing associate of the Company of Ateneo Dancers.

Sofia Galve is a cum laude graduate from the University of the Philippines–Diliman with a concentration in Speech Communication. She is also a beauty queen, events host, and financial planner.

Acknowledgments

We would like to thank the researchers and writers who contributed to this book, most especially Frances Roberto, Elyssa Lopez, Martina Ferrer, Sofia Galve, and Gia Soliven. We look forward to the day we read your own books.

We would like to thank Apress for giving us an opportunity to share the stories of Asia's best founders. Our publishing team at Apress was instrumental in seeing this book to completion, led by coordinating editor Rita Fernando Kim, acquisitions editor Shiva Ramachandran, and development editor Laura Berendson.

I would also like to extend my thanks to my team at Ambidextr (http://ambidextr.media/) not already mentioned, including Junie Agcaoili, Monette Quiogue, Joanna Viegan, Kyle Nate, Sofia Marteja, Cherry Bantiling, Gab Rovira, Toni Roman, and Robby Vaflor. I would also like to thank my team at Future Now Ventures, most especially John Orrock and Arvin Rafol, for their support and guidance.

I would also like to thank my amazing co-author, Gracy Fernandez, who drove the completion of the book and helped realize its full potential. It would simply not be the same without your foresight into the most impactful waiting-to-be-told founder stories across the region.

I would also like to extend my gratitude to the never-ending support of my family, including my parents (hi Mom and Dad!) and brothers, Mike and Nick. I miss you all and I will see you soon.

I would also like to extend my gratitude to my mother-in-law, father-in-law, and siblings-in-law, Sam, Chester, Boss, Gio, and especially Jezy, who helped review chapters and provide valuable feedback on the manuscript's progress, and baby Marga, who provided the inspiration to complete the book over its journey. We hope when you read it one day, you may see a glimpse of what you can achieve in time.

Most of all, we would like to thank all the founders who graciously gave their time in order to share their stories with us. We believe that your reflections and insights will accelerate the learning curve for the next generation of entrepreneurs in Asia. We would like to thank the respective marketing, communications, and public relations teams at the featured companies who coordinated the interviews with your founders.

In particular, we would like to express our gratitude to the following founders and their teams:

Winston Damarillo, Micaela Faith Beltran, and Nina Terol of Amihan—Thank you for sharing the two-pronged approach of GlueCode, which will be of interest to founders used to setting up operations in a single country. With your chapter here, we would argue that there is now officially a WD cannon: *Ready or Not, Ready or Not 2020, Asian Founders at Work,* and *The Durian Unicorns.* You can make a WD boxed set.

Chih-Han Yu, Susanna Hughes, and Doris Hsu of Appier—Thank you for sharing one of the most successful pivots in the book. The transition into being one of Asia's leading artificial intelligence companies will surely inspire other founders still experimenting with their business model. Can CrossX work for books and ebooks?

Achmad Zaky, Fairuza Iqbal, and Intan Wibisono of Bukalapak—Bukalapak is a textbook definition of an ecosystem enabler: You help sellers sell. Thank you for sharing your story, which will undoubtedly encourage more founders to serve the MSMEs who need help transitioning into the digital economy. Please bring Bukalapak to the Philippines!

Siu Rui Quek, Qiyi Liao, and Patrick Lim of Carousell—You believed in a mobile-first experience when everyone else in the space was desktop-focused. Your story will certainly push more founders to be first movers, even when doing so goes against all conventional wisdom. Thank you for giving founders the guts to give a literal elevator pitch when the situation calls for one.

Patrick Grove and Eric Tan of Catcha Group—Thank you for sharing the story of yet another one of your many successful ventures. We are eager to watch iflix become your sixth IPO. The world will be watching, in between, of course, binge-watching their favorite localized programs on your platform.

Mark Sears of CloudFactory—Thank you for sharing your insights into CloudFactory in particular and impact sourcing in general. I hope your model will encourage more founders across the world to be conscious of their entire product's or service's value chain.

Ron Hose of Coins.ph—Financial inclusion is a buzzword today, but you pushed for it in the Philippines when no one else did. Thank you for building a product that helps millions of Filipinos access the digital economy. We're eager to see what Coins.ph will do now with the backing of Gojek. We also think it's time you reward yourself with a postpaid plan.

Mohan Belani of e27—If one of e27's measures of success is the number of founders that you help, we believe the story you shared here will contribute to this effort. You somehow managed to navigate the delicate balance between building a business and serving resource-conscious startups. We look forward to everything coming full circle when the founders who read of you here will in turn contribute their own success stories to e27. Thank you!

Khailee Ng of 500 Startups—Your desire to help founders, both inside and outside the 500 Startups ecosystem, was palpable throughout your interview. Your unique perspective as a serial entrepreneur and investor with deep experience in Southeast Asia will guide more founders in search of wisdom. We hope more of them take away your emphasis not only on valuation, but on social impact. The world needs more founders who think they can change it.

Shao-Ning Huang and Lim Der Shing of JobsCentral—Thank you for sharing your whirlwind journey of building JobsCentral as this book's only co-founding couple. Although your example may be an edge case, it will help all founders have better personal and professional relationships with their co-founders. We are also sure you will continue to be a job creation engine, this time through the ventures fortunate enough to have you as angel investors.

Shing Chow and Tesh Kaur of Lalamove—You had no experience in logistics, but you made one of the region's top on-demand logistics companies. We hope your story will encourage more founders to make similar improbable leaps, and lead to more industries being disrupted with fresh eyes. On a personal note, we must especially thank you for LalaFood, which powered many of the writing sessions for this book.

Chatri Sityodtong, Tammy Chan, and Nanthini Ratnam of ONE Championship—While you may not yet be ready for the ONE Championship book, what you share here is considerable. As with your martial artists, your story to this point will inspire founders to compete with dignity and grace. Please keep us in mind when you're ready for the full telling of the ONE Championship story.

Ritesh Agarwal, Prasidha Menon, and Alok Kumar Dash of OYO Hotels & Homes—You mentioned that one of the best pieces of advice you got from Peter Thiel was to think in terms of scale. We think your story, with OYO Hotels & Homes now being the world leader in its category, is an embodiment of that ideal. Thank you for inspiring founders to focus on the biggest dent in the universe that they can possibly make.

Zac Cheah and Peko Wan of Pundi X—Thank you for weaving cryptocurrency into the fabric of everyday life. We are indeed eager to experience an era where transacting with crypto becomes as easy as buying a bottle of water. Pundi will lead the way in mainstreaming not only crypto, but the blockchain technologies that can similarly disrupt long dormant industries. This future cannot come fast enough.

Maria Ressa and Cecille Santos of Rappler—Facing death threats and bogus arrests, you have one of the most challenging day-to-day lives as a founder. Thank you for sharing your courageous story. We know it'll force more founders to pause and reflect upon how they can better stay true to their values.

Min-Liang Tan, Jan Horak, and Vanessa Li of Razer—As the foremost gaming peripherals creator in the world, Razer is the only true hardware company in this book. We hope your story will inspire more founders to think of where they can create value off-screen. Users will benefit from products created with the same eye for design and craftsmanship as that very first Boomslang.

Teresa Condicion of Snapcart—You are the foremost Filipina technopreneur. We are especially proud to share your story because it will encourage more *pinays* to more pursue careers in STEM or their own startups. We are sure your next venture will be this beacon for the country as well.

Willis Wee of Tech in Asia—Appearing in Tech in Asia is still a badge of honor for any tech startup in the region. Thank you for showing us the other side of this media entity and what it takes to build something that others take pride in. We hope to one day grace your pages not only as authors but as founders.

Akiko Naka of Wantedly—Recruiting and hiring is tough. Thank you for making it easier for businesses to find not only the talent they need, but those who will stay for the long haul. Next time we're in Japan, we can't wait to drop by for a chat and see how these visits ought to be done from the person who does them best. Please give us this honor!

Zeeshan Ali Khan, Ibrahim Suheyl, and Komayal Hassan of Zameen—Thank you for sharing the story of Zameen. While most would look at it as a two-sided marketplace, it's really a solution that enables people to find the most important thing in life: a home. Thank you for showing founders how they create products for our most significant life areas.

Chitpol Mungprom, Carter Lim, and Vilon Ho of Zanroo—You were our first interview for this book. Thank you for giving us the opportunity to share your story, even when this project was still in its earliest stages. It has been a pleasure to witness Zanroo's growth over the past two years in the marketing-technology space, and we have no doubt you will rise as one of Thailand's first unicorns.

Royston Tay of Zopim—Your story is one of the most colorfully and artfully told in the entire book. Thank you for sharing your insights in such a way that is sure to keep readers glued to the page, as you take us through a master class on customer experience, service, and success. We are eager to see your continued success in this space at Zendesk.

—Ezra Ferraz

Introduction

It has been almost twelve years since the release of Jessica Livingston's landmark *Founders at Work*, a blip in normal time but an eternity in tech. Although Silicon Valley still presides over the tech world as a kind of mecca, it is no longer the end-all, be-all for the aspiring founder.

There are now many hubs across the globe where founders can put up a startup and obtain the resources they need to scale. Many of these are in Asia, in places where Sand Hill Road is more lore than a location. China and India lead the way in producing successful startups, with over 150 and 25 unicorns respectively (as of this writing), but many countries in Asia are now boasting of their own vibrant tech ecosystems, ranging as far west as Pakistan and Nepal and as far east as Thailand and Hong Kong.

The tech landscape, in short, has shifted. We no longer live in a unipolar world revolving around Silicon Valley. Asia has risen to become just as important a region for global innovation, and its emergence over the last decade has necessitated the creation of *Asian Founders at Work*.

Broadly speaking, what works for a founder in Silicon Valley will be markedly different from what works for a founder in Manila, Philippines or Jakarta, Indonesia. There will be some similarities, but what the founder operating in one of Asia's emerging tech hubs needs are examples of fellow entrepreneurs who have successfully built tech companies in our own business contexts. To put it simply, we need more Jack Ma's (how's that for a shirt slogan).

Celebrating founders in Asia is important for two reasons. The first is the practical application of their own lessons. The question-and-answer format smartly chosen by Livingston and employed here frees the founder from the editorializing, frameworks, and other paradigms that most other business books use to box in subjects with their own preferred thesis or argument. What readers get is the literary equivalent of a fireside chat, one where you get the best seat in the house.

The journey of some of the largest tech companies in Asia illustrates just how differently companies are built in the region, as in the case of Gojek, a ride-hailing super-app founded in Indonesia and active across Vietnam, Thailand, Singapore, and the Philippines.

Gojek co-founder Kevin Aluwi shared that they simply started the company to challenge the stigma of motorcycle traffic drivers in Jakarta.

"They were stigmatized as untrustworthy and lazy people, and the simple but really perceptive idea that Nadiem had, through his personal experiences dealing with them, was that this stigma was not true," said Aluwi, who became co-CEO with Andre Soelistyo when Nadiem Makarim resigned from the position to join the new presidential cabinet in Indonesia in October 2019.

This stereotype, combined with Jakarta's legendary traffic, provided a unique opportunity to help the drivers earn more money. Unlike the vehicle offerings Uber was offering in different parts of the world at the time, the motorcycle drivers could cut through traffic much faster than a car, making them the preferred choice to transport people and deliver packages at scale.

Although there were already millions of apps on the market at the time, Gojek initially launched as a call-center model, with users having to call in to make their transport or delivery requests to dispatchers. Smartphones were just cost-prohibitive: an iPhone would equate to four to five months' worth of the average motorcycle driver's income.

When Gojek did switch to an app-based model in January 2015, they had to contend with another challenge that would surprise most entrepreneurs who were digital natives: almost 100 percent of drivers had never used a smartphone before. Gojek didn't just have to teach its drivers how to use their new app, but digital literacy in general.

"We set up training programs to get us going, but what was really cool was to see was how some of the tech-savvy younger drivers who were more tech-savvy becoming ambassadors and mentors to older drivers who wanted to join, and they walked them through this brand new world of mobile internet! These drivers really became the flywheel that helped us solve this problem," said Aluwi.

While Aluwi and the Gojek team were elated when the company became the country's first unicorn, they were just as proud for what it meant for Indonesia as a whole. He felt that it validated that Indonesia was an important emerging startup ecosystem, which increased investor interest in the country.

"Just as importantly, it showed that starting a company or working for a startup isn't a futile endeavor, which was a very common view by many in the country at the time," he said.

According to Aluwi, this next generation of entrepreneurs in Asia should treat recruiting, internal communication, and organizational development as some of the highest leverage activities that a founder can do, rather than relegate it to administrative HR work as he has often seen.

"I would actually argue that building a great organization and culture is one of the very few things a founder is uniquely positioned to do. Few others have the context and cultural authority to do so otherwise. I would say that organizational development and culture, product vision, and maybe fund raising fall under this category of being very founder dependent, but most founders in Asia I see disproportionately focus on the last two from what I can tell."

"If I could redo anything at Gojek, one of the few things I would change is how much attention I placed onto organization building and how much organizational debt was being accrued or paid off at any given time," he said.

Celebrating founder stories like Gojek's is important for just this reason. By learning about their successes, and more importantly, their mistakes, you stand to improve your own decision-making as you navigate your own startup journey in Asia.

The question-and-answer format smartly chosen by Livingston and employed once again here further enhances the possible practical application of lessons, freeing readers from the editorializing, frameworks, and other paradigms that most other business books use to box in subjects with their own preferred thesis or argument.

What readers get is the literary equivalent of a fireside chat, one where you get the best seats in the house. You can listen in on founders sharing their story in their own words, recounting all the highs, lows, and roller coastering in between that characterizes life as a tech entrepreneur.

The other major reason it's important to celebrate founders in Asia is for the inspiration, as cheesy as it may sound. The need for heroes does not stop in childhood, a fact we see in the idolization of tech luminaries such as Steve Jobs, Bill Gates, or Mark Zuckerberg. It's healthy to look up to people who can serve as signposts for our own path to success.

Even if Pakistan is different from the Philippines and Thailand is different from Taiwan, each of these countries is closer to one another—culturally speaking—than to Silicon Valley. It's this similarity that makes it easier to step into the shoes of an entrepreneur from a different market in Asia and glean inspiration that we can do what he did there, here where we are.

This likeness is evident in the story of Vijay Shekhar Sharma, the founder and CEO of Paytm, a fintech and ecommerce unicorn in India. He started the company in part because of his own personal experiences with financial exclusion.

"In the early days, I was not able to get small loans from banks. My family had a similar experience where my father could not get 'Rs 2 lakh' loan, which is basically $4000 in loans for something in the family," said Sharma.

Researching the problem further, Sharma learned that banks did not give out loans to people who did not belong to the formal financial system. To extend these Indians financial inclusion, the first step was not to sign them up for bank accounts—it was to make them part of the digital payment ecosystem.

Enabling businesses to accept digital payments and enabling customers to pay digitally can kickstart the journey of being a part of the formal financial system for both consumers and businesses. I learned about it in China and other Asian countries—how payment became the beginning of financial inclusion in the country," he said, adding that this is why payments were the foundation of Paytm before becoming a full-scale financial services company.

Sherma built Paytm around high frequency use cases, such as mobile top-up as well as Uber. The critical mass of users that resulted from these anchor use cases further attracted more businesses to the platform, which attracted more users, and so the virtuous cycle went.

One surprising anchor case was offline payments. "Many merchants were accepting payment through Paytm and were, in turn, making payments to their suppliers through Paytm much before we started targeting the full value chain. Our huge presence in the offline world made us a hugely popular name in India," he said.

As of this writing, Paytm is accepted by 14 million merchants, dwarfing the 2 million merchants that collectively accept cards from card networks and banks. The company now also provides savings, insurance, commerce, ticketing, credit, and wealth management services to their customers. For many businesses, Paytm is their first experience with a fintech product.

Despite the seeming ubiquity of their products, Sharma contends there is still so much more to accomplish.

"The growth opportunity present in front of Paytm is so large that whatever has been achieved till now is small in front of it. Every year, new products are being launched. We aspire to provide our services to 500 million Indians. This mission ensures that we remain ambitious," he said.

Sharma's story is relevant to the many entrepreneurs across Asia who also want to address financial inclusion in their own markets, or more broadly, founders who hope to launch a product that can scale in an emerging economy.

To this end, there are many definitions of success encapsulated in this book. There are those who exit via acquisition or IPO. Others reach unicorn status or even loftier valuations. Still others make their mark in terms of scale, disruption, or social impact. What they all have in common is the ability to concretize their particular vision of the world into reality. What can be more admirable— or indeed, heroic—than being the change that you wish to see?

Both current and aspiring founders have plenty of learn from the entrepreneurs profiled in this book. I myself am a humble testament to that. Halfway through writing this book, I saw an opportunity in the content marketing space and raised venture capital, drawing directly on the wisdom from the founders interviewed thus far. I have no doubt that readers will similarly be catapulted in new directions owing to the founders who were gracious enough to share their stories and insights here.

—Ezra Ferraz

Siu Rui Quek

CEO and Co-founder, Carousell

Siu Rui Quek *founded Carousell in Singapore in 2012 with Lucas Ngoo and Marcus Tan. Prototyped over the course of a Startup Weekend, Carousell is a consumer-to-consumer marketplace with a focus on mobile technology. With over 250 million listings, Carousell is one of the world's largest and fastest-growing marketplaces in Southeast Asia, Taiwan, and Hong Kong,*

Ezra Ferraz: Why did you choose to participate in the National University of Singapore's [NUS] Overseas College Program? Were you looking for the general experience of studying abroad like most college students, or were you actively hunting for business ideas?

Siu Rui Quek: I was very keen to go on the NUS Overseas College [NOC] program at Silicon Valley. I'd always wondered how companies like Dropbox and WhatsApp were able to create products that solve a global problem and change people's lives. So I wanted to go to Silicon Valley, in particular, to seek inspiration. And at the same time, I also thought it could help me overcome my fear of failure.

Compared to Silicon Valley, we tend to take fewer risks because of the stigma of failure in Singapore. As a result, we don't set the moonshot goals that startups in Silicon Valley do. Having the opportunity to go to the United States and be immersed in the risk-taking culture of Silicon Valley helped allay that fear. I'd always wanted to start my own company, so starting up right out of school was my litmus test for whether the NOC was a successful program for me.

© Ezra Ferraz, Gracy Fernandez 2020
E. Ferraz and G. Fernandez, *Asian Founders at Work*,
https://doi.org/10.1007/978-1-4842-5162-1_1

Ferraz: What were your formative experiences in Silicon Valley that led you to eventually founding Carousell?

Quek: We often hear of companies that seem to have found success overnight. But what we don't always know is the months of trying and failing that have gone into creating a successful product. Being immersed in the risk-taking culture of Silicon Valley helped me to see failure as a necessary part of the journey.

Ferraz: Were there any notable examples of failure that you experienced first-hand that drove home the idea that it's okay to take risks, and more importantly, that it's okay to fail?

Quek: I remember going to TechCrunch Disrupt in SF and seeing hundreds of startup booths, with many ideas similar to one another, and many were first time founders. There was this feeling of can-do vs worrying about failure. And you see conferences like FailCon that sees founders celebrate and share about their failed experiences publicly and almost proudly. There is also no stigma against hiring founders who "failed." In fact, it seemed to be a valuable add to the CV since presumably that person has had the experience and lessons learned.

Ferraz: Did you have any other formative experiences while in Silicon Valley?

Quek: Another lesson from Silicon Valley was to think of global problems and how we could use technology to solve them. Carousell may have started from a personal need of getting rid of stuff that's lying around. However, looking at the bigger picture and thinking about how we came to have so many things in the first place, it boils down to consumer trends. People are buying so many things, sometimes at unsustainable levels and often things they don't need, because everything is so cheap and accessible.

We see this as an incredible opportunity for us to take a mobile-first approach to solving problems, by using technology to make buying and selling simple so people can easily find new homes for things they have in excess.

The journey has been far from smooth sailing, but we've made it this far by staying laser-focused on our mission and believing that we're doing meaningful work, being adaptable and willing to learn, and brave enough to try and fail.

Ferraz: After your Overseas College Program, you returned to Singapore and participated in Startup Weekend Singapore 2012. What were your expectations of Startup Weekend going into it, and what was the experience of building the foundations of a startup during the event?

Quek: In March 2012, the three of us—Marcus, Lucas, and I—participated in Startup Weekend Singapore and built the first Carousell prototype in fifty-four hours to solve this problem. The basis of the idea was that selling should be as simple as taking a photo, and buying as easy as chatting. We had mountains of unused stuff that we didn't have the heart to throw away and the existing buy-sell forums were just not user-friendly.

If we were going to build something, it was going to be important to leverage the smartphone's strengths, as we noticed more people like us using the smartphone as the main device to access the Internet.

We already had this idea going into Startup Weekend—this concept we were building in our heads, so we saw the hackathon as our chance to be absolutely focused on building out a prototype in a compressed amount of time. We could concentrate on building it and hacking something together—just to show how it would look like if it worked.

Ferraz: Can you recall how you pitched your mobile platform for buying and selling at Startup Weekend Singapore? What kind of demo or prototype did you present to the judges and audience?

Quek: The really memorable part of Startup Weekend was that we almost didn't get in. Twice. There were eighty submissions, of which forty would be selected to give a one-minute pitch. We were actually idea number forty-one or forty-two. But thankfully, a couple teams pulled out, so we snuck in to be the last to pitch.

After the pitching, we fell just short again. We were idea number twenty-two. But thankfully, a few teams had consolidated. So we were the last team to be selected to actually build the product.

We demonstrated the prototype and won the competition, but in the grand scheme of things, the winning was secondary for us. What really inspired us to take the plunge and bring Carousell to life were the hundreds of people who told us they liked the idea through our Facebook, Twitter, and our Launchrock landing page.

Some even tweeted us to ask if they could download the app right away! It was intense and crazy, and we loved it. It showed how much the concept and the product resonated with some many people. That was the validation we needed to really take the plunge and launch Carousell after Startup Weekend.

Ferraz: So many Startup Weekend teams—even winners!—fizzle out after the competition is over. How did you sustain momentum after your victory? What were the first steps you took to creating both Carousell the business and Carousell the product?

Quek: We went into the hackathon with a passion to solve problems with tech, and already had the idea. Having validated that we were solving a meaningful problem, we took the plunge to go all in and make the idea a reality full-time.

Moving into BLOCK71 helped us to focus on the tasks at hand. Part of winning Startup Weekend was a dedicated space in the co-working space in BLOCK71.

The place was a focal point, and it became a habit to go there just for work, compared to our previous arrangements. There was a lot to do to get Carousell ready for launch. One of the first things we had to do was figure out what we wanted to do at the end of the three months.

That's when we really put our brains into building that first viable product. We prioritized the front end of Carousell and built the shell first, because we wanted to show people what it would look like. It was all just wireframes, and we had to decide on how the product should look, what the core features were, and where they would be.

Once we had that and something to show, we went to get feedback from flea markets and recruit sellers, before we started with the back end.

Between the three of us, we split the tasks. I'd decide on which features were essential. Marcus took care of design, ensuring the app came together in a way that was visually appealing. And finally, Lucas would work his magic and code on the back end and iOS app.

Ferraz: How would you compare your time at BLOCK71 with your time in Silicon Valley? How were the cultures similar? How were they different?

Quek: When we first moved into BLOCK71, it was still pretty quiet. I think it was probably half empty. When we moved out in 2016, they probably had five blocks and a waiting list. And today they must have eight or nine blocks full. So the experiment to start BLOCK71 worked out well. It's a great community to be part of because you have startups, incubators, and mentors come by, investors hanging around, and more. It's like a mini Silicon Valley, but of course on a much smaller scale. We loved the events on tech, design, and experience sharing.

Free food helps, too. We joke that we used to feed ourselves off the free pizza at the events in Silicon Valley, and we had the same in BLOCK71. We got help from successful entrepreneurs who were back in the grind doing their next startup, and it was great being peers with them, learning from their experience, borrowing their templates for employment contracts, and one even became our angel investor, and that was Darius. I guess the key difference was that Silicon Valley has a more robust ecosystem with many generations of repeat entrepreneurs, venture capitalists who had witnessed many scales and cycles, and things such as startup-specific lawyers, bankers, etc.

Ferraz: You credit a lot of Carousell's success to the community at BLOCK71. How was Carousell involved with BLOCK71? What kind of tips or strategies did they give you that helped Carousell grow your user base to the point that you were the number-one lifestyle app in Singapore?

Quek: Besides being our center of gravity for Carousell's initial launch, the co-working space was also a hotbed for many of Singapore's first startups. That's when we were introduced and formed relationships with the budding startup community in that area, such as Darius from 99.co and the Burpple founders. We would often get together to share our experiences and trade advice.

We recognized that we were all on the same path, coming across the same issues, be it around user acquisition, product design—you name it. Maybe someone had crossed that bridge before the other, and we could talk about the experience and what we would or would not have done differently.

Ferraz: What was the most important lesson that you learned from another founder at BLOCK71 that you directly applied to Carousell?

Quek: Definitely humility. Darius from 99.co was a startup hero for us in Singapore because of his successful exit with tenCube, and he probably didn't need to be back in the grind building another startup with his team. But you could see his dedication, grit, and humility building his startup. Been there, done that, but still absolutely committed. It was a great reminder for us founders to stay focused, work really hard, and keep learning.

Ferraz: When you tried to obtain a US $10,000 grant from NUS, one of the comments from the professors was that the idea of a C2C marketplace was not new. Can you now qualify his remarks? What was the landscape of C2C selling in Singapore at the time? How did you think your solution would be different?

Quek: For us, it was really solving a personal need that made us realize the potential for Carousell. We were addicted to our smartphones. We spent a lot of our time using the Internet via our mobile devices, but there were no apps for selling and buying that provided mobile-first experiences.

The alternatives for buying and selling online were often a tedious and convoluted process if you weren't a power user. We were convinced we could leverage the mobile experience and create an overall better experience that was simpler and familiar for many. So he was probably right. It's now new. But for us, it was all about reimagining Carousell from the ground up with a mobile-first experience without having to reinvent a proven and beautiful business model of online classifieds.

Ferraz: Though the professor initially rebuffed your idea, you persisted. Can you share the story of how you ended up in a literal "elevator pitch"? What did you say to him to convince him on the idea of Carousell?

Quek: We reiterated our passion for the idea and commitment to build the product we believed would provide a solution to a problem we cared about. We were definitely disappointed when the idea was rejected, but we simply refused to take no for an answer. We waited for the professor to exit the meeting room where we did our pitch. We chased him down and followed him into the NUS Enterprise office elevator for a literal elevator pitch.

He probably saw our passion and strong belief. It was enough to move him to eventually award us a US $7,000 grant the next day. We're incredibly grateful to our professor, who believed in us enough to take a leap of faith.

Ferraz: Outside of the evident passion it takes to pitch something in an elevator, can you recall what you said to him during those moments that may have made him reconsider the viability of a mobile-first classifieds?

Quek: I can't remember now. It has been over seven years! I think we just told him how we truly believed in this, and the fact that we were going to go all in and do this full-time proper.

Ferraz: Although your creation of Carousell was profoundly influenced by your trip to Silicon Valley, how did you actively try to differentiate your platform from other C2C marketplaces in the West as you started product development?

Quek: We were one of the pioneers in this space globally and there wasn't much available to reference and compare. We simply built an app based on what we felt would make a great experience. It helped that we were designing this app for ourselves! We felt that combining the simplicity of snap-list-sell, chat-to-buy, and a social discovery experience would be an overall better experience than the legacy products.

Ferraz: To get feedback, you would show user interfaces and mock-ups of the app to shoppers at flea markets in Singapore. What kind of responses did you get? And how did this feedback shape the product development of Carousell?

Quek: Those were some of the more intense days, where the three of us— Marcus, Lucas and I—would head out to weekend flea markets and distribute free bottles of water in exchange for feedback on our app and user downloads. We wanted to get real feedback from the ground to improve our product.

Responses were generally positive. Many sellers faced the same issues we did, in that online channels were simply too inconvenient to sell effectively. Others also preferred the social interaction of dealing face to face, which was why they opted to participate in flea markets.

Feedback covered pretty much everything, like which categories we should include, what the norms of dealing were, and how we should capture that experience on mobile.

Ferraz: How did you decide which feedback to ignore or follow through on? How did you prioritize the ideas you did want to implement?

Quek: It was a combination of gut and intuition, and also a firm belief that we would have to be convinced on the minimal set of features we needed to have to offer a great user experience, and that we would have to rapidly iterate and improve based on feedback and data.

Ferraz: In August 2012, you launched Carousell's iOS app. Even though growth plateaued for the first few months, what kinds of strategies and growth-hacks did you try in vain to get people to sign up and actively use the app?

Quek: Marcus, Lucas, and I were really inspired by Paul Graham of Y Combinator. He coined the phrase "do things that don't scale," and laid the responsibility of early growth at the founders' feet.

With that in the back of our heads, we were relentless in recruiting new users, whether it came to visiting even more flea markets and campus events or pasting flyers all over NUS noticeboards in the middle of the night.

Looking back, the early days were incredibly scrappy, but it was what got us off the ground to where we are today.

We learned the value of backing up the hard way. Just two weeks before our official launch, our entire database of initial listings and images were inadvertently deleted. Gone. Irretrievable.

After the initial panic subsided, we had little choice but to go back to all our early sellers and humbly ask them to relist and reupload all of those photos. We couldn't launch with an empty marketplace after all.

To our surprise, every one of them relisted, even though they were doing us a massive favor. That was a really significant moment for us, as it taught us the value of community. All those weeks of engaging these sellers, talking to them, and getting feedback, would culminate in their solid backing of us.

Ferraz: Can you recall any other notable examples of you or your co-founders doing something that did not scale in your earliest days?

Quek: We emailed every user who signed up to welcome them, ask them how they heard about us, and if they had feedback for us. We also replied to every customer support email ourselves, replied to every tweet and Facebook post. We also reached out to users one-by-one on platforms where people were buying and selling with a less than optimal experience. We were also regulars at SCAPE where they had flea markets, so we talked to seller by seller to get them on board, handed out ice water to passers-by to get them to sign up on Carousell, and even helped certain sellers take photos to upload listings for them. We did everything it took to get that next seller and buyer as we had no money for proper marketing.

Ferraz: What surprised you the most about your four hundred early adopters? Who were they? What kinds of items were they buying and selling?

Quek: When we launched, we had very few categories, as we recruited mainly from flea market sellers. So they were mainly selling knick-knacks, clothing, and fashion accessories.

What surprised me most about our first early adopters has to be their faith in us. In the startup life, nothing is ever smooth sailing.

The first one and half years were tough. At one point, we had seven new users a day, but then we had four hundred active users that we kept in close contact with. We emailed every single person who signed up. We built a relationship from there and discovered the target audience that resonated most with our product were those who were between fifteen and twenty-four years old and female, who had no assumptions of how online marketplaces historically worked. We were inspiring an entirely new generation of online sellers!

Ferraz: Once you knew that this was your demographic, did you try any novel ways of reaching them?

Quek: No. But we had to write content targeted at young women. We had to make it up and create content such as "Top 5 Peplum Tops" or "Top 5 Little Black Dresses," and we even sent out fashion-centric press kits to fashion publications and got coverage.

Ferraz: One of your early successes was convincing Facebook sellers to migrate to Carousell. What were the most common objections or concerns you got from them about migrating to Carousell? And how did you generally convince them that it was worth it to do so?

Quek: Facebook was just one of many avenues where we reached out to our community. Our approach was to communicate a solution to problems that people were facing. Specifically, Facebook was not optimized for buying and selling. The community there came about entirely organically. We convinced them to move over by communicating how we solved their problems and delivered a better experience.

I think one of the things we had going for us was how we were a mobile-native application built with the sole intent of making selling and buying simple. We made it easy to take a photo and list your item straightaway. Or if you were buying, it was simple to just start a chat that was already integrated in the app.

Ferraz: How are you continuing to convince Facebook sellers to switch over to Carousell, even with new commerce-focused efforts like Facebook marketplace?

Quek: We have one absolute focus at Carousell, which is to constantly reduce the friction in the buying and selling process. So we are continuing to make listings simple with AI to suggest titles, prices, etc. We are making discovery a lot more personalized. And we are also doing things such as introducing escrow payments to add trust and convenience.

Ferraz: After you became the number-one lifestyle app in Singapore, did you have to make a conscious effort to grow one side of the marketplace—that is, buyers versus sellers—more than the other? Or did the marketplace largely take care of itself?

Quek: During those three months leading to launch, we were focused on acquiring users and listings, curating the best quality ones, so when we launched, it's not an empty ghost town. We went out to talk to users at flea markets on weekends just to get feedback and recruit sellers. We reached out to a hundred or so sellers in the space of three months, of which we only ended up with seventy and more than seven hundred listings.

Even after launch, we made a conscious effort to keep finding and acquiring new sellers, because we knew that new listings would keep our marketplace fresh and varied. It was solid one-and-a-half-year grind before we saw the traction and the network effects. More than five years in, we are still less than one percent done in our mission to inspire the world to start selling. So we are still laser-focused and working very hard to inspire even more people to start selling with Carousell.

Ferraz: Is the general pattern that if you get good, high-quality, and diverse sellers, the buyers will always follow? Has anything surprised you about how the two marketplace sides have grown vis-à-vis one another?

Quek: I think as a startup you've always got to be focused given finite resources. From the start, we were laser focused on sellers since our value proposition was strongest for this group. We had a ten times better experience—snap, list, sell in thirty seconds. It was a strong and clear message. To mitigate the lack of liquidity early on, we focused on building single-user utility into the app. Even if there were no buyers on the Carousell marketplace then, we made it easy to create a beautiful listing and shopfront for sellers, and made it easy for them to sell to their network across platforms like Facebook, Twitter, and Instagram so they reach the largest number of prospective buyers with the least amount of effort. Eventually the liquidity on Carousell built up and the network effects kicked in.

Ferraz: As you began to expand into other markets, like Malaysia, Indonesia, and Taiwan, did you make any changes to the Carousell product—apart from changing the language and currency?

Quek: We are very focused on building the simplest and most inspiring community marketplace, where people can buy, sell, and connect with one another. Our philosophy is to make selling as easy as taking a photo, and buying as simple as chatting. That doesn't change when we enter new markets.

With that focus on communities, we make it a point to have regular community meetups wherever we launch. These meetups allow us to gather feedback from local users and address any unique problems they face.

By and large, we keep the Carousell experience uniform in the markets we launch in. We introduce basic localization, like languages and currency. When we encounter market-specific trends, we may roll out features to address them. For instance, we activated a scooter category in Taiwan because we saw a high demand for it. We tied up with 7-Eleven in Taiwan to introduce payments and shipping there first, before our other markets.

Ferraz: Did growing your user base in these other markets closely mirror what already worked in Singapore? Or did you have to resort to completely different strategies for user acquisition?

Quek: The cities of Southeast Asia are highly differentiated. We speak different languages and dialects, have different cultures and traditions, and transact in different currencies. Even the level of infrastructure for Internet access and speed, smartphone penetration, transportation, and logistics, vary widely across the region.

As a startup based in Singapore, we grew up surrounded by these differences and knew that we had to go local to be global. We have local teams in all of our markets to ensure that everything we do is relevant and resonates with our users in that country.

Our app is optimized to perform even in challenging Internet conditions and is flexible enough to allow buyers and sellers to use what makes the most sense for them in their market, rather than us imposing a certain way of doing things.

Ferraz: Now that Carousell is one of the top C2C marketplaces in Asia, can you share a story of how the platform has helped one of your users—ideally one that you have not shared publicly before—that affirms your decision to have built this product?

Quek: We regularly hear stories about the Carousell community, and it really drives home why we're doing this when we hear of the meaningful interactions between our users.

One great story is how one of our Carousellers was getting started using Carousell and successfully decluttered her room. She eventually took decluttering one step further by helping out at local thrift shop, and selling their items through Carousell. What's really special was that this wasn't any thrift shop. This thrift shop donates all its earnings to an orphanage in the Philippines!

The full story can be found on our blog. But it's stories like these—how our platform enables so many to help themselves as well as others—that really validates what we set out to do. That is to inspire everyone in the world to start selling.

Ferraz: In June of this year, Carousell entered into a partnership with Foursquare. Can you outline the partnership and explain how it has helped your users so far?

Quek: We believe in helping people fill their lives with more meaningful things and experiences. Transactions within the Carousell community also tend to be carried out in person. Foursquare and its expertise in location-based services helps us connect our Carousellers more effectively, making it all the more convenient to get the items they always wanted.

Ferraz: In a 2016 interview with Tech in Asia, you memorably said that you would rather serve a billion people than make a billion dollars and that you were only one percent done with your mission. What is your assessment now of where Carousell stands? How far are you from solving your mission?

Quek: Less than one percent done. To me, it's less an actual measure of success but more a reminder that there's still so much to do.

In fact, over seven years on, I still feel like we've barely scratched the surface. Yes, we've built some amazing communities all across the region, but now is when the real work starts.

We're still trying to build a meaningful and enduring company that inspires the world to start selling. That's the goal. We're still so far away from that.

In the earlier years, we chose to focus on getting the product right and growing our markets with the support of investors. Now everything in place, it's time to execute our longer-term plan of monetization and create a sustainable company.

Ferraz: Can you share the story of your acquisition of OLX Philippines, and how your M&A activity plays into your goal of serving a billion people?

Quek: We got acquainted with the OLX Philippines team, and we were aligned in our mission to serve the over 100 million Filipinos and inspire them to sell and buy so as to make more possible for the community. They had a deep experience in the markets having spent 13 years solving this problem, had a very passionate team, and we thought this was a great way to accelerate the impact we can make in the country, and join forces to make an even larger one together. We continue to be open to acquisitions to accelerate our mission, and partner with great teams to make this happen together.

Ferraz: What are the challenges of integrating the OLX Philippines community—which may not necessarily have been mobile-first—into the Carousell experience, which is mobile-first?

Quek: It is definitely a new muscle we are building. The community on OLX Philippines are used to a certain user experience that's largely web-first, while Carousell is largely mobile-first. So we've worked very hard, and continue to work very hard, to harmonize the experiences and offer the best of both worlds. It's definitely helped us build a new capability to offer an even better user experience to the rest of our community across the markets.

Ferraz: What unconventional advice do you have for entrepreneurs in Southeast Asia who want to succeed like Carousell?

Quek: We really don't think we are successful yet and are still less than 1% done. If there was any advice at all, you've got to be absolutely passionate about the problem you're solving. It's this deep sense of purpose that will keep you going through tough times, and there will be plenty in the journey. For instance, just because you're not seeing any results in three months or six months doesn't mean that your idea isn't working. It took us one and a half years before we saw any form of rapid growth in Carousell, but we were absolutely passionate about the problem we were solving, and we were convinced it was a big problem for many. Stay close to your users, hear their problems and challenges, and keep iterating and learning.

Shing Chow
Founder and CEO, Lalamove

In 2013, **Shing Chow** *founded Lalamove, then still known as EasyVan, in Hong Kong. Lalamove is an on-demand logistics company that allows consumers and enterprises to ship both large and small goods via a mobile app.*

Active across Asia, Lalamove is available in more than 100 cities across Greater China, India, the Philippines, Singapore, Indonesia, Malaysia, Thailand, and Vietnam. In many of these markets, Lalamove competes with other on-demand logistics providers, mirroring the fierce ride-hailing battle that played out in Southeast Asia several years earlier.

Chow has raised US $461 million from some of the region's best tech investors, including Sequoia Capital China and Hillhouse Capital Group. Lalamove's current valuation makes it one of Hong Kong's unicorns.

Gracy Fernandez: After graduating from Stanford with a degree in economics, how did you eventually find yourself in the world of high-stakes poker?

Shing Chow: When I came back to Hong Kong, I worked in management consulting. The nature of consulting is to provide advice to companies but I did not get to make any of the actual decisions. So, while the job was interesting, I always felt like I was on the sidelines and not making a direct impact. A philosophy I've always lived by is something I've coined "A.P.P". It stands for Ability, Passion and Prospects. I've always believed that it's important to align your ability and passion with something that provides you with prospects.

E. Ferraz and G. Fernandez, *Asian Founders at Work,*
https://doi.org/10.1007/978-1-4842-5162-1_2

In order to find true success, you need to be doing something that fulfills all three attributes. So, while I was good at consulting and it certainly provided prospects, I didn't find myself immersed in it—that passion was lacking. I actually started playing poker to kill time at work and ended up being quite good at it. Of course, I didn't begin with high-stakes poker. In fact, I was barely breaking even during the first four years. I couldn't go on that way so I decided I had to improve or move on from this. I read that one needs about ten thousand hours to become an expert. Not wanting to give up, I played for twelve hours every day, and over time, saw my earnings skyrocket from $1,000 [USD] a month to more than $150,000 [USD] per month. So, now, with poker being something I was passionate about, provided me with prospects and an activity I had become skillful in, poker became aligned with my A.P.P.

Fernandez: How did you come up with the A.P.P. philosophy?

Chow: I've always believed that, in order to succeed in anything, you need to have a good ability in something, strong interest and passion for it and the intensity to want to do well at it. Of course, it has to have a future, to ensure sustainability. However, the acronym, A.P.P, I came up with at an event where I was asked to give advice to students on how to succeed or accomplish their goals. This was after I had started Lalamove. So I wanted to come up with something catchy that they would remember and yet encapsulates my philosophy. A.P.P naturally came to mind and coincidentally it spells app too which is perfect for a tech company with an app like us.

Fernandez: What did you learn from high-stakes poker that would eventually be applicable or transferable to the world of tech startups?

Chow: It wasn't so much the poker-playing skills that were useful to the world of tech startups, but the values I learned throughout that time that I brought over to Lalamove. Our core values are grit, passion, humility, and execution.

Despite not seeing results in the beginning and taking a while to achieve success, I never gave up. That persistence taught me the importance of having grit in everything I did—hence the first value. What also kept me going was the passion I had for the game which really should form the backbone of everything we do. Lastly, and this is something I realized after playing for a while, it's important to be humble. It's easy to feel invincible and get carried away when you're winning in the game. However, that arrogance could eventually lead to complacency which may ultimately be your downfall. Going back to grit, having that hunger to succeed is always necessary. Even all this time at Lalamove, I've held on to that drive to succeed and want all the employees to have that, no matter how big or successful we get.

Fernandez: After your successful career as a poker player, what made you decide to go back to Hong Kong?

Chow: During the last few years of me playing poker, I was often competing in Macau, so I was dividing my time shuffling between Macau and Hong Kong. My decision to move back to Hong Kong permanently was more to do with my desire to do something more than poker. Poker is a zero-sum game. However, I felt a strong urge to do something more fulfilling and meaningful—something that impacts others and not just me.

Fernandez: On-demand ride-hailing was already popular for consumers at the time you founded Lalamove. How did you get the idea that businesses also needed on-demand logistics services?

Chow: Actually, the sharing of cars and vans through dispatch or call centres, was already taking place in Hong Kong way before the term "shared economy" was officially coined. They essentially operated as a shared economy already. I find this to be unique to Hong Kong as I had not seen it practiced anywhere else. This was even before the Internet so the matching of vehicles to consumers was done over calls. It literally operated like a call center and was a very analog process.

When Lalamove was established, as you mentioned, ride-hailing was popular but there weren't many companies trying to digitize logistics services. With internet penetration increasing across the region, I saw this as a great opportunity to turn the dispatch center concept digital.

Fernandez: In what ways did you feel that digitizing the experience would improve the user experience of booking a van?

Chow: There are so many advantages technology brings compared to manual methods. Digitizing helps map users with the drivers closest to them. A tech company can also scale much easier and faster as there are fewer on-ground considerations than a traditional business would have. Scaling, in turn, allows us to manage a bigger fleet of drivers and vehicles. Call centers in Hong Kong in the past only managed about 500 drivers.

Technology also allows us to gather data that can be used to optimize operations to benefit our various stakeholders. The vast amount of real-time data and intelligence generated through our app can provide companies like us with insights to improve processes or invest more into areas that need it. For instance, based on the various routes drivers have taken, we are able to suggest the most efficient routes for the quickest deliveries. We're able to track our fleet of drivers, allowing us to manage deliveries more efficiently and intelligently, ensuring they reach their destination on time. We're also able to anticipate consumer needs based on historical data.

The nature of having an app also means that users and drivers can send and accept delivery requests when convenient to them, know exactly how much it is going to cost, and pay through a variety of payment options. As long as there are drivers available, users can deliver items of any shape and size at any time.

They are no longer restricted by the schedule of the logistics company. Technology allows us to do all of that which, in turn, makes for an automated and seamless user experience.

Fernandez: As a non-technical founder, how did you go about developing an on-demand logistics app like Lalamove? What were the biggest challenges here, and how did you overcome them?

Chow: I studied computer studies in high school and did quite well, so I had an understanding of technology. The difference between poker and building your own company is that, while poker is an individual game where you only have to rely on yourself, running a company requires teamwork. You also have to trust the people you hire as you would need to rely on them quite a bit. On the other hand, it also means that you no longer have to take on all the tasks and responsibilities yourself.

As the startup culture wasn't that well known in Hong Kong then, my biggest challenge was getting people to believe in the idea of the company. Being such a new concept, naturally, there were concerns and doubts. Funding overall for startups was also on the decline in China at that time. The online-to-offline [O2O] industry wasn't popular then, and many such companies were going bankrupt. I also felt that originating from Hong Kong worked against us, as there were not many examples of successful home-grown startups that investors could reference from. That perception made it hard to hire good people.

That said, you just need that one investor to believe in your vision and company. I was lucky to have developed a good background and network, which helped in building that trust and credibility with investors.

Fernandez: Given the dire economic situation at the time, how did you pitch and recruit your early employees?

Chow: The biggest obstacle I had was the perception that it wasn't possible to build a unicorn from Hong Kong. To be fair, there weren't any major startups in Hong Kong at that time, much less unicorns. So I had to convince them otherwise and change this perception. My approach was quite straightforward in that I talked about the Lalamove business model which was already a valid one since the logistics industry is already a well known one and we also had the "vehicle call center" concept I mentioned before.

The focus of my pitch was the change the internet is bringing to businesses and how I see it transforming the delivery and logistics industries. The startup scene may have been new in Asia but in the US, companies like Airbnb and Facebook were already seeing worldwide success. I put out some job advertisements and also relied on connections from friends. There are always going to be people who are more courageous and open to trying something new, and these were the type of people I was looking for. Passion is contagious. A small but enthusiastic and hardworking team can work wonders and I was fortunate to meet some very talented and driven people to form my core team.

Funny enough, none of my closest friends wanted to join. No idea why! So I talked to acquaintances and asked if they knew anyone who'd be keen. The Hong Kong tech scene has grown by leaps and bounds since then though so you get tons of people who are actually seeking out startups now!

Fernandez: More importantly, how did you convince investors to invest in Lalamove, at a time when, as you say, most online-to-offline businesses were going bankrupt?

Chow: It's a matter of finding one investor even though hundreds before may have rejected you. It's almost like finding a wife—you just need a market of ONE! I managed to find that one that believed in my vision. I'm actually not sure what exactly convinced them—I was just happy in the investment! I had met at least a few hundred before that.

Fernandez: Why did you initially start with vans for your logistics solution rather than, say, motorcycles or trucks?

Chow: Vans were popular in Hong Kong at that time. Motorcycles not as much. Vans are also large enough to accommodate a variety of goods so they're ideal for logistics services. However, we moved soon to include other types of transport to cater to the various countries we were expanding to. In every country we expand to, we always make sure to incorporate the local vehicles into our offerings, for example tempos in India and pickup baks in Jakarta. We even offer a variety of sizes for trucks and vans in certain countries. This mindset of adaptability is extremely important if you want to build a big global tech firm.

Fernandez: For consumers, adding a new vehicle type seems simple, but I'm sure there are both online and offline considerations for each new vehicle class you add. What are the challenges of adding a new vehicle class? Is there something different from offering motorcycles from, say, vans?

Chow: Adding different vehicle types opens us up to new industries and customer segments. For example, the F&B industry usually uses motorcycles for everyday deliveries or food orders. Factories rely on vans or trucks as they usually have large amounts of shipments. Sometimes customers would be different.

Adding a vehicle type isn't difficult as long as there is supply which means there are plenty of drivers using such vehicles. Of course, you'd have to come up with a suitable pricing model and update relevant marketing and corporate materials but those aren't challenging tasks. It's more about finding the relevant customer segment. Adding supply is always easier than adding demand. The vehicle types vary by cities too and they would be in the best position to determine the demand.

Fernandez: How did you introduce your technology to drivers and ensure they had the technological literacy to be able to use it effortlessly to serve customers?

Chow: Technology is taking over most parts of our lives, so most people are mobile-savvy. With many countries in Asia having some of the highest internet penetration rates, most people here are mobile-savvy. Technology is taking over most parts of our lives anyway so not much education was needed. Mobile phones becoming much more user-friendly over the years also benefited us. We also invest constantly into making the user experience on both our user and driver apps as intuitive and seamless as possible. So I would say that our app is quite easy to use.

Driving for Lalamove is also an attractive prospect for many vehicle owners looking for extra income on a flexible schedule, so not much persuasion was needed on that front either.

We do offer training for our drivers though, but this is more centered around ensuring that they are well equipped to provide the best service to our users.

Fernandez: Can you go into more detail about how Lalamove helps drivers earn more income, and in turn, enjoy a better quality of life? Perhaps you may want to share the story of one particular driver who Lalamove made a particular impact on.

Chow: With Lalamove, drivers have the flexibility to accept delivery orders as and when it's convenient for them. You can put in as many hours as you want. We have drivers doing this part-time, during their free time, as they have full-time jobs. They can also drive full-time if they wish. The app clearly lists out all the delivery requests available at that time, including drop-off locations, so drivers also have plenty of control over the types of orders they accept. We let users schedule orders in advance so drivers are able to select a few orders to fulfill and manage their time accordingly. This allows them to handle more orders in a day and, as a result, earn more income. There is also full transparency as earnings are shown in the app per job.

We always come across so many instances of drivers telling us about the impact we've made in their lives. Personally, I remember one I met at a press conference we organized in Beijing. He came from a surrounding province but had been working in the logistics industry in Beijing for 15 years. When Lalamove established itself in Beijing, he decided to drive with us full-time and had been doing it for a few years, being able to fulfill many orders in a day. He told me that his earnings from the few years with Lalamove allowed him to get an air-conditioner for his home to beat the hot Beijing summer. This is a prime example of how we help drivers take control over their time and income, and as a result, achieve a better quality of life. He also joked that, because he spent so much time driving, he had less time to argue with his wife! So I guess the extra income helped stabilize his relationship!

We think of our drivers as partners, hence you'll see us using the term 'driver partner' as they're an important part of our business. While technology can certainly help companies like Lalamove improve operational and business efficiencies, the human touch is still essential in providing a great user experience. The professionalism of our drivers is what encourages customer loyalty. To that end, our drivers undergo in-person training to get them acquainted with our company and the job. They are essentially an extension of the Lalamove brand. They're also entitled to a variety of incentives such as petrol rebates, discounts for mobile phone plans, and even get invited to a variety of events we organize for them.

Fernandez: What was the initial market reception from enterprises to a tech-enabled solution like Lalamove, who may have been used to using more traditional and manual logistics solutions?

Chow: Our users, both corporates and the man on the street, found Lalamove's solution a lot more convenient and flexible. With our platform, it's easy to track drivers and the movement of your goods, for instance. It provides people with the power to automate their deliveries. Ultimately, it allows you to order a delivery almost immediately and get it completed within an hour. A solution like Lalamove allows enterprises to scale according to their needs. Traditional logistics solutions can often be quite expensive as there are costs associated with warehousing and fleet maintenance for example. That may be hard for a smaller retail or online business to afford.

With a tech-enabled solution like Lalamove, businesses have access to our fleet of professionally-trained drivers and can arrange deliveries on-demand or ahead of time. We also offer various types of API integrations which means that companies can easily automate a high volume of delivery requests and track orders. This makes it easier for companies to scale their deliveries without the hassle of managing their own fleet.

Fernandez: How did your breadth of business and career experience help you with building Lalamove better than, say, someone who only might have had experience in logistics?

Chow: I feel that my lack of logistics experience actually helped me. I made decisions based on my logic rather than how they may traditionally be done in the logistics industry. In a way, that led me to doing things differently than how they had been done before. One example was having our drivers stick the Lalamove logo onto their vehicles which was great for brand awareness. I relied on data, instead of opinions, to make decisions.

Fernandez: Do you feel a logistics person would have overlooked the brand awareness component of the business? Can you share another example of how you did something different compared to how a person with a logistics background would have?

Chow: Since I've never been in the traditional logistics industry, I can't know for sure how a logistics person would think. However, I think a traditional logistics person wouldn't think of scaling the company as quickly. This is something a tech-based company would do and know that it's possible. It wouldn't be as easy for a traditional logistics company as they'd have other aspects to consider such as fleet management and warehousing. Expanding to new markets in a matter of months is practically unheard of in many traditional industries but is doable in the startup and tech world.

Fernandez: In less than six months since your launch, you had already expanded to other countries in Southeast Asia. How were you able to achieve this kind of stratospheric growth that all founders dream of?

Chow: Growth really is a necessity if you want to survive, especially as a tech company. We already had that mindset. Being able to scale was a priority for us from day one so we made sure to keep working towards it.

Fernandez: In the wake of companies like Honestbee, how do you make sure your scaling is organic growth—of people genuinely wanting your product—rather than artificial growth, spurred on only by a large warchest and effectively buying customers?

Chow: There are certain constraints we place on the local city teams to ensure organic growth. We have to make sure that we are scaling to provide value and investing in aspects of the business that can create long term success. Ultimately anything we spend money on has to make business sense. We have to ensure that it is aligned with our business goals and have long term prospects. In the startup world, it's common for companies to focus on increasing brand awareness in the beginning no matter how much their initiatives may cost. We place emphasis on building a profitable business and have been since we started. If our revenue is higher than cost, it means we're creating value and being sustainable.

Fernandez: When you expanded overseas, what was the most difficult market to operate in, and why? How did you address these difficulties?

Chow: We expanded to Japan within our first month of founding, and unfortunately, had to pull out. It is such a unique country in terms of culture, language, and regulations, and we did not have the right internal capabilities to succeed there. Till today, we don't have any operations in Japan.

Fernandez: What exactly was it about Japan's culture, language, and regulations that made it difficult to succeed here?

Chow: It was really more to do with the fact that we were unprepared, with no internal capabilities whatsoever to manage the market. When we expanded there, we didn't even have an app so we didn't know how to manage the business. Being so new, we also didn't have a structure where we can manage a regional company. We were small and inexperienced. You may wonder why we chose Japan. Well, it's one of the biggest markets in Asia and has a lot of potential but us going in there when we did was too premature.

Fernandez: Even though you are no longer active in Japan, did you apply the lessons you learned from your stint there to your other markets in some way?

Chow: We learned that the pacing of expansion is extremely important. With growth being extremely important to us, we're always excited to move into new markets and we want to do it quickly. However, as Japan taught us, being too hasty can end up being a detriment. There are various aspects we consider before expanding into a new market. We take into account the product market fit, market size and our internal capabilities. This includes having an internal system and a big enough team to support the expansion.

We've made a lot of mistakes but most of those mistakes were necessary. Even expanding into Japan, it cost us money but we learned. In hindsight, we should have expanded into Mainland China earlier, and established ourselves in Beijing. However these mistakes are all necessary to learn. It's impossible to make the right decisions all the time. It's always about learning from mistakes, or critical errors. That learning process is more important than trying not to make mistakes. However, I feel that everything has worked out in the end.

Fernandez: Now that Lalamove is more established, do you think you'd ever go back into Japan?

Chow: Definitely. Japan still holds a lot of potential being such a large country. We are in a more prepared place now, having expanded to many other countries. We also have a much bigger, more experienced and varied team now.

Fernandez: Has there ever been a moment when you seriously considered exiting a market, but ultimately decided not to? How did you turn things around in this market?

Chow: With the exception of Japan, we've not faced such a situation so far. Learning from our experience in Japan, we've been prepared and fully dedicated to the other markets we've expanded to.

Fernandez: How did the entrance of other on-demand logistics companies, like Transportify in 2014, influence your business direction or product roadmap?

Chow: I believe it's more important to make business or product decisions based on what is best for our drivers and users. They are the end users of our product, after all. There are always going to be competitors anyway so making business decisions based on them may cause us to lose sight of our unique selling propositions. What our competitors are doing doesn't influence those decisions.

Fernandez: Has the entrance of other competitors made it more challenging to recruit drivers? How did you in turn respond?

Chow: Our main focus was increasing efficiency in our business operations and our app. Increasing productivity means we can do more with fewer drivers. A more efficient product also means we get more users which provides drivers with more delivery requests. Recruiting new drivers hasn't really been a problem. The key is to ensure that Lalamove is the preferred company for them to keep driving with. The best retention tool is to ensure they're earning enough income and are happy driving with Lalamove.

To that end, we treat our drivers with respect. For instance, we organize "Star Driver Nights" every year in various countries where we treat our drivers to good food and fun performances. It's a chance for them to let their hair down and get to meet the Lalamove team and other drivers. It's also an opportunity for us to reward them for all the hard work and dedication they've put in into providing great service to our users. Initiatives like these are a result of the mentality that we have where we treat our drivers as partners. They go a long way in making our drivers feel like they are an important part of Lalamove's success.

Fernandez: Some of your competitors operated in many other logistics verticals, like sedans or SUVs. Why did you choose to stick to your core offerings of trucks, motorcycles, and vans?

Chow: Trucks, motorcycles and vans allow for delivery of various types of goods, from documents to larger items, and are also the most commonly found so it's what we continue to stick to. We do localize our offerings by market. For example, in Jakarta, we also deliver by vehicles called Pickup Box and Pickup Bak. In Singapore and Kuala Lumpur, we offer delivery by car.

Fernandez: As you built out Lalamove to be a regional company, what are your top hiring criteria?

Chow: Lalamove's core values are humility, passion, grit, and execution, and it's important that the people we hire display these qualities. Of course, the expertise they bring with them is important, too. They have to have the knowledge to do the job well, but the right attitude will set them apart and help propel Lalamove to greater heights.

Fernandez: Do you keep an eye out for people—like you—who may not have a background in logistics, so may have new insights to bring to the space?

Chow: It's not that we close ourselves off to anyone with a logistics background—we do have employees who come from logistics but not a lot. Our employees come from a variety of backgrounds but a number have a technology or operations background. It's important that we remain open-minded in hiring. Where they come from does not matter as much as the skills and expertise they bring with them. Lalamove is not a traditional logistics company so having that background isn't crucial for us.

Fernandez: Why did you wait so long to announce that you were a unicorn? What was the thinking or strategy at play here?

Chow: Sometimes, knowing that you have achieved success makes people complacent. I want all of us to feel like an underdog all the time. There's still so much we have to accomplish.

Fernandez: How do you keep your team members feeling like an underdog, even though the company is now routinely praised as one of your country's few unicorns?

Chow: We still have strong competitors, some of whom, are also unicorns and much bigger and better funded than us. While we are brand leaders in certain countries in Asia, such as the Philippines and Thailand, we still have a long way to go in many other countries to be market leaders. We also want to be a global company and we're far from that. In terms of fundraising amounts, some of our competitors have raised more.

So, while we have achieved some success, there is so much more to accomplish and we never want to rest on our laurels. This is the same mindset that's constantly communicated to the team. My goal is to build the largest on-demand logistics company.

Fernandez: What unconventional advice do you have for founders who want to build a tech company as influential and as successful as Lalamove?

Chow: I'm always afraid of giving advice, as success depends on a number of factors. Often, it is a combination of the opportunities you get, luck, and your circumstances. It's hard to copy and duplicate companies, and oftentimes, that doesn't make a business successful. It's important for entrepreneurs to understand themselves and know what they excel in and are passionate about. Finding that niche is more critical. Essentially, they need to find their own A.P.P.

Fernandez: Since finding the middle ground between what a person excels in and what they are passionate about is so crucial, how do you advise that founders can better or more efficiently accomplish this self-discovery?

Chow: I would advise them to try many different things. You can't put yourself into a box. Success involves a lot of trial and error. I've tried many things too—some successful and others a complete failure. You may end up stumbling upon things that you are passionate about. For instance, I never expected to be a poker player. It's important to be brave and step out of your comfort zone.

Khailee Ng
Managing Partner, 500 Startups

Khailee Ng is one of the most successful founders from Southeast Asia. In 2011, he sold daily deals site GroupsMore to Groupon, as part of the latter's entrance into Malaysia. Just two years later, Ng sold social curation and news platform Says.com to Malaysian media giant Media Prima Bhd.

Now, as one of four managing partners of 500 Startups globally, Khailee also oversees Southeast Asia as a region. Ng is one of the few venture capitalists with direct experience in the region as both a founder and an investor. His track record in this role is equally impressive. Of the 180 investments Ng has made, three are already unicorns: Grab, Revolution Precraftd, and Bukalapak.

Gracy Fernandez: Let's start with how you began your journey in tech, and what kept you going.

Khailee Ng: I'd like to think my journey did not begin with me. I'd like to start with my father. He grew up dirt poor in a rubber plantation, where his ten older siblings and parents toiled to save up for him to go to college, so he could become an engineer. Save up and buy me a computer.

When I first figured out how to use the computer to create websites, I sat in front of my computer for nineteen hours. I was fifteen years old. At the time, I heard that one could even earn money from making websites. So I flipped newspapers to find advertisements that didn't have a website URL. I rang them up, asking if they wanted a website built for them. I tried not to sound like I was fifteen years old.

© Ezra Ferraz, Gracy Fernandez 2020
E. Ferraz and G. Fernandez, *Asian Founders at Work*,
https://doi.org/10.1007/978-1-4842-5162-1_3

Eventually, I went from building websites to building web companies. Many of them didn't make enough money to be considered a huge success. But two of them turned out well. One was a news site that became the most visited online media group in my country and a listing that on my country's stock exchange. This company was then acquired by the largest media company in my country. Another was an early e-commerce company that was acquired by Groupon. I was thirty years old.

I thought about my father's journey of hard work. I worked hard, too, in my own way. But how did I create wealth that otherwise may have taken his generation a lifetime to accumulate? I had the Internet. I didn't need to "know the right people" or "go to the right school." All I had was ideas. And the Internet.

What if more people knew this? And used it? Traditional capitalism had historically created a wealth divide. It doesn't have to be that way! Tech can allow the opportunity for more people to be creators in this world. More people would win!

This is what keeps me going, especially in creating a truly global venture capital platform.

Fernandez: They say every successful tech startup has a bet-the-company moment, where a decision can shape its entire future, for better or for worse. What was this moment for you at either SAYS.com or GroupsMore? What were the possible choices, and why did you choose to go with the option you did?

Ng: Sure. Here is one story.

I walked into the office one day. I was greeted with alarming looks from my colleagues. One spoke up, "Did you see? Facebook has banned our website URL and shut down our Facebook page."

You see, SAYS.com didn't begin as a news website. It began as an online research panel. This meant one could be paid to answer an online survey. I would monetize from companies who wanted customer insights. Once I hit a ceiling of monetization with the companies I served, I asked them, what could I do to make more revenue? They told me, market research budgets tend to be much smaller than advertising budgets. So I decided to pay my users to share advertisers' content on Facebook. While this move grew revenue, Facebook didn't like that I gave its user base ways to generate income from their Facebook feed.

After it banned SAYS.com from appearing in Facebook, it was as though I walked into the office and lost my entire business. And I did. All advertiser revenues dried up in the days that proceeded. My team had this "what-do-we-do?" look. Some days I didn't even go to work. I stayed in bed, so distraught, I couldn't even cry.

Some days, I got up. I worked with the team to come up with a new business—one where we would become a news website that had content so compelling, that it would go viral. We thought that advertisers would pay us to help them generate such genuinely newsworthy, shareable content that we didn't need to pay anyone to share anything or sell a single banner ad. We only tolerated good content—content so good, that users wanted to share it.

As we pursued this vision—one day, three months later—Facebook lifted the ban. SAYS.com quickly grew to become the most visited news site in our country. Along the way, we had more and more winning content campaigns with our advertisers. We not only saw revenue in the millions, but we were also double-digit profitable. We were well on our way to an IPO.

The decision I am most proud of is that we got through the trying times without letting go of a single staff member. And not a single staff member left during that time. It's almost as if we had made a shared and unspoken decision to get through things together.

Fernandez: After also exiting GroupsMore that went to Groupon, what made you decide to pursue venture capital versus creating and trying to exit another tech startup?

Ng: Yes, we had a lot of traffic from SAYS.com that helped launch GroupsMore's leadership in the group buying space. From start to exit it was four months total. I did think a lot about starting more startups. However, I started angel investing first. And I was hooked. I get an immense thrill from creating things with people. Venture capital was the eventual path after I ran out of angel-investing money! [Laughter.]

Fernandez: When you joined 500 Startups, the VC firm had already been around for some time. How did you decide that 500 Startups was the right fit for you over other VC firms, where you could have started your venture capital career?

Ng: 500 Startups started in 2010. I joined them in 2014. You see, I am a bit of an unintentional entrepreneur. My passion comes from creating things, seeing ideas to fruition. It's pretty magical to think that you can quite literally think things, and they can become real. Entrepreneurship and venture capital are two different vehicles for seeing ideas come to life. At times, they may be the most effective vehicles. At times, an effective vehicle may already exist.

When I was touring Silicon Valley, I met with many firms. They were incredibly effective at funding Silicon Valley and folks who would move there. I cared a lot about others who were not connected to Silicon Valley. 500 Startups was the only firm I met that would go out of their way to find and invest in entrepreneurs that didn't pattern-match, or have a connection with Silicon

Valley. They were the first Silicon Valley firm to go to the far reaches of Europe, Asia, and even Africa. Again, this was before many countries even had startup ecosystems. They had already built a brand that had proven that global investing could be a profitable and scalable endeavor.

To me, 500 was an effective vehicle for creation. To 500, I must have been a stranger from Malaysia with a big dream. Yet, in the same way I saw something in them, I am glad they saw something in me—enough to have me work with them to build their platform.

Together, we created multiple market-specific funds across the world. While I started with home, in Southeast Asia, 2,200 companies, 74 countries, and multiple unicorns later, including many non-US unicorns, we have an even more effective platform for creating the kind of prosperity that the Internet economy enables, benefiting many people in many different parts of the world.

Fernandez: Prior to working at 500 Startups, you were a very successful serial entrepreneur. What formative experiences did you have that shaped how you would eventually invest in, mentor, and advise founders at 500 Startups?

Ng: Six years ago, I asked myself the same question. When 500 Startups first asked me to join their fifth accelerator batch as their first entrepreneur-in-residence, I asked, "Why me? Both my exits were in Southeast Asia. What do I have to teach Silicon Valley founders?" I was immediately told three things. One, a large number of founders in Silicon Valley aren't from Silicon Valley. Two, new companies are born and built under resource constraints, and what I have done in the resource constraints in the nascent Southeast Asian ecosystem would be highly relevant. Three, the future of startup success in a global world would benefit from non-US experiences, adding diversity of context and ideas.

Hence, I would attribute one or two formative experiences, but a collage of "random" experiences, some my own and many my portfolio companies share with me. I'd like to think whenever an entrepreneur feels stuck, I would have 50 ideas to help him or her find a way forward!

Fernandez: Can you share any examples of resource constraints that you experienced at your two previous startups that would eventually be formative in helping you quickly coming up with 50 ideas when advising founders faced with a problem?

Ng: The 50 ideas comment is an extension of my personality type as an "ideas" person. I don't think there's an explicit set of experiences from the startup days that would extend into a specific solution to a new startup as every new startup's context is different. The role of the ideas and examples is to stir creativity and see a new way forward!

Fernandez: What were your first one hundred days like at 500 Startups? What was the most challenging part about making the transition from being a founder to being an investor?

Ng: I started with 500 Startups as an entrepreneur-in-residence, which at the time meant that I would be helping portfolio companies as though I was working with them, well, as an entrepreneur. That gave me a chance to be a partner and a peer. I learned a lot from working with these founders. As I eventually wore the investor hat, I never really took off the entrepreneur hat in that sense. I helped Grab hire their first technical employee, wrote and launched their first mobile-responsive landing page, and introduced them to their first institutional investor. While I may not have been as involved in all the companies I invest in, I am always ready to do whatever it takes. In many ways, I feel what my founders feel. And that is very important to have that basis of mutual respect and understanding, especially when investing at the seed stage.

Outside of investing, I spend time building my team, platform, process, and strategy as a managing partner of 500 Startups globally. And that is true company building work. I would like to think I have found the best of both worlds!

Fernandez: Outside of Grab, what other companies have you been plugged into as kind of an on-demand, CXO, and what did you help them?

Ng: For Carousell, I made their first Malaysian hire, Office Space. For Bukalapak, I helped them court and hire their COO. But for many companies, I create platforms for other mentors to help them with growth, B2B sales, and even founder wellness. I'm good at some things but many other people are far better at other things, and 500 provides economies of scale and mentors to engage many of the right people to give help to my founders.

Fernandez: Can you share the story of the first company you invested in at 500 Startups? What was the process like for a founder-turned-investor?

Ng: I can talk about the first set of companies I invested in. That makes more sense to me, as they were all evaluated, reviewed, and invested around the same time. One fell apart in a few months. Two are alive, but still finding their way to an exit. Another was Carousell, now worth US $550 million, Bukalapak, around $3 billion, and Grab, which at this time is worth $15 billion. In many ways, I felt like I did not know what I was doing. I went with a good part of my gut. The same feeling I got when I believed in an idea as an entrepreneur. Oh, and rejecting the many founders on the way to investing in some was much tougher than I thought. I badly wanted to help them. I felt for them. But I had to be clear with them and responsible for the money entrusted to me to invest. In some cases, I would offer advice and connections where relevant, but nothing benefits them more than a clear and fast answer, and feedback why. That way they can move on more quickly.

On another level, I benefited so much from my peers at 500 Startups. I could dig in and research the past deals they've done in other markets. I had a lot of benchmarks and input from them.

Fernandez: Can you share an example of how experience in other countries helped you make an investment into a similar business in another market?

Ng: One of our Mexican investments was in a company called Yaxi. They proved that taxi-booking can be as valuable as "black car" booking, which was Uber and Uber clones at the time. It helped me make the case for the Grab, then called MyTeksi, very quickly.

More importantly it also helps us to see what is a "no." We veered away from some business models because of what was learned about the models in other markets.

Fernandez: What is the toughest part about mentoring and advising founders? How do you make this investor-founder relationship successful?

Ng: I ask myself, how does this get done well, at scale? Assuming that I will be the primary mentor and advisor to founders creates limitations on how effective the firm can be at scale. The benefit of having a large portfolio the way 500 Startups does is that we have the economies of scale to run programs. We have run B2C and B2B growth programs, bringing down legendary talent from the likes of Facebook, YouTube, and Lyft, and in multiple geographies. In Southeast Asia, for example, we have flown in fifty mentors, with eighty-eight companies participating, clocking in over two thousand hours of hands-on growth work! I wasn't involved in mentoring and advising. But the team put together a successful program that did.

We noticed that founder burnout, stress, and depression were a real thing. We sought out experts. We found the Director of Emotional Wellbeing Research at Yale and his partner, a successful life coach. We tried and introduced their programs to founders in Southeast Asia. We got feedback like, "We canceled our divorce after practicing the tools we learned," and "I was cured of my three months of insomnia and now manage my mental health way better," all the way to entire management teams of our founders seeking more coaching. Again, when I embrace my personal limitations, I unlock unlimited potential. This is what I believe 500 to be, not a VC firm, but a VC platform.

Fernandez: Can you delve deeper into this problem, so people can better appreciate your innovative solutions? How have you seen founder burnout, stress, and depression negatively affect both founders and the companies they lead?

Ng: The divorce and insomnia examples are listed below. But across 500's two-thousand+ investments, there have been two founder suicides. That's two too many.

On a basic level:

1. Founders may tend to over-personalize, internalize, and energize issues in business as issues in themselves, or their lives.

2. Tools and tactics to regulate awareness, communication, vulnerability, and strength are very helpful, but are not the first things they ask for. They just spend more time at work.

3. Having a foundation of friends, health, and family gives strength. But it is also the weakest part in most founding journeys with this "all in," "go big or go home," over-glorification of over-working culture.

There is another way. Very rarely is a startup a quick sprint. We're playing the long game here. It is better to have foundations and tools. You'll need them. You don't want to pick them up the hard way. That's what the drive to run these programs is about.

Personally, when I was going through having my entire business wiped out at SAYS.com, from the Facebook URL ban, I had to put up a strong front every day, but I felt broken inside. That takes energy. Even after we created the new business, I felt it may happen again at any time, and I didn't feel secure. The thing is, I still did not talk to my team about it. I only told them much later when I broke down, and they asked me "why didn't you tell us earlier, we all could have doubled down and helped, shared the burden". This is a familiar story that all founders can relate to. And I'm here to say, you don't have to turn your problems into your entire universe. On the contrary, you have a universe of resources and help for you to overcome any problem at all. Anything.

Fernandez: 500 Startups is also like a startup in that you directly and indirectly compete with other VC firms. What did you do to further define or differentiate 500 Startups from other VC firms?

Ng: Many VC firms do the work that I believe in—bringing the prosperity of the Internet economy to more people. That being said, it is easy to keep leaning on doing what had worked in the past, to base future investments to familiar patterns. I had witnessed a VC panel once, where a VC said he would only invest in founders that came from Harvard, Stanford, and so forth, and founders who worked in Apple, Google, and so on. Fair strategy! But that should not be the only strategy. If every VC did that, we would further the wealth divide, and limit the prosperity that tech can bring to people. That may make a VC rich, but rob many of opportunity. This does not mean my strategy is to invest in the most uneducated and inexperienced founders. It just means that I believe that talent and opportunity come in many forms, and it is my job to see through that. I joined 500 Startups because they live those values, too.

So here is how we differentiate. The first is by the diversity of founders we want to invest in, who they are. We are proud to have a good blend of gender identities—especially being a female-led, majority female management firm, with staff of multiple ethnicities, sexual orientation, spiritual beliefs, upbringing, etc. The second is by geography. Aside from investment activity in 74 countries, we were the first Silicon Valley VC in many countries. The third is by problem set. We don't just want to solve for conveniences in cities. We have invested in the rural solutions, space tech, biotech, robotics, health, agriculture, and food. We have partners who develop their own theses of what opportunities are out there, and we pride ourselves in daring to invest in new areas. So far, this has yielded superior financial returns for our funds, as less crowded areas have lower entry valuations. And when we strike it big, we may sometimes be the first and only VC firm in those companies.

Fernandez: When someone doesn't have the rubber stamp of having graduated from the Harvards of the world or worked at the Googles of the world, what heuristics do you use to quickly identify talented founders from different or even unconventional backgrounds?

Ng: I consider things on two levels. First, is what the business needs. Every business may succeed based on industry know-how, relevant experience, or something specific or technical. The next level is personality, attributes, the hustle, the independent thinking, the action bias, the charisma. Both of these levels are independent of school or company.

Fernandez: Can you share the story of a founder with an unconventional background that you backed? How did you find this person, and what impact has their startup made so far?

Ng: So many stories. I will take Bukalapak since they're a well-known company. All of their founders are local graduates. The primary founder, Zaky, did not work in a well-known company. His co-founder, Fajrin, was at BCG for a bit, but Zaky got it going before convincing Fajrin to join. Today, Bukapalak not only helps four million sellers across Indonesia increase income, it extends to offline "warung" operators who are small mom-and-pop stores that procure items and sell top-ups, close to a million of them and many in rural areas. They know and care about local because it is in their DNA.

Fernandez: 500 Startups has its various local arms. What are the challenges of scaling a VC firm globally and securing good deal flow from around the world? How do you overcome these challenges?

Ng: When I first began, I was traveling a lot, often alone. Have you watched the movie The Martian? The one with Matt Damon, where he was stranded on Mars and would only communicate sporadically with NASA's headquarters on Earth. Well, that is how I felt. And that may be how some of my colleagues feel sometimes. How do one hundred fifty people in twenty offices, many who travel often, collaborate and stay connected? This is a question I ask myself often. The times we do get together, we have endless conversations and so much to catch up on. The daily slack channels and video conferencing helps, too. Day-to-day work is largely distributed, autonomous, and led by local entrepreneur-turned-VCs like me. That is the easy part. The harder part is to learn from one another and feed off each other's energy. To celebrate together. Staying close while being distributed is still a work in progress! I call it scalable intimacy.

As for deal flow, we tend to have very good deal flow because of referrals from our existing network, and our visible brand voice. However, when we delve into new geographies and areas, we need to work hard to say, "Yes, we invest in agritech!" or "Here's who we are in your language!"

Fernandez: Some VCs have pointed out that the problem with getting referrals from your existing network is that you will end up with people who more or less resemble your current or past founders. How do you actively find the "hidden gems" who may not currently be part of the tech community, but may prove to be great founders and also contribute to your diversity initiatives?

Ng: When we landed in Jakarta, we worked with a Indonesian angel investor who happened to be a popular actor. We did a press release in the local language and we gave him an email address people could 'spam'. We found some really strong deals where the founders didn't speak English as the first language. This is one of the many things we do to stretch beyond our comfort zones.

Fernandez: 500 Startups is turning eight this year and is now on its twenty-fifth batch of startups. What trends have you noticed, particularly among your Asian startups and founders?

Ng: First, is that our well-known accelerator program in Silicon Valley has become one part of our business. The larger part has become direct seed investing via our many funds. The biggest trend we have noticed along the years is that our Asian founders may not be as interested, relatively speaking, in learning from Silicon Valley. These days, they want to learn from China and India, too. Now they just think bigger in terms of numbers, users—scale, scale, scale.

Once upon a time, innovation was Silicon Valley. Today, innovation is more and more a global story. And this is beautiful.

Fernandez: 500 Startups is a household name for any tech founder in the world. What do you still want the firm to achieve, especially in Asia?

Ng: A film director I admire, Ang Lee, once described his work as "a never-ending dream." When I read that essay, it really moved me—for a few reasons. Firstly, I identify with the creative spirit. I describe it as always flowing—kind of like a life force of growth, renewal, and connectedness. One can even call it love. It feels to me the work I have been involved in ever since I wrote poems on paper, wrote music on a guitar, or wrote code that became websites, or wrote business plans that became companies... I've been connected to this force, this creative spirit. It feels very much like a never-ending dream. That being said, the world can feel like a never-ending nightmare for some. Terrorist attacks are on the rise. Some locales and governments are in the dark about enabling a digital economy. Many super-talented founders are either focusing on the wrong problems or are not being focused on by venture capitalists. The world is full of nightmares that can be turned into dreams.

I would like to see the platform of 500 be of service to a broader audience. Our firm has a separate unit for ecosystem development. We have pioneered VC education courses co-taught with schools like Stanford, Berkeley, and INSEAD. This has sparked the education and even launch of multiple new VCs amongst its hundreds of alumni. Our ecosystems development unit has even been engaged by governments to help wire up their ecosystems. But the world is welcoming of endless opportunities to serve. I would love not just 500, but the larger tech industry to direct its power not just to earn, but to serve. I guess, one can only dream.

Fernandez: Can you go into more depth about ecosystem development? How is building a tech ecosystem in a particular market similar to and different from growing a startup or a VC platform like 500 Startups? What exactly is your involvement in this unit?

Ng: I am not involved here. Our ecosystems unit runs our education business, where we've created courses to teach VC and accelerator management with Stanford, UC Berkeley, and INSEAD. We graduated 500+ candidates from 60 countries. We have a government's business there that has helped multiple cities and government kick-start angel investment, accelerators, etc. We also do similar things with huge corporations. It's a very different business from the investing side, which 500 is known for.

In the early days in SE Asia, we collaborated with corporations and governments to run many programs, on top of investing, to kick-start the ecosystem. There are many regions in the world which are not like SE Asia, and they are prime places for ecosystem development work.

Fernandez: Now that you have seen both sides of the coin as an entrepreneur and an investor, what would you say is the essential component of any successful startup?

Ng: In the beginning, it is the founders. As the startup grows, it is the culture, the tribal norm that is set by the founders. The coding and encoding of a culture can be not-too-different from writing software. There are if-then statements, rules, and processes that repeat. If wired up well, companies can be a force of change, be adaptable, and true to their mission. If the coding isn't clear and robust, but instead messy, it is easy for a company to falter, or be led astray, especially by the shareholders who creep up in ownership. What may have started as a mission-driven firm may end up maximizing profits at the expense of others, as many firms do.

We are entering an era of truly mission-driven companies. I have seen high leverage founders who run companies who are successful enough to choose their investors, and stay in control of the mission. These are the companies that will continue to change the world for the better.

Fernandez: Assuming every successful startup founder has these qualities, what would you say separates the average successful founding team from those who go on to be truly transcendent in their particular space, such as the unicorns you have backed?

Ng: Sometimes high-quality founders just aren't enough. There are market and timing considerations, too.

Fernandez: What final words of advice would you like to offer the founders who will read this book, many of whom dream of one day having the backing of 500 Startups?

Ng: As this book is being published, the barriers to building winning companies, getting access to capital, advice, and talent will continue to decrease. Creating companies and building a scalable company will be the easier part. How does one do that and be in good mental and physical health? How does one be kind to people? Grow and preserve service to family and friends? Lend a helping hand to folks outside your industry or value chain? Give back?

Being solely achievement focused and wealth focused is pretty passé. I urge founders to be good humans. Look at your companies as vehicles of creation and service. Look for a broader set of people to care for and a broader set of problems to solve.

Fernandez: How do you keep founders from focusing on wealth or the "exit"? As you point out, tech innovation is one way to bridge the wealth divide, but focusing solely on that may be counterproductive. In the same way that you have life coaching, do you find that you also have to coach founders to not be money- or exit-focused?

Ng: Keeping folks from focusing on wealth is absolutely not the point. The idea is expanding the sphere of compassion to be caring of employees, vendors, suppliers, customers, your own friends and families, and maybe other stakeholders. And for the mission-driven ones, *all this is good business. You will make even more money just by being good.* It is not one or the other. People too often get that wrong. We have to delete that idea. Delete, delete, delete. We do both. We make money and do good things. We make even more money by doing even more good things. Real examples in our portfolio include kitabisa.com which crowdfunds for personal causes and charity. Millions of dollars a month go to uplifting people and lives! Outside of our portfolio,

Impossible Foods attacks climate change by giving an alternative to beef consumption—cow farting and cow feeding are some of the largest environmental hazards. Over time, I believe more companies focused on mission and impact will rule, and all of the other companies will also be more mission and impact oriented.

Fernandez: What are the biggest trends to look out for?

Ng: Many times, we think of the future of humankind in terms of technology. Technology and economy aside, there are bigger questions and macro trends to not lose sight of. For example, not too long ago, concepts such as human rights were not the norm. In fact, in some places, disgusting concepts like mass killings or slavery were norms. It still exists in this day and age. So, what norms will be changing in this generation? Our shared consciousness is already becoming acutely aware of gender and racial biases. What's next to evolve? Will slavery and mass killing of "non-cute" animals—chickens, pigs, cows— become the next concept to be disgusting? Will the sole pursuit for economic power give way to the pursuit of service to others? Or will things get worse before they get better? Will the rise of multiple superpowers in the world be breeding grounds for terrorism?

We think of being "founders" in terms of the companies we will build. Yes, we are in an age where the economy is the primary conversation, and money talks. Yet, previous generations had religion, warfare, or survival to be the primary conversation. Not the economy. So if not the economy, what will be the next in this tapestry of time?

I think it is important to ask non-technology questions and to tune in to the evolution and direction of cultural norms. I think it is not to get over-identified as founders, or VCs, or "tech people." We are all humans, after all, only conscious in this form, in this short blip of time. Let's at least remember that. And hopefully, make this experience uplifting for each other.

Royston Tay

Founder, Zopim

Royston Tay *co-founded Zopim in Singapore in 2007 with Wenxiang Wu, Yang Bin Kwok, Qing Ru Lim, and Julian Low, who all met while studying abroad at Stanford University through the National University of Singapore Overseas College program.*

Having caught the entrepreneurial bug, they worked on several ideas before settling on their most promising one, Zopim, a Live Chat product for the many small businesses just coming online. After graduating, they lived a Spartan lifestyle for more than two years, subsisting on US $410 per month as they tried to develop the product. When the co-founders decided to switch to a freemium model, they were surprised by how many of their existing customers converted to the paid product. Within a few years, Zopim was used by 120,000 websites in over 100 countries.

In April of 2014, Zendesk acquired Zopim for US $29.8 million, partially in cash and the rest in common stock. Tay was absorbed into Zendesk as general manager of Chat, and Zendesk had an initial public offering on the New York Stock Exchange just one month after the acquisition in May of 2014. Tay worked at Zendesk for more than three years before leaving in late 2017. Today, he's an active angel investor and startup mentor in the Southeast Asia startup scene.

© Ezra Ferraz, Gracy Fernandez 2020
E. Ferraz and G. Fernandez, *Asian Founders at Work*,
https://doi.org/10.1007/978-1-4842-5162-1_4

Gracy Fernandez: You happened to meet your co-founders during the NUS Overseas College Program. What formative experiences did you have together while abroad that would later inform your thinking around Zopim?

Royston Tay: The NUS Overseas Colleges [NOC] program has created a steady stream of entrepreneurs who went on to create household names, like Carousell, Shopback, 99.co, and MoneySmart. It's no exaggeration to say this program changed all our life trajectories from ordinary undergraduates to passionate, determined entrepreneurs.

Zopim's story is no different. Before NOC, I was en route to graduating with honors in engineering, before joining my friends in engineering or consulting jobs. In 2005, I was accepted into NOC and headed out to Silicon Valley for a year. It started off badly. I interned at a decent startup, but my job as QA engineer was dead boring. I did get really good at playing ping-pong. I signed up for extra classes at Stanford, which I was neither hard-working nor clever enough to excel in.

But there was this other group of NOC students who barely talked about work or school. Every night, instead of heading home, they were out there attending events and meetups, and networking, organizing, pitching their startup ideas, and *pretending* to be startup founders. "That's better than pretending to be a QA engineer," I thought.

I joined the group's leadership team. Everyone got fancy titles. I was the VP of Mentorship. Armed with our fancy personas, we hosted events and meetups where established founders or early employees of red-hot startups like Facebook and YouTube shared their experiences with us wannabe entrepreneurs. It was intoxicating to finally feel part of the hallowed scene.

NOC also gifted me my co-founders, who were already brilliant coders and hustlers. I was the least accomplished of the lot. Somehow we clicked and spent weekends dreaming up ideas and developing prototypes. We would pitch them and invariably get shot down. Upon returning to Singapore, it seemed natural that we would continue doing that together. Of all the mostly crappy ideas we had, only one didn't get shot down as much. That was how Zopim started.

On reflection, one lesson stood out—entrepreneurs aren't made overnight. Unlike many other professions, there isn't a career ladder leading there. Especially for young inexperienced founders, pretending to be an entrepreneur while finishing up a degree, or working a second job to keep the lights on is a necessary rite of passage. It's tiring, exhausting, and demoralizing to have ideas and prototypes ridiculed by others. But if you can't stomach that, or somehow see the sadistic thrill of it, you won't be able to embrace all the crazier challenges that comes after.

Fernandez: Can you share the experience of doing a literal "elevator pitch" to famed venture capitalist Tim Draper?

Tay: Tim happened to be in Singapore, and someone organized a closed-door pitching session for him. We weren't cool enough to be invited, but we were shameless enough to show up. He was larger than life, living up to his reputation by breaking out into an impromptu rendition of a song he wrote for startups. Thankfully, he's much better at his actual day job as a VC.

The pitch was in a speed-dating format, a handful of entrepreneurs had about five minutes to pitch their ideas to him before another group was rotated in. It was Tinder on steroids, if he liked the idea, we could follow up for the next date. There were two of us at that event—Wenxiang, one of my co-founders, and me. We had several ideas at that point, so to maximize our chances, he pitched Zopim, and I pitched something else. I don't recall Tim listening much to the other pitches, but he really liked Zopim and wanted to see our prototype. We had written exactly zero lines of code at that point but confidently promised to show him something "soon." A couple of emails later with his PA, our second date was set two months later.

Fernandez: How did you and your co-founders manage to build a prototype in as little as two months? What did Zopim look like at this time? What features did it have, and which did it lack?

Tay: Right from day one, we wanted Zopim to be an easy way for anyone with a website to easily chat with customers on it. "Why would you not want to chat with every hot lead?" was the thinking.

It wasn't a new idea. "Live chat" had been around for a while, but it was very expensive and complicated to set up. Only Fortune 500 companies with large IT and support teams could afford to use it. Riding on the wave of emerging web technologies at that time, we believed two radical improvements would disrupt the industry, making "live chat" available to all.

Firstly, we believed it was possible to build a chat widget that anyone with no coding knowledge could install on any website. Secondly, it was possible to build a fully web-based chat application, so businesses no longer had to download any software. They could chat with customers on any computer with a web browser.

Today, these are industry standards, but back in 2007, these were big technical challenges. A good chunk of the two months went into deep research, showing up for end-of-semester exams and general procrastination.

Two weeks before, we finally holed ourselves in a dark dingy room to code day and night. Being engineers, our first eureka! moment was when we finally managed to send the first message from our experimental widget to our experimental web application, and back.

We had cracked huge technical challenges under the hood, but other than that, Zopim had none of the features that eventually made it commercially successful. It was also ugly as hell. We spent our last few days frantically slapping lipstick on the proverbial pig, coding up till minutes before our second date with Tim. Junliang—another co-founder, who was still in Silicon Valley—was waiting outside Tim's office when we finally released the demo to him.

Needless to say, we bombed it. Tim politely spent fifteen minutes with us and said, "Come back when you have more traction."

Fernandez: So many tech entrepreneurs choose to drop out of school once they get their winning idea. Why did you choose to work on Zopim while still pursuing your undergraduate degree?

Tay: Dropping out of school to start a company is a very Western concept. Since this book is Asian Founders at Work, we should advocate "Asian" standards—graduate with honors and build successful companies!

On a serious note though, the startup incubation arm of our university, NUS Enterprise, was very supportive. We were literally full-time entrepreneurs without having to drop out. We had free office space on the college campus, courtesy of NUS Enterprise. We spent almost all of our waking hours at work, skipping most lectures and doing the absolute bare minimum to graduate.

More importantly, we avoided having to explain to our families what we were doing. In their eyes, we were still students going to school, not unemployed bums trying to do this "startup thing." Startups weren't so cool back then.

Fernandez: Even if you did not end up raising from Tim Draper early on, you ended up getting investment from the iJam grant. What are the advantages of raising grants early on as opposed to seed funding from angel investors?

Tay: Let's be honest, we weren't exactly picky about funding. Back then, Southeast Asia had virtually no investment scene. There were few startups and even fewer investors. It was the classical chicken-or-the-egg problem. In the decade since, Singapore did fantastically well to engineer a vibrant startup ecosystem.

Early on, the government had to artificially stimulate startup growth using grants and matching investments. The timing was perfect for us. We became the second startup to receive the iJam grant.

Raising grants came with challenges. The grant sizes were small, which meant we had a shorter runway to achieve lift-off. We turned that to our advantage by instilling a culture of frugality, which lasted all the way past profitability and even after our acquisition.

Without raising venture money, we were also in full control of our company and had little dilution. When Zendesk acquired us, almost ninety-five percent of the proceeds went directly to the founders and employees, giving most of our early employees a deservedly lucrative payday.

Even though we had a good outcome, grants are no longer critical stimulants today. Our startup ecosystem is attracting great founders and a glut of investors. With market forces effectively picking out winning ideas and teams, ambitious startup founders should pit themselves against the best in the capitalist arena instead of relying on grants. But, should the music stop and venture funding becomes harder to come by, I hope Zopim's story will remind entrepreneurs that bootstrapping to sustainable fast growth and profitability is still very possible.

Fernandez: You and your co-founders famously lived off an allowance of around SG$500 for two years. What were the lifestyle sacrifices you had to make in order to live on this shoestring budget?

Tay: I'm an advocate for starting up young. One of the reasons is that we didn't need much and the opportunity cost of starting a business was low. In plain English, we didn't have lucrative jobs to walk away from, and we hadn't acquired a taste for the "high life."

Like many Asian families, all of us were living with our parents, who graciously continued housing and feeding us. Being comfortably middle class, we weren't expected to put bread on the table yet. Five hundred dollars was just enough for a bunch of fresh college graduates who spent all our waking hours in a free office, eating cheap meals on a college campus.

Acquiring a social life was tricky, especially if we wanted to meet up with non-startup friends. Understandably for them, having been cooped up in office for the week, and having disposable income for the first time, weekends meant loosening the purse strings and enjoying life. Those were perks we couldn't afford. We couldn't travel far for holidays. We couldn't plan for marriage, housing, much less kids. We never had more than a thousand dollars in our savings account. Watching peers and even younger friends zoom past us in living standards wasn't easy.

But I don't want to make it sound tougher than it was, because it really wasn't terrible. We surrounded ourselves with startup friends who were in the same predicament. We became awesome at throwing low-budget, high-fun parties. Knowing how poor we were, our incubator, NUS Enterprise, often hosted events for entrepreneurs with free booze and food. This camaraderie and sense of purpose in what we were doing everyday more than made up for the perceived struggles of being poor. I still look back at those days with a lot of fondness.

Fernandez: At some point, you gave your co-founders an ultimatum about their commitment. Can you share what led up to that moment, and how it went?

Tay: More than a year after meeting Tim Draper, our product had launched into free beta, but with less than a hundred active users. In the meantime, most of our startup friends had cracked major monetization or funding milestones.

The engineer in me was still excited about coming to work to develop features and improvements for a growing customer base. But the entrepreneur in me couldn't ignore the reality that we were a slow moving train wreck. Given we were targeting small and medium-sized businesses [SMBs], we needed hundreds of paying customers to barely break even. At this rate, we would run out of cash long before we got there.

As a coping mechanism, we desperately ploughed longer hours into work. One founder even moved into office with all his worldly belongings so he could work at night. In the morning, employees would tiptoe into an office that resembled the stinky living room of a mad scientist, which isn't so far from the truth. Work started to feel laborious and highly inefficient. We had voluntarily stopped taking salary to stretch our runway and keep employees. "This isn't fun anymore," was probably how we all felt. One of us had to say it, but only we as a team could fix it.

I gathered all the founders in a quiet meeting room and shared my sentiments. I was planning to leave in one month unless we figured out, and committed to a plan that could get us to the next level.

I never came close to following through. The founders responded amazingly. We decided to roll our final dice of designing, developing, and launching pricing with our remaining short runway, something we've procrastinated for years. We also needed to spruce up the working environment. Evicting our live-in founder and all his worldly belongings would take too long. We needed a temporary, free co-working space that had AC, coffee, hot desks, and blazing-fast Internet. NUS Enterprise swooped to our rescue once again. Or rather, we swooped into the open meeting area outside their administrative offices, squatting there for months, often first in, last to leave in our mad race to the finishing line. Not only that, they helped us extend our runway with a bridge loan to tide us through a few tough months. Something we're eternally grateful for.

In retrospect, one downside of not taking venture capital was not having someone to kick our asses when we needed it, to hold us accountable to key milestones. Without "adult supervision," we had to find ways to manufacture a collective sense of urgency. "Ultimatums" aren't sustainable, thankfully we eventually became great at keeping ourselves accountable without resorting to it.

Fernandez: After building your prototype and fundraising, what further changes did you make to the product to introduce it to actual customers?

Tay: As newcomers, we knew we were a decade late to building enterprise features that allowed massive customer support teams to work efficiently. Instead we focused our attention on the wave of small businesses starting to sell online. Our barebones prototype already made setting up and using live chat easy, which was better than expensive alternatives. So we very quickly launched our free beta, thinking users would give us feature suggestions in return for free usage.

Over time, the growing pool of beta users pushed us to invent features no one had thought of. For instance, many of them used Zopim to chat with customers while fulfilling other duties. Logging into our app was too troublesome. We found ways to send messages to their favorite messaging apps and let them chat with customers without even logging into Zopim. Back then, it was Gtalk, MSN, Yahoo!, Skype—the ancient predecessors of today's WhatsApp, WeChat, Slack.

Eventually, these features snowballed to make our official pricing launch a successful one.

Fernandez: You have stated that its Zopim's customer-centricity that has allowed it to succeed. How exactly was the company customer-centric in its earliest days?

Tay: Customer-centricity means putting customers at the heart of business decisions. This might be easy to forget in larger enterprises where employees are far removed from customers. But startups rarely have this problem, they are either customer-centric or they die.

Like many startups, we did things that didn't scale in the early days, as long as it kept customers happy and gave us a better understanding of their needs. It helped that our software was designed for that. In the early days, we stalked every customer on our website to chat with them and solicit feedback. We were so enthusiastic they often thought we were bots. Sometimes, their bug reports or feature suggestions seemed so important that we'd implement them on the spot and push it out while chatting with them. Later on, even though we hired a dedicated support team to handle questions, we made sure everyone in the team continued serving customers at least one hour a week, bearing the full intensity of customer complaints in real-time. No better way to build empathy!

What set us apart from many startups was that many SMBs used Zopim as their first customer support software. Therefore, we also had the opportunity to introduce new standards for customer-centricity via our software design. For instance, we made our chat widgets prominent and welcoming. Customers on a website could start chatting with live agents within one click, instead of being inundated with prequalifying questions designed to scare users away. Our customers loved this.

We also encouraged our team to adopt a slightly irreverent style of conducting customer service through live chat, mixing in messaging lingo and emoticons, while staying responsive and professional about the task at hand. That allowed us to establish an instant friendly rapport with customers in ways that wasn't possible through email or phone support.

Today, this emphasis on making it easy for customers to get help, either via self-service, automation or through a friendly and personable human agent has become the standard.

Fernandez: You were tasked with creating the business dashboards for Zopim. Did any of the metrics that business leaders wanted to see surprise you, and why?

Tay: To understand the metrics that our "business leaders" look at, it's necessary to take a short detour. Zopim was unlike other Enterprise startups of that era. We didn't build a sales or marketing team until we were comfortably profitable. Our early growth engine revolved around virality. That is, we achieved exciting growth numbers while spending zero dollars on marketing and sales.

From the start, we wanted Zopim to be a great product for SMBs at a free or low price point, so any business that needed live chat would choose Zopim without a second thought. In return for this fantastic deal, we insisted on keeping the "Zopim" branding on the chat widget, with little exceptions. This meant every time we signed new customers, they were effectively advertising for us to users and competitors on their websites. When we say our product sells itself, we truly mean it.

Given this backdrop, we weren't fixated on Monthly Recurring Revenues numbers like other Software-as-a-Service companies. It was important, but still a by-product of our viral funnel improving over time, which were the numbers we examined closely. For example, an unusual metric we tracked was the "rate of referral" from our widget to our website. Another metric that our product managers insisted we constantly improve was the Net Promoter Score, which measured how satisfied customers were with our product.

It's no coincidence that customer-centric companies look at similar metrics. The difference is how we see these numbers translate directly to revenue growth.

Fernandez: Once you introduced the paid subscription, why were you surprised that adoption of Zopim was higher than it was when it was a completely free product?

Tay: It's common sense that the cheaper a product, the more likely customers would afford it. Nothing is cheaper than free, therefore if customer adoption was low while Zopim was free, it would be disastrous to launch pricing. This was our naive thinking for two years.

Turns out this thinking applied mostly to consumer-products. Businesses on the other hand valued reliability and quality. First impression matters when they evaluated products. A "free beta" didn't inspire a whole lot of confidence. Prospective customers were worried we might lock them into an expensive pricing once they started using us. Or worse still, terminate their service when we ran out of money.

Over the years, we've learned to think about pricing as a feature of our product. As with developing product features, we put in as much love into designing an elegantly simple pricing plan which extracts a fair value from the smallest to the largest customer.

After repricing Zopim a few times since, this initial surprise has given way to quiet confidence in our ability to deliver great value even at higher prices.

Today, there are already plenty of pricing blog posts guiding entrepreneurs on key pricing considerations. Our personal revelation was that even with a ton of pricing research and surveys, the only way to learn with certainty is to actually roll out pricing changes. In a fast growth startup, newly minted features and evolving buyer profiles mean pricing plans and price points have to be tweaked every so often. A healthy SaaS startup should review their pricing every two years at least. Just be responsible to old customers by "grandfathering" them appropriately.

Fernandez: You initially turned down another acquisition offer prior to the Zendesk deal. Why did you decide against the deal?

Tay: We never ran Zopim thinking of any particular exit strategy. We believed as long as we ran the business well and customers loved us, opportunities would come along. True enough, over the years, we received several offers.

There was one offer that stood out. It was from an 800-pound gorilla in our space. I was at an event where their founding CEO was speaking. He is a pioneer in our industry and still someone I highly respect today. As he was leaving, I went up to introduce myself. To my surprise, he's heard about us and had wanted to reach out. We quickly found ourselves bonding over drinks, which led to talks of a potential acquisition.

Despite our mutual respect, there were several reasons it didn't work out. Valuation was one, but the fundamental reason was that he didn't believe our self-service business model of winning customers would scale. He predicted we would hit a sales plateau in a year and be forced to compete with his company for enterprise deals, involving expensive marketing and sales teams.

We respectfully declined his offer and proceeded to blow past his "plateau" several times over. Today, enterprise companies like Zendesk, Atlassian, Zoom, and Slack have proven that it's possible to build highly efficient sales and marketing operations around the same product-centric, self-service approach that we were built upon.

Fernandez: How did the potential acquisition by Zendesk present itself? What was the discussion like with you and the co-founders when choosing whether to push through with this deal?

Tay: To give some background, Zendesk's first product was a highly popular help-desk software. It wasn't a new product category, but they were growing phenomenally because of their "beautifully simple" product philosophy and self-service business model, an approach that resonated with us. Some of the hottest tech companies back then like Twitter were using them for customer service. We were also customers and had always admired or stole liberally their UX design patterns.

One day, I received an email from a Zendesk email address. Two of their senior executives wanted to fly to Singapore to meet us. There wasn't a stated agenda. I replied, "Yeah, sure," and within two weeks, we were hosting them in our cozy little office.

They quickly made their intentions clear. They viewed live chat as a fast-growing, highly complementary space to theirs. They tried building their own chat product, but it was so shitty—their words—that their salespeople often recommended other products. Zopim was one of the top names. What did we think of being part of Zendesk?

As a marriage of two product categories, it was a match made in heaven. Live chat was indeed fast-growing, but a tiny industry compared to help desk. We had many joint customers, and our integration feature with Zendesk was hugely popular. In our own business plans, we forecasted having to enter the help-desk industry to compete with Zendesk at some point in the future. Two market-leading brands working together would certainly shake up the space. We didn't discuss valuation at the first meeting, but I remembered looking at their cash balance thinking they'd never be able to afford us. I left the door open and said we were happy to explore it only if the offer made sense. In the meantime, we had a thriving business to run.

A few months passed before they reached out again. This time to invite us to meet their entire senior management team in San Francisco. Everything checked out. We passed each other's "beer buddies" test. We sat down with their VPs across many departments and shared best practices. A lot of mutual admiration was built up over this intense short period. There was still the problem of valuation.

Their cash position hadn't changed much, but something else had tilted the equation significantly. They revealed they had filed privately to go public on the NYSE. If everything went according to plan, their shares would soon be tradeable, making a part-cash, part-stock acquisition more attractive. It also introduced a lot of uncertainties into the negotiations. Suddenly, we had to put on our banker hats and decide for ourselves if the valuation of their shares made sense. The tables were turned one afternoon when their CFO pitched us like investors, running us through their numbers to convince us that their valuation was fair.

Even though the deal was worth a widely reported US $30 million, which fell short of what we had in mind, we were bullish that after IPO, Zendesk would continue growing, and the value of the deal would increase if we held on to the shares. This leap of faith was thankfully justified with their shares today worth many times what their CFO pitched to us.

We flew back to Singapore with the term sheet in hand, but it was only the start of an intense three months of negotiations, due diligence, and flipping back and forth on whether to follow through with the deal or not. The dilemma was obvious. We were on a good growth trajectory, and so staying independent was a great option. On the other hand, being part of a fast-growing company allowed us to be more aggressive in our growth plans without worrying about funding and other execution risks.

Two months in, with Zendesk growing weary of our indecision, we locked ourselves in a hotel room, resolving to only leave the room with a unanimous decision on taking or rejecting the deal. Nine hours later, we emerged from the room bleary-eyed but with a decision. I think what tipped us over was that being part of Zendesk would shorten our learning curve as entrepreneurs scaling a company. Our employees would have the opportunity to learn from some of the best minds in Silicon Valley as well.

Fernandez: So many founders dream of an "exit" that is often a literal one— they leave the company they founded with significant cash or stocks. Why did you and your co-founders prefer to stay on post-acquisition for such a long period?

Tay: That's the impression many non-startup friends had as well. "Why are you still working? Why aren't you sipping martinis in the Bahamas?"

People in the tech scene usually know an acquisition often requires founders to stay on a few years to properly integrate their products, employees, and processes into the parent company. The acquirer often paid up part of the acquisition proceeds over a few years. If we left early, we would be leaving money on the table. It's aptly known as "golden handcuffs" in our industry. For us, it was three years.

Beyond the monetary aspect, because we had such a tight-knit team in Zopim, the founders took it upon ourselves to ensure we stayed to lead everyone through the tough process of melding our strong product identities and culture with Zendesk's.

Fernandez: What was the most challenging part about adjusting to the newly merged companies post-acquisition?

Tay: We definitely underestimated the challenge of integration. If we had done our research, we'd have known most M&As fail by default. The first few years was the toughest period for the founders. We gave ourselves a lot of pressure to sustain Zopim's growth rate, while at the same time integrating our employees and products. It was two full-time jobs squeezed into a day. In the early days, it was common for us to attend conference calls in the wee hours, followed by a full day at work. We often reflect that we've never worked ourselves so hard before, even compared to our founding days.

With hindsight, it's obvious that we didn't have mid-level managers who could "tango" with Zendesk's managers on important decisions. We had great employees, but they weren't adept at building relationships, understanding a wider array of stakeholders and power structures, negotiating compromises and acquiring resources. They were builders not managers.

Ultimately, this power vacuum created an us-versus-them mentality, which often required a founder's involvement to find a compromise. That was often me, since I headed up product development, marketing and sales. If I could do this all over, I would have hired senior managers to run those departments much earlier, reporting to me so I'd still have final oversight over decisions. Since then, I've seen how great managers triage problems, find elegant solutions to complex challenges, and enable rank-and-file employees to focus on doing the things they love.

Today, despite the hiccups at the beginning, through lots of goodwill and sheer will from both Zendesk's and our team, the acquisition is undoubtedly a resounding success story in the landscape of M&As.

Fernandez: Culturally, what did you make it a point to keep, continue, or maintain at Zendesk from Zopim, post-acquisition?

Tay: We were a younger team, so we made it a point to keep the environment cozy, casual, and fun. This meant allowing employees to continue coming to work in shorts, flip flops, or walk around bare-foot if they wanted to. Other than that, our employees shared a close transparent relationship with the founders. We tried to build this up over time with the rest of Zendesk leadership. Whenever senior executives flew over, there would be intimate, no-holds-barred town halls. The Q&A often threw up unfiltered awkward questions which were gamely answered by the leaders.

Fernandez: Were there any challenges in consolidating Zopim—the brand that you had spent years building—into the Zendesk mother company?

Being a close-knit company, we had developed our branding and mascot not just to appeal to customers, but also to represent us. Not surprisingly, it was emotional for employees to let go of this identity, even though we shared plans to merge the brands very early on.

It helped that we were able to keep the brand for almost two years before rebranding Zopim as Zendesk Chat. By then, we were mentally prepared. Not only that, our branding teams also did a fantastic job of rebranding Zendesk from a monolithic product brand to a brand capable of supporting multiple products. This meant that Zendesk also retired their own beloved branding and mascot that served them well for almost a decade. We were in this together.

Rebrands are often on the receiving end of vitriol and hate from customers, but Zendesk's was a resounding success. The design team deservedly won an award in 2016 for this rebrand.

Fernandez: What was the most surprising part you experienced in preparing Zendesk for IPO?

Tay: The preparation for acquisition and IPO happened simultaneously. Zendesk listed very shortly after our acquisition went through. So my job was to make sure we didn't mess up the IPO inadvertently. For a scrappy startup running out of Singapore to suddenly be ready for an American IPO from the financial and legal perspective was crazy already. And this was on top of the intense negotiation over acquisition.

We had lots of professional help of course, but I remember there was a never-ending checklist of things we had to complete. One example stuck out. Before the acquisition, our self-service model had won us customers from all corners of the world, which included a tiny handful of customers from a country sanctioned by the US. Even though it was inadvertent, it put us in serious breach. We had to quickly terminate those accounts in advance of the acquisition and gently nudge them towards other solutions. Zendesk's legal team got reprimanded sternly on our behalf and we were often teasingly reminded of it.

All in all, it was well worth it. For not messing up the IPO, I got to represent Singapore and Zopim on the NYSE podium. I also introduced Wall Street to the new Asian phenomenon then—the selfie stick!

Fernandez: Now that our communication is splintering across multiple mediums like social media, chat, and other platforms, what role do you see Zendesk having in this environment?

Tay: Consumer behavior changes all the time and businesses are always trying to engage customers on their favorite media. To always be at the bleeding edge, we assign small teams to work closely with customers to co-develop new products based on these emerging behaviors. For instance, to help businesses chat with customers on multiple social media and messaging platforms, I led a small team in Singapore to experiment with a product called Zendesk Message. Some of these products eventually fail, some take off, some are merged with existing products, but we always learn a great deal being on the frontline.

What doesn't change is that as businesses grow, they need a centralized set of customer records that captures the entire history of every customers' interactions, regardless of where it happened. They also need a robust engine that automates interactions where possible, and hands customers to the right employees at the right time via the most appropriate media. At the core, this is what Zendesk provides across our multiple products.

Fernandez: Beyond using Zendesk of course, what advice do you have for founders in Asia on becoming more "customer centric"?

Tay: As mentioned earlier, in the early years of a startup, founders naturally spend a lot of time with customers to develop product-market fit. Customer-centricity is rarely a problem. Beyond a certain size though, day-to-day management, meetings with ever-growing groups of stakeholders and fire-fighting tend to consume founders or CEOs. Customer face-time decreases as good hires take up sales, product and support managerial roles. This is natural, but if left uncalibrated, it's easy for customer face-time to slip down to zero for founders.

In Zendesk, one of the founders used to keep reminding everyone that every time we huddled inwards for internal meetings, our asses were facing customers. True to our values, the founders and senior executives often lead by example by scheduling time for customer visits, especially when they travel beyond our San Francisco headquarters. At town halls, they often reflected on what they've learnt on such visits to encourage employees never to stray too far away from the people footing our bills every month. Nothing beats leading by example.

Fernandez: What unconventional advice do you have for startups who want to build an organization as successful as Zopim?

Tay: Especially for founding CEOs, my unconventional advice would be find time to be "bored." For most people, it feels great to develop an expertise in one particular field, subsequently immersing themselves in work that they're good at and enjoy. Personally, once I catch myself slipping into this "state of flow," it often means I've figured out the work enough to hire someone to replace me.

It's scary to not have my scheduled filled all the time, but it gives me time to think and be curious about challenges happening elsewhere in the company, in the industry, in the world. Quite often, this led me to clear-headed decisions on what our company and I needed to focus on next.

It's no surprise that many high-powered executives set time aside for down-time and meditation. Steve Jobs himself said, "Boredom allows one to indulge in curiosity, and out of curiosity comes everything."

Chatri Sityodtong

Founder, Chairman, and CEO, ONE Championship

Chatri Sityodtong, *an MBA graduate from Harvard Business School (USA), founded ONE Championship in Singapore in 2011 after a successful career on Wall Street. He returned to Asia to launch ONE Championship because he wanted to unite the region by creating Asia's first global sports media property to celebrate Asia's greatest cultural treasure, martial arts.*

A lifelong martial artist with over 35 years of experience as a student, fighter, teacher, and coach, Sityodtong leveraged his deep martial arts experience into Asia's largest sports media property with over 100 events to date across Asia, including Tokyo, Singapore, Dubai, Manila, Jakarta, Bangkok, Taipei, Kuala Lumpur, and Beijing.

Sityodtong managed to raise institutional capital from some of the world's most renowned investors in tech and media, including Sequoia Capital, Temasek Capital, and Greenoaks Capital. With over US $275 million in funding today, ONE Championship is one of Asia's hottest unicorns with plans to become a US $100 billion company in the future.

Ezra Ferraz: Most people don't necessarily associate Wall Street with entrepreneurship. What did you learn on Wall Street that would later serve you well as a founder?

© Ezra Ferraz, Gracy Fernandez 2020
E. Ferraz and G. Fernandez, *Asian Founders at Work*,
https://doi.org/10.1007/978-1-4842-5162-1_5

Chatri Sityodtong: Wall Street taught me a lot about leadership, capital allocation, business models, capital markets, and much more. Of course, I also learned a lot when I launched my US $500 million global hedge fund. That being said, I would say my foundation as an entrepreneur started when I launched my first startup in Silicon Valley at 27 years old. For the vast majority of my business career, I have been an entrepreneur, making ONE Championship a natural step in terms of size and scale of opportunity.

Ferraz: Can you perhaps share a story of a purpose-driven entrepreneur you met while still working on Wall Street?

Sityodtong: I would say that the entrepreneurs that I admire most have remained quite consistent, whether it is Richard Branson, Steve Jobs, Jeff Bezos, or Elon Musk. I admire different things about different entrepreneurs. However, I identify most with purpose-driven founders like Steve Jobs and Elon Musk. For me, success is intrinsic to what it is that ignites our souls. Ultimately, a true entrepreneur seeks to make a positive impact on the world.

Ferraz: What was the exact light-bulb moment when you learned that you wanted to create ONE Championship?

Sityodtong: I wouldn't call it a light bulb moment per se, but it was something that had been building up for a while.

I owned a US $500 million global hedge fund when I decided to retire at 37 years old. On paper, I was on top of the world. I had everything in life and more. Inside though, something was missing in my soul. No one knew it, but I knew it. All the money and material things in the world could never fill that void. I was not living my definition of success. I was living society's definition. It was painful to admit, but I had climbed to the top of the wrong mountain. I remember vividly how scared I was to walk away from the life that I knew in order to chase something that I truly loved. My family and friends told me that I was stupid and crazy. My mom tried to dissuade me by reminding me of the days my family and I lived in poverty. She told me not to take my success for granted.

In life, we don't choose what we love. The heart wants what the heart wants.

Martial arts has been my greatest passion in life since I was a kid. I've been a part of martial arts as a student, a fighter, a teacher, and a coach for almost 30 years. It changed my life in so many ways. It gave me courage, strength, discipline, humility, work ethic, and so much more. Above all, it gave me a warrior spirit to conquer adversity and a desire for continuous self-improvement. Without a doubt, I owe a lot of my success in life to martial arts. While I am still involved in other businesses today, there is no question what lights up my soul.

Martial arts is what I love. Martial arts is who I am.

If there is one thing that I can share from my journey, it is that the world has it wrong. Success does not create happiness. Happiness creates success. Do what it is that ignites your soul. If you love what you do, it will emanate in everything you do. Happiness is your reward. And success will inevitably follow. Ultimately, I'd rather be a failure at something I love than be a success at something I hate.

I feel blessed that ONE Championship is now Asia's largest global sports media property with a global broadcast to over 145 countries. Even though it has only been eight years since I started ONE Championship, it feels like a lifetime of blood, sweat, and tears.

Ferraz: Why did you feel it was important to unite Asia with a martial arts sports league like ONE Championship?

Sityodtong: Asia had never had a multibillion dollar sports media property before ONE Championship. As an Asian, I wanted to unleash real-life superheroes who inspired the world to dream more, do more, and be more in life.

Of course, as a lifelong martial artist, I wanted to celebrate Asia's greatest cultural treasure and the deep-rooted values of integrity, humility, honor, respect, courage, discipline, and compassion with the world. Asia has been the home of martial arts for over 5,000 years, and I want to showcase the beauty of authentic martial arts.

Ferraz: Why do you believe martial arts is one of the biggest achievements of Asian culture?

Sityodtong: Asia has been the home of martial arts for over 5,000 years, and there is a homegrown martial art in almost every country in Asia that is a part of society, culture, history, and tradition. There is nothing greater than martial arts to unite the entire continent of Asia. Even today, millions of parents send their children to martial arts schools to inherit integrity, humility, honor, respect, courage, discipline, and compassion. In many ways, Asian values are passed down generation to generation through martial arts.

Ferraz: Most people are already daunted by the prospect of starting a much simpler startup compared to a global sports league. What were your first steps in creating ONE Championship?

Sityodtong: I am far from perfect as a leader, but I take pride in creating a true meritocracy for everyone at ONE Championship. I believe that everyone should be afforded the equal opportunity to be the master of his/her own destiny. I believe in fairness. I believe in the simple law of karma. Do good, and good will come back to you. Do bad, and bad will come back to you. At my companies, we don't care about paper qualifications, CVs, race, gender, religion, sexual orientation, social status, nationality, color, or any of society's typical bullshit. I embrace diversity of every kind. We welcome people from all walks of life and from any and all backgrounds. I believe that everyone should have the power to control his/her future based on integrity, character, and performance. By the same token, I have zero tolerance for hatred, prejudice, politics, ass-kissing, back-stabbing, etc.

ONE Championship is a celebration of Asia's greatest cultural treasure, and its deep-rooted Asian values of integrity, humility, honor, respect, courage, discipline, and compassion. Our mission is to unleash real-life superheroes who ignite the world with hope, dreams, inspiration and strength. Through the power of media and the magic of storytelling, we have the precious opportunity to unleash role models, celebrate values, ignite dreams, inspire nations, and change the world.

Leaders must stand for a certain set of values, and do everything possible to defend, nurture, and protect those values. Values are the bedrock of the greatest companies on the planet. When a leader and his/her team have shared values, aligned goals, and a common mission, wonderful things can happen. The secret sauce for any company is its culture. Values create the foundation for a great culture. And a great culture inspires extraordinary achievement. At ONE Championship, there are 6 core values (in order of importance) that drive the culture:

- **Integrity:** Do the right thing even when no one is watching. No one is perfect, but try your best to do the right thing. Don't lie, cheat, or steal. Do your best to live in a way that would make your mom proud.

- **Happiness:** Spread happiness. Try to be a source of positive energy and happiness for yourself and your colleagues. Positive energy is what changes the world for the better. Happiness is what creates extraordinary performance.

- **Excellence:** Excellence is doing your job above and beyond the call of duty even when no one is watching. Hold yourself and your colleagues to the highest standard of excellence.

- **Continuous Self-Improvement:** Try your best to learn, grow, and improve 1% a day in every area of your life. No one is without flaws or weaknesses. We are all imperfect. We are all works-in-progress. Be intellectually honest with yourself so that you can always improve. Use constructive criticism as an opportunity to unleash your potential.

- **Teamwork:** Put the needs of the team ahead of your own. If you look at history in any sport, world championship teams are made of selfless individuals who put the team ahead of themselves.

- **Loyalty:** Loyalty is black and white. If you want everyone to invest 1,000% of themselves into your success, you must be loyal to everyone. No one will give 1,000% to you if you are not loyal. It is the simple law of reciprocity. Be worthy of your teammates' loyalty. Be loyal to your team and your team will do everything in its power to see you succeed.

Ferraz: Apart from building out your team, can you go more into the operational side of starting a sports media property? I'm sure people would be curious on where one even begins to build this kind of entity.

Sityodtong: Content is everything. The key to any media business is to create compelling, viral content. It means a sharp eye for detail and a creative mind for storytelling.

Ferraz: How did your own background in martial arts inform how you shaped the league?

Sityodtong: "IKIGAI" is a profound Japanese concept on the art of living. The fundamental belief is that life only truly begins when you discover your IKIGAI and start living it with honesty and authenticity. The direct translation for IKIGAI is "reason for living" in English. The Japanese believe that everyone has an IKIGAI, but that it requires deep soul-searching and true self-reflection to find it.

My IKIGAI is to unleash greatness in the world through the power of martial arts. Martial arts has been my greatest passion in life since I was a child. Since Day 1, our mission at ONE Championship has been to unleash real-life superheroes who ignite the world with hope, strength, dreams, courage, and inspiration. Ultimately, I want to help alleviate the injustices of poverty and inequality around the world.

Ferraz: Can you share more in-depth about how ONE is pro-fighter? Perhaps contrasting it with common sports league practices around the world that you wanted to do differently or reform.

Sityodtong: ONE Championship has a payscale that ranks among the highest in the world. On a personal note, I am full of appreciation and gratitude that our athletes have embraced ONE as their partner in their success. I don't take this responsibility lightly. As their CEO, I promise to work harder than anyone in the world to see that their dreams come true. I am far from perfect as a leader, but my heart is in the right place. Like many of them, I also survived poverty and adversity. I have been in their shoes and I have walked their path. Martial arts is what I love. Martial arts is who I am.

Ferraz: Apart from geography and audience, how did you try to define ONE Championship as different from other martial arts leagues?

Sityodtong: My global competitors sell fights. In doing so, they espouse violence, hatred, anger, controversy, and unruly behavior. Often, their athletes are caught in scandals of domestic violence, drugs, felonies, and more. On the flip side, ONE Championship builds heroes. Through the magic of storytelling, the power of media, and the beauty of our heroes, we inspire millions (and eventually billions) to dream more, do more, and be more in life. We ignite hope, celebrate values, create dreams, inspire nations, and change the world.

Ferraz: If you were to think about your events as a "product," what did you determine to change after launching your debut product "Champion vs. Champion"?

Sityodtong: I have personally spent thousands of hours on our in-stadium product as well as our live broadcast product and shoulder content. I am obsessed about delivering the world's best experience for our fans.

Ferraz: Can you share an example of something new you implemented to ONE Championship by thinking about what it would take to beat you?

Sityodtong: Whether it is our culture, our product, our brand, our team, or anything else, we are always looking to learn, grow, and evolve. The greatest advantage that ONE Championship has is our ability to adapt and execute at speed and scale.

Ferraz: What were the challenges in striking the initial deal with ESPN, and how did you overcome it?

Sityodtong: Like I said, the first three years of ONE Championship was filled with failure and rejection. Rejection after rejection, but eventually things began to turn up. Eventually, we had one broadcaster in the Philippines, ABS-CBN, the largest broadcaster in the country, who gave us a chance. They saw the numbers—people love the content, our kind and our brand of content. After ABS-CBN gave us a chance, after that first broadcaster believed in what we could do, we continued to ride that, and we were able to get more broadcasters by delivering the numbers.

Ferraz: Publicly, ONE Championship looks like it was a winner from the start. What was your company's darkest moment, and how did you turn things from the brink?

Sityodtong: As I said, during the first three years, we were not getting anyone to believe in us. But once that one broadcaster took a chance on us, it was all downhill from there. All we needed was someone to believe in us, and they did, and we have delivered since. Soon, more and more began to believe, and now we are the biggest martial arts organization in the world.

Ferraz: Any sports league is defined by its stars. What have been the challenges of attracting the best fighters to your league, and how are you addressing them?

Sityodtong: In the beginning, in the early days of ONE Championship, it was really hard, because we were just a startup. I was fortunate to have met some renowned, world-class martial artists and contacts in the business. They were a massive help in attracting some great stars and talent. Once we were able to get some big names and really good athletes on the ONE roster, we started to get attention and recognition from other world-class competitors who wanted to join the ONE family and compete in our promotion.

Today, we have the biggest collection of martial artists and world champions across multiple martial arts. Guys like Demetrious Johnson, Eddie Alvarez, Giorgio Petrosyan, and Nong-O Gaiyanghadao. All of them are massive stars in their respective fields. All of them are world champions. All of them are world-class martial artists. These big names just show the quality of the athletes that we have on the roster, and that's just the start. Now, many fighters also want to sign with us.

Ferraz: What are the most important considerations for world-class martial artists in choosing a sports property to participate in, and can you share how you cater to these considerations?

Sityodtong: It is everything. To the world's best martial artists, they want a home. They want a global platform that will showcase their skills, their achievements, and their stories to the world. Of course, money and other economic opportunities are also critical.

Ferraz: Many sports leagues have succumbed to negative spectacle—i.e., tacitly encouraging fighters to fight or talk trash at weigh-ins. How have you strived to balance the need to market events with traditional martial arts values?

Sityodtong: The biggest misconception about martial arts is that it is about fighting and violence. Unfortunately, some organizations in the West have tarnished the image of Asia's greatest cultural treasure by turning it into a bloodsport spectacle fueled by hatred, anger, drugs, controversy, trash talking, humiliation, and even criminal behavior. It is disturbing to see these organizations espousing and rewarding corrupt values and showcasing it as "martial arts" in order to profit. As a lifelong martial artist, I am deeply saddened by the lack of integrity and authenticity. It is a mockery. It is a disgrace. It is a lie.

Asia's greatest cultural treasure has been a way of life here for over 5,000 years. Through the practice of martial arts, we inherit the deep-rooted Asian values of integrity, humility, honor, respect, courage, discipline, compassion, and much more. Martial arts is the journey of continuous self-improvement mentally, physically, emotionally, and spiritually. It is the warrior way of life. It is the teachings of philosophy and values. It is the bedrock of society and harmony. Equally important is that martial arts empowers us with an unbreakable warrior spirit to conquer adversity. No one is perfect and no one is meant to be. We all fall down. We all make mistakes. We all fail. Martial arts has the incredible ability to change lives, to turn weakness into strength, to mold fear into courage, and to transform the ordinary into the extraordinary.

As the CEO of Asia's largest global sports media property, I think deeply about my responsibility and ONE Championship's power to shape and influence values, culture, and society across our footprint of over 145 countries. It is the reason why I personally select heroes who exemplify the best of humanity to represent the face of ONE Championship such as Angela Lee, Bibiano Fernandes, Rich Franklin, Renzo Gracie, Aung La Nsang, Eduard "The Landslide" Folayang, Giorgio Petrosyan, Brandon Vera, Martin Nguyen, Alain 'The Panther' Ngalani, Yodsanklai Fairtex, Amir Khan Ansari, and several others. It is not a coincidence that ONE Championship invests the vast majority of our marketing budget on these select few athletes. These men and women not only rank among the best martial artists on the planet, but they are exemplary role models for the world. When children put up posters of our heroes in their bedrooms, parents can feel safe and happy. Families can celebrate our heroes for their values, their achievements, and their life stories. You see, life is not about making money at the expense of humanity. No, life is about making the world a better place for humanity. For me, our mission is sacred at ONE. We have the precious opportunity to unleash real-life superheroes who ignite the world with hope, strength, dreams, inspiration, and courage. Through the beauty of storytelling and the power of media, we inspire millions (and eventually billions) to dream more, do more, and be more in life. We ignite hope, celebrate values, create dreams, inspire nations, and change the world.

Ferraz: Has there been any pressure from partners, such as broadcasters, to include even a little of the negative spectacle? How do you resist such pressures?

Sityodtong: Yes, of course. However, ONE Championship refuses to succumb to any negative pressure. Ultimately, ONE Championship is a celebration of Asia's greatest cultural treasure. As the CEO of Asia's largest global sports media property, I think deeply about my responsibility and ONE Championship's power to shape and influence values, culture, and society across our footprint of over 145 countries.

Ferraz: As ONE Championship grew, how much did you try to make your company's internal culture mirror the culture of martial arts? How did you try to make it differ in any way?

Sityodtong: When children put up posters of our heroes in their bedrooms, parents can feel safe and happy. Families can celebrate our heroes for their values, their achievements, and their life stories. You see, life is not about making money at the expense of humanity. No, life is about making the world a better place for humanity. For me, our mission is sacred at ONE. We have the precious opportunity to unleash real-life superheroes who ignite the world with hope, strength, dreams, inspiration, and courage. Through the beauty of storytelling and the power of media, we inspire millions—and eventually billions—to dream more, do more, and be more in life. We ignite hope, celebrate values, create dreams, inspire nations, and change the world.

Ferraz: Do you offer any kind of training in martial arts as an optional perk to employees?

Sityodtong: Yes, all of my employees are provided with free martial arts training.

Ferraz: When did you raise your first financing? How did you convince some of your investors—who ordinarily invest in tech startups—that ONE Championship could produce a similar sort of return?

Sityodtong: Farallon Capital Management was my seed investor when I launched my global long-short equity hedge fund in 2005. I remember feeling like the luckiest startup hedge fund manager on Wall Street because Farallon, one of the world's most prestigious hedge funds with an impeccable reputation, an incredible 20 year track record, and $20 billion under management, chose to be the 1st and largest investor in my fund. It also took a small equity stake in the business. A few years prior, I had the good fortune of meeting David Cohen, Farallon's Chief Investment Officer and one of its managing partners at the time. In the smart money circles on Wall Street, David had a reputation—which he still enjoys today—as one of the best risk arbitrage and value investors in the industry. When I launched my fund, David was the one who led the investment from Farallon. Goldman Sachs also took me on a global roadshow across North America, Europe, and Asia where I met over 100+ institutional investors to raise more capital. To cut a long story short, my hedge fund eventually had $500 million in assets under management.

When I look back at that experience today through the lens of entrepreneurship, I can see 5 key lessons on the art of capital-raising:

1. Live with integrity. For me, integrity means doing the right thing even when no one is watching. Do your best to live in a way that would make your mom proud. Integrity is essential for success in life and it is no different for investors. Before Farallon invested in my fund, it did a

massive amount of due diligence on my character, my values, and my past. Of course, they looked into my achievements in life too, but integrity was first and foremost.

2. Surround yourself with greatness to unleash your greatness. I was fortunate that Farallon Capital Management decided to back me. I was lucky that Goldman Sachs chose to take me as a client. I was blessed that Ernst and Young agreed to be my auditors. For a startup fund, these blessings from prestigious, best-in-class companies helped to create a strong foundation in terms of brand, intellectual property, systems, processes, resources, and network.

3. Dream big. Act small. Irrespective of one's position in life, I believe that it is best to act small. What does that mean? It means work for every penny as if your pockets were empty. It means hustle for every deal as if you had nothing in your bank account. It means fight for every inch as if your company's existence depended on it. To this day, I work, hustle, and fight as if my life were hanging in the balance. I don't take anything for granted. Dreams are great, but nothing beats old-fashioned hard work.

4. Create your own luck. There is no doubt that luck plays a huge factor in life and in business. When I was living on $4 a day in poverty at the lowest point of my life, I could never have imagined that I would be living the life of my dreams today. As much as I would like to take full credit for my achievements, the truth is that I have been the recipient of a lot of good luck and extraordinary blessings in life. Always remember that a single person can change your destiny in the way David Cohen did for me. When you meet people from any walk of life, my advice is to be genuine and to be kind. People can feel authenticity. People will remember kindness.

5. Be transparent. As an entrepreneur, I have learned that telling potential investors the good, bad, and ugly about my business is the best way to build trust. Every company has flaws. Every company has challenges. Every company has risks. Investors respect it when you walk them through the negatives and explain how you intend to overcome those negatives. So, when speaking to investors, my strong advice is to be open and transparent at all times.

In summary, it doesn't take magic to raise capital. Anyone can do it. Just remember that integrity, hard work, and transparency will go a long way to maximizing your chances of success at raising capital.

Ferraz: For the vast majority of your investors, it was likely the first time they invested in anything sports- or martial arts-related. What were their most common concerns, and how did you convince them otherwise?

Sityodtong: I think all smart investors look for world-class leadership, an attractive business model, a powerful product, a strong economic moat, and a huge addressable market. Luckily, ONE Championship has all of those elements and more.

Ferraz: Compared to other founders, you don't only actively promote your company or product, you are very much active in sharing your experiences as a founder and promoting entrepreneurship in general. Why do you feel this is important to do?

Sityodtong: I believe it is important for me to share my experiences with the world for the next generation. If you are not fighting for something bigger than yourself, then you are dying for nothing. I truly believe it. In many ways, entrepreneurs are artists and romantics. We believe in dreams. We believe in love. We believe in expressing our souls through our work. At the end of the day, we all die. Nothing remains, except for the impact we make on others. The knowledge that we left this Earth better off than how we found it is perhaps the immortality we seek.

Ferraz: You have mentioned that you don't feel the world is yet ready for a ONE Championship book because you are far from done. What is your vision for ONE Championship's future?

Sityodtong: When people congratulate me on building a US $1 billion property in ONE Championship, I don't feel that my team and I have done anything yet. We are literally just getting started. My vision is to create a US $100 billion property, the world's most valuable sports media property. Of the 7.5 billion people on this planet, only 6% are entrepreneurs. It is a job that requires 24/7/365 of a person's mind, body, and soul. I would say that 90-95% of all start-ups fail eventually. The historical odds of creating a US $1 billion startup are 1 in 10 million startups. With all these crazy numbers, many people question why entrepreneurs do what they do.

It is simply not rational.

For me, entrepreneurship is one of the greatest adventures in life. Yes, it is true that the economic rewards in entrepreneurship are handsome. However, if you ask true entrepreneurs—such as Elon Musk, Richard Branson, or the late Steve Jobs—what drives them, it is not money. It is the thrill of the adventure. A true entrepreneur yearns to change the world, to defy the odds, and to make a positive impact on the lives of others. Money is simply a by-product.

Ferraz: Is there a traditional end-game for One Championship like other startups who dream of exiting via acquisition or IPO?

Sityodtong: Yes, I plan to IPO ONE Championship in the future.

Ferraz: What is your number-one piece of advice to founders in Asia in any field?

Sityodtong: Embrace failure, live with resilience and grit, understand that there will be doubters and naysayers, and do what it is that ignites your soul. The journey never ends.

Willis Wee

Founder and CEO, Tech in Asia

In 2010, Singapore Management University alumnus **Willis Wee** *founded Tech in Asia in Singapore after recognizing a gap in the global coverage of technology and startups. Most media outlets focus on Silicon Valley startups, even though Asia is increasingly home to the world's most promising tech companies and has a growing regional readership eager to learn about them.*

Wee started Tech in Asia as a blog known as Penn Olson before evolving it to the full-fledged technology news site that people know today. Tech in Asia covers tech news from China, Hong Kong, India, Indonesia, Japan, Malaysia, Vietnam, the Philippines, Singapore, and South Korea. Startups in these markets are featured in the publication because of its high-level readership. In addition to its news, Tech in Asia also has a job marketplace and a signature events series.

Wee has raised more than US $12 million to date, including backing from Y Combinator and Facebook co-founder Eduardo Saverin. After exploring a blockchain-based product, Wee ultimately added a subscription for Tech in Asia readers in 2018. Wee predicts that the change will cause page views to drop, but revenue to increase on a per-user basis.

Gracy Fernandez: What did you feel was missing in coverage of the Asian tech ecosystem that made you decide to put up Penn Olson?

© Ezra Ferraz, Gracy Fernandez 2020
E. Ferraz and G. Fernandez, *Asian Founders at Work*,
https://doi.org/10.1007/978-1-4842-5162-1_6

Willis Wee: Back in 2009, I was reading a lot of different publications that covered tech and entrepreneurship. I consistently found that a lot of the stories were Silicon Valley–centric. Asia was severely underrepresented. For example, innovative companies like Alibaba, Rakuten, and Tencent were growing aggressively, but it felt like they were neglected and often misunderstood.

Fernandez: Can you share an example of how one of these Asian tech companies was misrepresented in Western coverage, so readers can better feel the gap?

Wee: Alibaba was always seen as a copycat of eBay but in actual fact, it has innovated a lot more than eBay in its user interface and fintech applications.

Tencent's WeChat was seen as a copycat of WhatsApp. But today we know that's not true. It's a super app—basically helping users to do anything A to Z.

On the surface, these companies look the same but underneath, it's a whole different animal.

Fernandez: How did you try to amend this gap in coverage?

Wee: Penn Olson started as a social media blog. But my interest in entrepreneurship somehow got me connected to entrepreneurs across Asia. My pitch was simple: "Have coffee with me, share your stories, and I'll turn the conversation into a story on my blog." People like to share their stories, and we were probably one of the first to give them attention. So founders introduced me to more founders, and that was how I got plugged into the community.

As I was still in college in 2009, Penn Olson remained as a side project for a couple of years before I decided that it could be something I could do full-time. It was doing pretty well as a side project. I made profits via banner ads and reinvested the profits to hire more freelance writers.

Fernandez: How did you manage to raise funding for Penn Olson—a startup in a field that is not necessarily known for high returns?

Wee: I didn't plan to raise money. I didn't even know what a VC was. In early 2011, I got connected with Willson Cuaca of East Ventures on LinkedIn. I asked him if he was okay with explaining to me what VC was all about. We met at a McDonald's near my university, and he asked me, "What's your MAUs?" "What's your mission?" "What's your product roadmap?"

I candidly answered as I chewed on my hamburger. Willson said he wanted to invest because he believed that a publication like Penn Olson would do a lot of good for the nascent tech and startup community in Asia.

He asked me to send him a pitch deck by the end of the week and invited me to Jakarta, Indonesia, to participate in one of East Ventures' startup events. Through the event, I got to meet more founders and get a feel of the local startup community in Indonesia. I also met with all the partners at East Ventures.

When we returned to Singapore, they offered me a check, and I took it. I was 24 years old and had minimal work experience. So there was nothing to lose. Everything concluded within two weeks. In March 2011, we incorporated Penn Olson as a proper business entity in Singapore.

Fernandez: How did you figure out what to ask for if, as you say, you were very young and still learning? Did you seek guidance from anyone or look to resources anywhere for more knowledge on the fundraising process?

Wee: There wasn't much of a negotiation. I just tried my luck to ask for more—from US $100K check to $150K and also a better valuation—and they quickly agreed. I didn't push for more as I'm already thankful for them taking a chance on me.

Fernandez: As you come from a sales background, what did you look for in your first writer and journalist hires?

Wee: I care a lot about the quality of our reporting. So naturally, I look for experienced journalists who can help us build a solid foundation. Equally important is that they have to believe in our mission, which is to build and serve the tech and startup community in Asia.

Fernandez: Were there any interesting ways that you vetted both for their talent in journalism and their belief in the Asian startup and tech ecosystem?

Wee: Not really. Those were the early days and we were an unknown. So, anyone who wanted in, we believed, just needed to have a strong conviction.

Every story published creates opportunities for the founders and stakeholders or helps to demystify and inform readers what's going on in the industry.

We are bridging the information gap through journalism. Information is key to supporting a thriving community. Our first few hires were Rick Martin, Charlie Custer, and Steven Millward. Charlie still freelances for us, and Steven is still with us full-time. I'm forever grateful for the work and dedication they put in.

Fernandez: When did you realize that Penn Olson could evolve from a blog into a major publication?

Wee: Even though I was aggressively pursuing stories, building events, and the community, I didn't think much about turning the company into a major publication.

But as the ecosystem matures, we learned that there is a lot more demand for well-researched and investigative journalism. There is a lot more money at stake, so that's very natural. But a well-researched piece takes weeks or even months to produce. So clearly, we had to change our business model, and subscription was the way to go. In hindsight, it was a great move, but it wasn't easy switching from free to a subscription model.

We tried doing subscription as early as 2014, but the lack of seamless payment technology like Stripe made it extremely difficult. While we always aspire to produce great stories, writing for paying subscribers today really pushes us to evolve from a blog into a major publication. We are slowly getting there.

Fernandez: Can you share more about this initial attempt to do a subscription model in 2014? How long did the experiment last, and when did you know that the subscription model would not work for you because it was ahead of its time, technology-wise?

Wee: The experiment lasted for about 6 months. Additional thoughts: First, there was a lot of friction having users to subscribe using PayPal. They had to go through several screens and confirmation before they could subscribe so naturally the drop off rate was high because internet users are impatient in general. Second, tech aside, it was ahead of its time because the market wasn't open to paying for quality content. Third, to be fair, we didn't do a great job on content either. We were creating compelling content but just not enough volume to keep users sticky.

Fernandez: What was the most challenging part about rebranding Penn Olson into Tech in Asia, and how did you manage it?

Wee: There was an attachment to the Penn Olson brand and also concerns that it would hurt our overall brand, SEO, and traffic. But everything went smoothly. Our product team made sure SEO and links remained intact. I had to convince the shareholders that the rebranding would bring a lot more clarity on what we stand for and serve as a stronger foundation for the business.

Fernandez: Can you share about why there was a need for the re-branding in the first place? When people heard the name Penn Olson, what did they usually think the company did?

Wee: There was a need to rebrand because people couldn't really connect the brand name to what we did.

Penn Olson was thought about along this line: "As we pen down our thoughts, we learn. And it's awesome to learn."

I started Penn Olson with the idea to turn it into a marketing agency but it turns out that I'm a lot more passionate about tech and startups in Asia.

Fernandez: What were some of the early unsuccessful digital marketing strategies that you employed to increase the readership of Tech in Asia? What did you find ultimately worked?

Wee: There was a period of time where digital media companies were obsessed with page views. The logic made sense—more views, and therefore, more ad money. We got caught into it as well. In hindsight, we prioritized the wrong things. We produced videos, short stories, and graphics that brought in tons of views but had very little value to our users.

Fernandez: Can you explain this in greater detail? What was the nature of the content that was attractive enough for readers to click on, but not substantial enough to give them value?

Wee: The content was a mix of short one-minute videos made very quickly via simple software and pulling in stock images. They could also be a simple image with a founder's quotes.

It's not necessarily bad content. It's good to have some of these to help explain things very quickly and concisely. But flooding our channels with such content doesn't reflect the quality of journalism we aspire to reach.

Furthermore, we couldn't monetize the millions of views because clients doubted the quality of the traffic, and there are always more prominent platforms, like Facebook and Google, where they could park their ad dollars.

Thankfully, at Tech in Asia, we built a culture to always step back and look at our strategy. While the vanity metrics—i.e., views—looked great, it made little business sense. We couldn't figure out the unit economics. Users were telling us that our content quality suffered and our newsroom wasn't proud of its work. It was also challenging to communicate with our shareholders because no one likes to see a growth chart going down. Some felt uncomfortable as we moved toward the subscription model, but thankfully, were willing to back the decision.

What worked for us was to go back to our roots of producing well-researched content. The beauty of the subscription model is that you clearly understand what content users are willing to pay. It created a virtuous cycle within the organization. Our newsroom feels validated, the product and data team's work directly helps them produce better content, the users are happy, and the subscription revenue allows us to reinvest in quality journalism.

Fernandez: What made you realize that Tech in Asia needed to evolve beyond being a publication and evolve more into a product?

Wee: Tech in Asia covers all things tech and startups in Asia. It had the privilege to be part of YC. So naturally, we tend to treat our publication like a software product.

Having a product mindset helps. For example, we measure and grow our subscription business like any SaaS company, looking at growth through an AARRR [acquisition-activation-revenue-retention-referral] lens.

The book Don't Make Me Think by Steve Krug also influenced the way we look at products. Whether it's a landing page, an event, or even a pitch deck, we tend to ask ourselves if it is easy enough for users to understand and enjoy what we built.

We also use the Google Design Sprint methodology if we want to test hypotheses quickly.

Fernandez: What was the first non-media product—Tech in Asia jobs, events, etc.—that Tech in Asia launched, and why?

Wee: As our user base grew, we had people ask us to organize meetups and events. I was skeptical back then. I didn't know much about running events and was worried about the high upfront costs. There was a lot of risk for newcomers like us. Putting in hundreds of thousands of dollars and expecting a positive return on investment is ambitious.

But I chose to listen to our users and went ahead.

So on February 2, 2012, my birthday, we organized the very first Tech in Asia Conference in Singapore. We hosted about eight hundred people. We were very humbled to see people gathered together because of Tech in Asia. Seeing people connecting at our events convinced me that nothing beats face-to-face meetings, and events are likely one of the better channels to get connected with people in the industry.

In 2016, we launched Tech in Asia Jobs to help startup founders hire—for free—through our platform. We believed we had the right audience, so we built something simple to kick-start the product. Understandably, there was a lot of skepticism from the industry in the beginning. People were asking the difference between Tech in Asia jobs and other job portals. My answer has always been the same: We believe that our audience is uniquely suitable for employers hiring in the tech industry.

We started monetizing Tech in Asia Jobs in early 2019, and are happy to see that employers are willing to pay to hire through our platform. Most importantly, we believe that the jobs product is very aligned with the mission of the company as we help to bridge the talent gap in the industry.

In early 2019, we also rolled out Studios, Tech in Asia's branding and marketing agency. It's a vehicle to create compelling stories for our audience with selected brands. We believe our branded content stories uphold the Tech in Asia quality, but they aren't necessarily stories that our newsroom would pursue. For example, a video documentary series featuring a prominent VC's ten-year history of investing in some of the most powerful companies in the region is exciting but isn't a story that our newsroom will place as high priority.

In a nutshell, for Tech in Asia, here's how each product aligns to our mission. Media—bridging the information gap. We provide you with the latest news and analysis on all things tech in Asia. Jobs—bridging the talent gap. We match tech professionals with the right employers. Studios—bridging the connection gap. We build brands among Asia's tech influencers.

Fernandez: What are the challenges of managing a company with multiple online and offline products? How do you overcome it?

The challenges are mainly to create synergies among the products that do not dilute our core roots, which is digital media and journalism. So as an organization, we are very clear that digital media is the top priority. Without it, our studios, conference, and jobs products wouldn't flourish.

Fernandez: Can you give examples of how you've tried to create synergy between your various online and offline products?

Wee: First, we spent a lot of resources building and maintaining our data warehouse so we can track and understand our users better on the news and jobs fronts. With data, we believe we can give what users want with a lot more accuracy. Second, with that setup, we then attempted to build our own event management platform. The idea is to have our users register and pay for events through our platform. Not just our own event, but every tech/startup event across Asia. If we had that going, we could successfully have both online and offline data on our readers, know what they read, what job excites them, and what events they attend and all of that information will give us insight to serve them better.

Fernandez: Can you share the story behind your acquisition of SGEntrepreneurs?

Wee: Gwen and Terence have the same mission and vision as we do, so it is easy to chat very deeply. The acquisition talks proceeded very naturally. We found that it was more efficient to combine resources and efforts to build a publication focusing on tech and startups in Asia.

Fernandez: How did you first approach them with the idea of an acquisition? Were they the only media company that you were considering?

Wee: We started with a two-way candid conversation, asking questions like: What motivates you? What are your struggles? How can we do better for the community? Knowing their thoughts and numbers help us decide quickly that they are good people and it is a lot more effective to just work together. Which then led on to acquisition talk very naturally.

They were the only one we considered because their content and ours are aligned. There has been very strong mutual respect.

Fernandez: Many acquired founders leave shortly after being acquired, but in your case, editor Terence Lee is still a major player at Tech in Asia. How did you manage to integrate the SGEntrepreneurs team so successfully into the team and culture at Tech in Asia?

Wee: Tech in Asia is super transparent. When we hire or acquire, we speak very candidly about our strengths and weaknesses as an organization.

Fernandez: What did you identify to them as the strengths and weaknesses of Tech in Asia when speaking to the SGEntrepreneurs team or other potential acquisitions?

Wee: Tech in Asia allows people to experiment, lead, and own projects. So you'll get a lot of satisfaction from getting your hands dirty, doing great work. We are a company that treats every team member as an adult. That means we let people decide when they want to take leave and work, and this is reflected in our unlimited leave and flexible hours policies. These are policies which have been there since day 1. We are also extremely mission-driven and our mission serves as a guiding compass.

Our weaknesses are that we suffer from the typical startup curse. We are profitable, but because we are relatively smaller and always taking calculated risks to reach greater heights, we occasionally get ourselves into trouble. As we try to improve things, people often find that there is a lack of processes which can be frustrating at times.

Fernandez: What else did you do with the SGEntrepreneurs team that led to their successful integration?

Wee: We also deeply discussed growth and career paths and different scenarios should we win or lose as a team. All these chats helped people to know what they signed up for. It prevented shocks, and therefore improved talent retention. In fact, Hendri and Glenn, the founders of Gamesaku, an Indonesian gaming blog we acquired, are still with us even though we stopped our gaming publication.

Fernandez: What are the challenges of managing a remote, multicultural team spread out across many markets and time zones? How have you addressed this?

Wee: One of the key challenges is that we are not able to meet face-to-face, and that sometimes makes relationship and trust building a little harder than usual.

To address that, we invested in communication software like Slack, use a lot of gifs and emojis to express ourselves, and also try to bring many team members together at our conferences. To build trust, we share a monthly report, which includes very sensitive data, such as bank balances, profits and loss, and so forth, to all team members, so they get the same level of information as our shareholders and management.

We also have an unlimited leave policy. People can report to work at any time they want. We trust that every team member is a responsible adult and will know when to rest and work.

Fernandez: What were the challenges of having to de-prioritize coverage of some regions, even to the point of having to shut down coverage of certain markets?

Wee: The challenges are that we may miss out on potential future growth. Take India, for example; it's a growing market, but our internal data tells us that it's not what our readers want to know as of now. So de-prioritizing it may limit our future growth in that market.

Fernandez: Most founders would dream of having an investor as influential as Eduardo Saverin. How did you manage to get in touch with him? How did you manage to successfully pitch him on the idea of Tech in Asia?

Wee: Eduardo's friend AJ reached out to speak with me when I was at YC. Then I had a few calls with Eduardo, and he bought into our mission. After YC, we were lucky to have Softbank leading our financing round, and Eduardo participated. He also participated in our following round, which was led by Hanwha. It's been a great experience working with Eduardo, and we are lucky to have him and Elaine, his wife, talking to us whenever we need second opinions.

Fernandez: Unlike most Y Combinator startups, Tech in Asia joined the program as a later-stage startup. What was the experience of attending Y Combinator like as a later-stage startup?

Wee: It was a great experience to see how companies in different stages think, plan, and grow. I don't feel there's much difference, since we entered YC through a new product named Techlist. It was a company database subscription business, which we then pivoted to Tech in Asia Jobs.

Fernandez: YC is such a dream for many startups, particularly from Asia. Can you share more about the experience? What was the program like?

Wee: The program allows us to get an inside look at how some of the brightest people in Silicon Valley think and grow their businesses. Here are some of the things I really enjoyed:

1. *Focus on giving what users want.* It's fundamental to all businesses, but not many people truly understand it. The effort put into understanding and meeting user needs is enormous and seeing how some of the best YC companies did it gives you the motivation to provide a 7-star experience for your users.

2. *I metric + compound growth.* There are so many things to track and founders often get confused and track the wrong things. YC helps to simplify that and asked founders to pick one metric and try to focus on the small things and grow 5% every week to achieve compound growth.

3. *Talking to investors.* Basically, if you want to raise money, ask for advice. If you want advice, ask for money. It's very true.

Fernandez: What did you learn from your experiences at Y Combinator that you sought to apply to Tech in Asia once you completed the program?

Wee: Make something people want. That's the YC motto. I think it's ingrained into me and hopefully throughout Tech in Asia. It's so simple but yet hard to achieve. A lot of founders build products and companies for different reasons. But the most successful companies tend to be the ones that created products that people really want.

Fernandez: It was reported that Tech in Asia was considering an ICO earlier this year. What was your initial thinking behind this idea, and why did you ultimately decide to abandon it?

Wee: It started as a side project between a colleague and me. We asked ourselves questions. What makes us think that startup A is worth reporting over startup B? Who gets to speak at our conference? Which article should we feature?

A lot of these decisions are made centrally by Tech in Asia's staff and not by the community. So, we were thinking about how do we make Tech in Asia truly for the community and by the community. We were influenced by the whole blockchain hype in 2017 and 2018, too. So we studied and believed blockchain could potentially be a technology for us to decentralize Tech in Asia. Our white paper goes more in-depth on the topic of implementation.[1]

We decided to abandon it because there were a lot of internal struggles. It was hard to get alignment across all teams because it caused a lot of disruptions. In mid-2018, our core businesses also suffered, which made it very challenging to go ahead with the project.

Fernandez: Can you share more about this? What were the major arguments, both in support of decentralization and against decentralization of Tech in Asia?

---

[1] https://docs.google.com/document/d/1RdEPKHQDaaPzxC2LyuuyS28Wqfnf4IWQghz KeFMdkMQ/edit?usp=sharing

Wee: The major argument is whether Tech in Asia's reputation will suffer if our project tanks. Even if we can get past that, decentralization will disrupt a lot of our current workflows. For instance, some questions we think a lot about are: How do our own reporters compete with community writers for fair incentivization? Similarly, what will happen to the engineering team? Our engineering team will have to evolve quite drastically. Does that mean we can't go ahead with the subscription model?

Basically, a lot of the discussion focuses on "why break things if it works well?" At that point in time, I was convinced that decentralizing Tech in Asia was possibly one of the best things for the community.

In hindsight, we are lucky that we didn't launch. We did the right thing. While I do think that the theory makes a lot of sense, as far as I can see, the actual implementation of decentralization isn't feasible.

Fernandez: What unconventional advice do you have for founders in Asia who want to build a platform as successful as Tech in Asia?

Wee: "If you know your *why* in being an entrepreneur, then you will just have to embrace both the highs and lows, and enjoy the process." I recently heard this from a fellow founder. I think it's so simple yet insightful.

Ritesh Agarwal

Founder and CEO (Global), OYO Hotels & Homes

In 2013, 18-year-old **Ritesh Agarwal** *founded OYO Hotels & Homes in India. The company began as Oravel Stays, a platform for listing budget accommodations, around the same time that Agarwal was accepted to the Thiel Fellowship.*

After seeing a larger opportunity in real estate, Agarwal pivoted the company to the OYO Hotels & Homes we know today. It is now one of the world's fastest-growing chains, with more than 13,000 franchised and leased hotels and 6,000 homes and spaces, altogether totaling more than 450,000 rooms. The company is active in more than 500 cities around the world.

Backed by top investors, such as SoftBank Group, Greenoaks Capital, Sequoia India, Lightspeed India, Hero Enterprises, and China Lodging Group, OYO Hotels & Homes recently raised US $1 billion, thrusting the company into unicorn status. Now at only 25, Agarwal remains determined to continue upgrading sub-quality real estate.

Gracy Fernandez: You founded Oravel Stays—the predecessor to OYO Hotels & Homes—when you were only eighteen. What background did you have in entrepreneurship that gave you the confidence and know-how to build your first startup at this young age?

Ritesh Agarwal: I started my entrepreneurial journey with Oravel Stays in 2012 after graduating from high school. I was eighteen back then and didn't have any experience with entrepreneurship. Right after finishing school, I came to the northern half of India to a place called Kota in Rajasthan. This was

© Ezra Ferraz, Gracy Fernandez 2020
E. Ferraz and G. Fernandez, *Asian Founders at Work*,
https://doi.org/10.1007/978-1-4842-5162-1_7

the time when a lot of new age companies were being built. I used to take weekend trains and come to Delhi to listen to these entrepreneurs. I listened to a lot of fantastic entrepreneurs, and I wished I could work with one of them. I wanted try to build a company, and that's how Oravel Stays came into being.

Ever since I was in school, I wanted to become an entrepreneur. As a young kid, I sold FMCG products, SIM cards, and what not. So my upbringing has been slightly different from the traditional technology, media, and telecom [TMT] founders. I started by selling SIM cards and telecom products, and I learned a heck of a lot doing that. Even today, a lot of conviction-based learnings come from the days when I was selling SIM cards and FMCG products to the small mom-and-pop stores in my hometown, Rayagada, a small town in the eastern Indian state of Odisha.

Fernandez: Did any of the lessons you learned selling SIM cards and FMCG products stay with you and eventually help you later on as a tech founder?

Agarwal: Yes. I think two big lessons from those days have stayed with me all these years. The first lesson was the ability to understand customer needs in a holistic and nuanced manner. I was selling SIM cards and FMCG products to small mom-and-pop stores in my hometown and often they would not be aware of all of the latest products available in the market or their features. They would often not be able to cater to changing customer demand triggered by advertising on TV and other mass media and would stock a limited inventory.

The second big lesson I learned was the value of perseverance which, in my view, is an irreplaceable trait. There is always a light at the end of the tunnel. Too many people give up early without realizing that impactful or big things take time. It's important to keep putting in effort. So the belief of every overnight success is a five-year-old story.

Fernandez: What problems were you trying to solve with Oravel Stays that other accommodation providers were not addressing? You did a lot of first-hand research for Oravel Stays yourself. What did you learn about this business by staying at different accommodations providers?

Agarwal: Going back to the early days, right after Oravel, I had made friends with a lot of homeowners. So I stayed with one of them every day for almost three months. This is how I stayed at almost a hundred places. I realized that there was a fantastic untapped opportunity wherein ninety-six percent of hotels across the world have less than one hundred rooms, especially in India. However, every hotel or chain is focused on making a difference to hotels that have one hundred rooms or more. So I felt this is a very exciting opportunity, and I should invest in this direction. That is what inspired me to set up the first OYO hotel.

My downside was going back to the university, which is not a very big downside after all! I felt even if there is a ten percent chance of success, I'll take it. Whenever I have had two opportunities—risking it versus regretting it, I would invariably choose to risk it because I never want to regret that I didn't pursue something that I really wanted to do. So that's sort of what inspired me to start the first OYO hotel, and the first asset was a success. We went from nineteen percent to ninety percent occupancy in the first month.

Fernandez: What was it about your business model or user experience that enabled occupancy to make such a dramatic jump?

Agarwal: When I look back, I think it was due to the focus on customer experience. We invested in essentials such as linen and flooring, basic renovation, customer service at reception, room service, hygiene, and maintenance of the hotel. We also listed it on our website and marketed it to target customers through offline channels, where word of mouth played a strong role. Gradually, we saw an increase in occupancy and then we had hoteliers in the neighborhood reach out to us to understand what we were doing differently. The rest, as they say, is history.

Fernandez: After launching Oravel Stays, you received a $100,000 grant as part of the Thiel Fellowship. How did you spend the money?

Agarwal: I invested all of it in OYO to help build the business. It was my personal money, and by the time I got the fellowship amount, we already had early investors in Oravel Stays. But I felt the company I am building is personal to me, and I would dedicate whatever resources I had to build it. Even after six years, I continue to be personally very committed to the mission in the long term, and I think I am lucky to have the opportunity to take such a long-term view.

Fernandez: Outside of the cash grant, what else did you gain from the Thiel Fellowship in the way of knowledge, networks, or other resources?

Agarwal: I am thankful for the time I spent in the Bay Area. The mentorship I received from the Thiel Fellowship and the quality of ideas I was exposed to were on par with the best business schools. But the icing on the cake was that I got a chance to learn everything while pursuing my dream. Getting mentored by Peter Thiel really changed my worldview and gave me a new perspective on entrepreneurship. I realized that thinking big and solving at scale were very important. I realized thinking and having a big mission is important. No matter how small your company is or which corner you run your business in, nobody in the Bay Area wants to be the biggest business in California. Everybody has the dream of being the most impactful company in that segment worldwide.

Fernandez: Apart from thinking on a much larger scale, what else did you learn from Thiel that has shaped how you think?

Agarwal: The other key learning from the Thiel Fellowship was to understand the real significance of innovation. For any business and startups in particular, it is vital to inculcate the spirit of curiosity and lateral thinking to succeed in the long run. At times, we tend to get carried away by what we think are good ideas, but in reality, they may not serve the customer's purpose in any way. It is crucial that we understand the customer's requirements and direct our efforts toward providing the best possible solution to their requirements.

While one is in the process of coming up with a truly innovative solution, it is essential to keep an open mind. One should accept failure, and be willing to learn, unlearn, and relearn again.

Fernandez: Why did you finally decide to pivot Oravel Stays to OYO Hotels & Homes?

Agarwal: Oravel Stays was a platform for listing diverse accommodations, like small assets, vacation homes, and so forth. We had a significant amount of assets in early days, and since those owners became friends, I started spending time staying with them while between school and university. During such trips, I discovered the disconnect between the demand and the supply of quality living spaces.

While I was travelling across India on a shoestring budget and had to lodge in some of the not-so-great guest houses, I realized that I was looking at the wrong end of the rope. The problem wasn't the lack of available budget hospitality options. It was that the majority of mid-market and economy hotels, whether branded or unbranded, lacked the minimum baseline standards of quality and service delivery. This meant that the solution wasn't merely aggregating hotels on a website. It was to upgrade the experience and take responsibility for fixing it.

I wanted to fix this problem by using design, technology, and talent. That's how OYO was launched in 2013, with the promise of delivering chic, well-designed, stay experiences. Today, OYO is the world's third-largest and fastest-growing chain of hotels, homes, managed living, and workspaces. Unlike a booking platform, or a hotel room aggregator, or an online travel aggregator, OYO Hotels & Homes is a chain of hotels just like all the other hotel chains world over.

Fernandez: Can you go into more in depth about how you upgraded rooms? What were the most common issues with them, and how did you solve each of these?

Agarwal: Typically, we have a list of parameters for identifying hotels which can be part of our chain. Once we identify a particular hotel, we often end up upgrading the rooms by investing in multiple areas which could range from fixing seepage issues, deploying quality linen in the room, ensuring the bed size and mattress are per our standard specifications, Wi-Fi and room hygiene is in order apart from ensuring that the AC and TV are operational. Additionally, the upgrade also involves investing in training the staff and having a dedicated OYO captain assigned for the hotel who regularly audits compliance to OYO's standards. We have set a new benchmark in transforming and renovating assets in a record time of within 14 days, which is a stark contrast to the industry standard of up to 90 days.

Fernandez: What were the challenges of pivoting your business model and rebranding?

Agarwal: The challenges were many when we decided to pivot from a listing platform to a full-fledged hotel chain. I remember the first property we started with—the occupancy was around nineteen percent. The property was not run in an efficient manner.

Invariably, these hotel owners in India had a different full-time business. The hotel was often their passive investment. On the consumer side, finding a clean, comfortable place—there was either a sixty or seventy, or maybe a one hundred–dollar hotel room that you could get. Or everything you got would be broken. You would get unclean places. People not willing to attend to, let alone get places that were beautiful, exciting, and inspiring emotion.

So on the supply side, there was a fundamental problem of yield generation along with the asset owner wanting to get away with the daily hustle of managing the hotel. On the consumer side, the consumer wanted a space that was well organized and well designed and at a price that is fair and attractive to the Indian consumer.

I realized very early that growing without having the secret sauce or competency that is truly special for you is very hard. And invariably, that would enable competitors to come into the market. The only true competitor leverage is being able to have secret sauces and competencies for making sure that you can do the same thing better than everybody else.

Just to give you some context, today, we are opening upwards of eighty thousand rooms a month, on an average, globally. The reason we are able to do that is that there are some things very special we do at OYO, and those things make us better than what others can replace or respond to. So the belief of every overnight success is a five-year-old story and being able to continuously invest in the same thing every day just to make it a little bit better than yesterday is what I have learned over a period of time.

It is very critical to ensure that I am doing the right thing—whether it is with our customers, asset owners, team members, profits, or margins. Regardless of any metrics, I make a decision based on all the learning that I have gained over the years and the deep thinking done on long-term aspirations. And then do the right thing. Let me cite a couple of examples.

In 2015, we had a lot of complaints regarding our customer service. We made the hard decision to stopping growth for four months, no matter what our shareholders said. And I feel it was one of the best things we did.

In distribution, we partnered MakeMyTrip, Ctrip, Meituan, and a lot of other OTA leaders worldwide. And I think it was one of the best things we did while making sure that our direct distribution channels continued to grow.

Fernandez: And what did you do during those four months?

Agarwal: We focused on identifying key problem areas and finding solutions that are scalable.

Fernandez: How did you convince hotel owners to partner with OYO Hotels & Homes?

Agarwal: India is a supply-constrained market, not just for hospitality but for most consumer services when it comes to the organized sector. When we launched in 2013, the demand for high-quality, affordable accommodations in good locations was already there. The problem largely lay on the supply side, where there was a fundamental problem of yield generation along with the asset owner wanting to get away with the daily hustle of managing the hotel.

In the initial days, convincing hotel owners to associate with OYO was a herculean task. Being a completely new, untested business model, hotel owners were skeptical about the value and prospects we offered. Soon, they started seeing repeat customers and greater revenues. They also noticed how hotel operations, revenue management, and CRM became more efficient and convenient via OYO apps. They were then convinced.

Fernandez: To encourage growth, did you undertake any activities that don't scale, similar to how the Airbnb founders took photos of all of their early rooms or condo rentals, which ended up driving bookings?

Agarwal: I can share an anecdote in this regard.

Lightspeed Venture Partners was one of our earliest investors, and we had around thirty or forty hotels in Gurgaon in late 2013. We were doing really well in terms of occupancy. For those who are not from India, Gurgaon is a part of the Delhi/NCR region. So, funnily, when the asset's occupancy was increasing and all, as an entrepreneur, I did all the hard things. I picked up phone calls, responded to emails, and everything under the sun to run the day-to-day operations. I used to really like picking up phone calls and so on. Bejul Somaia, a partner at Lightspeed Venture Partners India, used to host me for a monthly lunch. During one of these lunches, he told me that he heard from someone that I have been taking phone calls from customers. I replied that I love doing that. So Bejul retorted, "That's fantastic! We have found the leader for the customer service department of OYO. Let's now hire a CEO!" That's when I understood that I should start building a strong management group sooner rather than later. This approach is not sustainable.

Since then, we have invested in the management needed to take OYO to the next level. I am so thankful to Abhinav Sinha and Maninder Gulati for their unflinching support in the early days. We recruited some of the smartest and one of the best leadership teams among young companies across the world. We have recruited in India, China, the United Kingdom, Indonesia, and the Middle East. I think we are very happy with the results of the leaders we have recruited. Do note, we have never lost any single senior leader in the history of our company. That is the second thing we have been very happy about.

Fernandez: Since you have a variety of models for working with partners—including franchising, leasing, and operating hotel units—to what extent do you take ownership over any customer service issues?

Agarwal: Irrespective of whose fault it is, we take collaborative responsibility and work toward resolving the issues.

In the service and hospitality industry, one needs to be constantly evolving to meet changing consumer demands. At OYO, customer experience is of utmost priority to us, and hence, we take feedback seriously and constructively. We believe that when it comes to experience, there is always room for improvement, and it can be achieved if one listens to the customers carefully. We have a robust ground team that is supported by innovative technology to ensure that we offer a consistent and quality customer experience. Our social response systems are super quick, and we respond within minutes of receiving a complaint.

We have been able to deliver good hospitality, which has helped us to scale up rapidly. Today, approximately ninety percent of our business comes from repeat and word-of-mouth customers, which is a testament to our popularity. Having said that, we will continue to learn and improve.

Fernandez: When you first raised venture capital in 2015, what vision did you sell your investors on, especially as there is no shortage of solutions in the accommodation space?

Agarwal: Our mission and vision have not changed since we started. Right from day one, we were committed to our mission of delivering a chic hospitality experience at hard-to-ignore prices with a focus on creating beautiful living spaces and changing the lives of over 3.2 billion middle-income people globally. When we launched in 2013, the problem wasn't the lack of availability of budget hospitality options. It was that the majority of mid-market and economy hotels, whether branded or unbranded, lacked the minimum baseline standards of quality and service delivery. This meant that the solution wasn't merely aggregating hotels on a website. It was to upgrade the experience and take responsibility for fixing it. I wanted to fix this problem by using design, technology, and talent. That's how OYO was launched in 2013—with the promise of delivering chic, well-designed, stay experiences.

Our vision is to be the most loved hospitality brand in the world. We are pretty optimistic that we will get there soon, especially when we see that over ninety percent of our business comes from repeat and word-of-mouth customers, which can be attributed to a seamless product experience, efficient operations, and solid distribution capabilities—all powered by innovative technology.

Fernandez: Many tech companies in markets as large as India or China have the luxury of focusing entirely on the domestic market and growing large entirely through those countries. OYO Hotels & Homes expanded internationally relatively quickly, with expansion to Malaysia in 2016. Why did you decide to expand globally so soon?

Agarwal: At OYO, we genuinely believe our mission is to bring better living spaces for the Indian who comes off of a train, the Chinese who comes in on a flight or a bus, or the European who goes skiing. It doesn't really matter who that individual is. There are over 3.2 billion middle-income people, and they all deserve a better living space.

In 2016, Malaysia was the first overseas market we entered, and today, we are present in eight hundred cities in eighty countries.

We decided to expand overseas early in our journey because we wanted to see if we could make a positive difference in the markets where the budget hotel segment was highly fragmented and there was scope to provide a differentiated and quality offering at affordable prices for customers. We approach every new market not as an Indian startup setting up shop in the country, but like a local entrepreneur building and localizing the OYO business model to make it work in that market. We understand that each market is unique in its own way, so we localize the product experience and interiors of our buildings, and our overall approach. This is another example of innovation at OYO.

As for our rapid international expansion, we have made this possible by investing in four key competencies in the last five years—the ability to scientifically identify and onboard strategic buildings within a shorter time period than others, renovate and upgrade living spaces in record time by leveraging our design and engineering talent, sustained demand generation across offline and online channels, and lastly, immersive technology that redefines the hospitality experience at every customer and hotel owner touchpoint.

This helps us bring in operational efficiencies through revenue management, dynamic pricing, service quality improvements by staff training and management, and so forth. Through this, we are able to drastically improve the quality of customer experience and help our franchise owners offer a unique value proposition to customers. While doing this, we are also able to ensure a much higher occupancy—sixty-five percent to eighty percent on an average—across our network hotels and self-operated brands, like the OYO Townhouse, leading to better financial returns on all of their hard-earned investments. This gives us the unique ability to attain growth at scale, where the company runs like a well-oiled machine.

Today, OYO Hotels & Homes is South Asia's largest, China's second-largest, and the world's third-largest and fastest-growing chain of hotels, homes, managed living, and workspaces. We have 23,000 hotels, 125,000 vacation homes, and over one million exclusive rooms spread across eight hundred cities in eighty countries.

Fernandez: Can you share more about some of the unique ways that you've localized the OYO Hotels & Homes' rooms, experience, or brand to certain markets?

Agarwal: Our teams across the world have observed local nuances with respect to the hotel industry in each of the countries where we operate. These observations help us in localizing and personalizing the experience for our guests. For instance, given local practices and beliefs in the Philippines, most hotel rooms keep a copy of the Bible in a drawer or on a table in the rooms for guests. In Indonesia, most hotel rooms have the Qibla sign, also known as Arah Kiblat in the local language Bahasa. The arrow sign signifies the direction in which the daily prayers should be offered. As Malaysia hosts a lot of Indian tourists, the hotels provide information on the nearest Indian/South Indian restaurants because the country has several dosa points. Moving West, in the UK, the majority of the hotels have tea-making facilities readily available for guests. This is unlike what hotels offer in other international markets. Traditionally, all hotel rooms in the UK will contain a copy of the Bible. A majority of UK hotels also avoid having a room 13, not necessarily because the Brits are superstitious, but because other nationalities would stay at these hotels and they would like to keep all guests happy. In China, most hotels can accept payment by QR code and even pre-book by QR code scans because of the high level of online payments in the country.

Fernandez: How did you expedite the process of upgrading and renovating rooms? There certainly must be some interesting, MacGyver-like solutions here, given that other hotel chains were unable to achieve this quality improvement themselves.

Agarwal: Technology is our core differentiator and drives our operations everywhere. Our deep renovation capabilities backed by proprietary technology-led products have enabled us to add 80,000 exclusive keys to our chain every month at a global level. We have set a new benchmark in transforming and renovating assets in a record time of within 14 days, which is a stark contrast to the industry standard of up to 90 days. We also have a 1,300+ strong team of civil engineers and designers in India, China, and other international markets. We utilize an AI-led design approach while evaluating guest feedback and identifying their most preferred designs. Our efforts are supported by in-house design labs [OYOXDesign and Townhouse Design Team]. Our full-scale, capability-led model allows us to undertake a 360-degree transformation and renovation while upgrading the existing structure of an asset, from flooring, plumbing, air conditioning, painting, and electrical fixtures to a utilities upgrade.

Fernandez: What challenges did you encounter as you started to expand overseas? Some of which are markets decidedly different from South Asia.

Agarwal: Operating in multiple geographies and bringing a consistent product is both exciting and challenging. Today, there are OYO customers who actively stay with us in almost all the countries we have opened.

We respect that each market is unique in its own way, so we localize the product experience and interiors of our buildings, and our overall approach. The macro environment for OYO to operate in any country remains that the majority of the hotels are unbranded and operate at sub-twenty-five percent occupancy, versus the branded ecosystem at seventy-five percent.

We believe that for any company trying to make a big impact globally, they should understand the potential that the market will offer, and customize the offerings and services based on the needs of that specific market. This research will give you a proper outlook as to how best you can run your business in the market and design for the most important stakeholder—the customer. Hence, companies who invest in understanding the complexities of the market, and are working toward solving a significant problem pertaining to that market—rather than bringing in a product or service that worked elsewhere, will definitely stand a chance to do big in the industry.

We are proud that in every country where we have opened OYO hotels, we have been able to increase the occupancy from twenty-five percent to sixty-five percent in less than three months on an average, with as high as ninety percent–plus consistent occupancies. Take, for instance, the OYO Sarkawi Residence in Jakarta, OYO Townhouse Sussex Gardens in London, or OYO 101 Click Hotel in Dubai.

For us at OYO Hotels, in a nutshell, we do the same thing in all the markets. We go to the unbranded building owners and we sign franchise, lease, or revenue management agreements to have them join the OYO family. They benefit from our transformational and renovation capabilities, operational expertise, technological know-how, talent, and wide distribution network.

On an average, every hotel that takes OYO's franchise or gets leased by us as a part of the OYO chain of hotels, is able to maintain occupancy of approximately sixty-five or seventy-five percent, which is an approximately twenty to thirty percent increase. We make this possible by investing in four key competencies—the ability to scientifically identify and onboard strategic properties within shorter time period than others, renovate and upgrade living spaces in record time by leveraging our design and engineering talent, sustained demand generation across offline and online channels, and lastly, immersive technology that redefines the hospitality experience at every customer and hotel owner touchpoint. This helps us bring in operational efficiencies through revenue management, dynamic pricing, service quality improvements—staff training and management, and so on.

Through this, we are able to drastically improve the customer experience at affordable prices, while ensuring a much higher occupancy, and significant growth, leading to better financial returns on all of their hard-earned investments for asset owners. When both the asset owner and the customer win, then we win.

However, the approach to pitch an asset owner and to acquire a new customer is always localized. We were lucky to have a strong team of OYOprenuers across multiple geographies who analyzed the demand-supply gap, and accordingly, came up with the right offering. We will continue to use our technological prowess along with our customer and hotel owner-oriented innovations to consistently scale up in every market.

Fernandez: So not only are your hotel units themselves localized, but the way you obtain partners is as well. Can you share some of your more unique approaches to unit acquisition around the world?

Agarwal: As the business is localized to suit the needs of the market and the hoteliers, we are able to organically connect with a like-minded hotelier who sees value in our business model.

Fernandez: As you grew both domestically and internationally, how did you develop the processes by which you vet the accommodation providers to ensure a consistent experience no matter where they stay?

Agarwal: We manage to ensure a consistent experience for our guests across all of our 23,000-plus hotels and 125,000-plus holiday homes by means of investments in CapEx to renovate a hotel's infrastructure to bring it to OYO standards. We provide skilled hospitality staff to our hotels and invest in technology to make the day-to-day operations at our hotels run smoothly.

Let me go through these in detail.

We have invested thousands of crores in CapEx, appointed hundreds of GMs to oversee operations and the customer experience across our 23,000-plus hotels globally. We invest in the asset alongside the hotel owners and provide free design and consulting to upgrade the infrastructure and design of the hotels. Our focus on design-driven online conversion leads to better reviews and therefore higher business while also solving for infrastructure issues to deliver better customer experience.

With a thirteen hundred–plus OYOpreneur-strong team of civil engineers and designers, OYO Hotels has powered the transformation of thousands of buildings across territories while promoting sustainable infrastructure in the hospitality sector. We utilize an AI-led design approach while evaluating guest feedback and identifying their most-preferred designs. Our efforts are supported by in-house design labs—OYOXDesign and the Townhouse Design Team. Our full-scale, capability-led model allows it to undertake a 360-degree transformation and renovation while upgrading the existing structure of an asset—from flooring, plumbing, air conditioning, painting, and electrical fixtures to utilities upgrade.

We have twenty-seven OYO Skill Institutes operating globally, through which we train hundreds of hospitality enthusiasts into skilled professionals. They are not just absorbed into OYO Hotels but by the hospitality industry at large. We provide trained staff at our hotels and support the existing staff of our hotel owners with contemporary knowledge and skills in the hospitality sector.

One of the most important aspects is our investment in technology. Technology has always been a key differentiator for OYO. As an intersection of real estate, hospitality, and technology, OYO has twenty-plus technological products that power various business verticals, and has helped the company build capabilities that make it possible to add over eighty thousand rooms every month under its portfolio. At present, OYO offers multiple app-based solutions for its customers, employees, and hotel owners.

Fernandez: This level of knowledge management is incredibly robust. What advice do you have for other founders on how they can build strong knowledge management practices for all their stakeholders?

Agarwal: Knowledge management is a critical aspect for organizations that are scaling fast. OYO is one of the most physically distributed companies in the world today with its operations in 800 cities across 80 countries. A massive amount of knowledge gets captured through various means on a daily basis. I think it is important for founders to ensure that they spend some time with the frontline staff and interact with them directly to be able to understand things on the ground in a nuanced manner.

A lot of knowledge sharing happens with seasoned OYOpreneurs from India moving to strategic roles when we expand into new geographies. They help percolate the learnings and most importantly the culture at OYO in the new market.

Knowledge management initiatives that are focused on corporate strategic business goals can provide significant return on investment [ROI] and long-term competitive advantage by improving the total customer experience. We leverage technology in a big way to draw learnings from trends emerging from our customer interactions on a daily basis around the world.

We have a dedicated Learning and Development function where employees are trained in various business-focused skills and the knowledge and tools to be able to perform their jobs even better.

Fernandez: Like Airbnb, do you have a north-star metric that you obsessively focus on as a measure of overall growth?

Agarwal: We have two business metrics—Net Promoter Score and Sellable Room Nights—that we religiously monitor and focus on as a measure of our business. While Net Promoter Score indicates customer experience and loyalty, Sellable Room Nights indicates the supply of inventory and eventually the occupancy and yield. However, from my perspective, the north-star metric that I am focused on is the impact we are making globally—our mission of delivering beautiful living spaces and changing the lives of over 3.2 billion middle-income people. Fifty million guests hosted at OYO so far. Three hundred thousand direct and indirect employment opportunities created so far.

Fernandez: Why did you decide to raise money from and partner with Airbnb?

Agarwal: Strong global strategic relationships like this support our mission and help drive collaborative efforts in the right direction. Airbnb's strong global footprint and access to local communities will open up new opportunities for OYO Hotels & Homes to strengthen and grow while staying true to our core value proposition. We're excited by the possibilities and committed to bringing benefits to the millions of travelers who can now rely on Airbnb and OYO Hotels & Homes to find a home away from home.

Fernandez: Where were you when you learned that OYO Hotels & Homes' valuation made it a unicorn, and what did you do next?

Agarwal: We have never looked at valuation as a measure of success. We look at the impact we are making, and measure it by the scale of having over one million rooms—hotels and homes—under management and over 500,000 heads resting on OYO pillows every night, on an average, and the 300,000-plus direct and indirect employment opportunities we have created worldwide. That is the measure of our success.

Having said that, I am deeply committed to it and so is the entire OYO leadership team. I can say with confidence that OYO is a multi-decade effort. I have a fiduciary duty to our shareholders to ensure that we create more value for them. We remain focused on execution to create great-quality living spaces, and that is what we enjoy the most.

Fernandez: You are already a market leader in your space. What do you want to accomplish with OYO Hotels & Homes for both your accommodation providers and your users?

Agarwal: I always say it is still day zero. I am only twenty-five and have a long way ahead. Each time I see an OYO in a new city across the world, it fills me with great joy and enhances the drive to keep going forward in the future. Looking back over the last six-plus years, I believe our passion, perseverance, and grit helped us grow to where we are today.

We are already the third-largest hotel company in the world, with over 1.1 million rooms as a part of our chain of hotels and vacation homes. With the $2 billion share buyback, I think the company is well placed to achieve exponential growth while redefining the future of living. The capital received through a forthcoming primary round will help boost OYO's expansion plan in India, the United States, China, the United Kingdom, the European Union, and Southeast Asian markets. OYO is increasingly evolving into a real estate company with over a million rooms under its management globally, but our focus is to change the lives of over 3.2 billion middle-income people worldwide by creating better living spaces. Our vision is to be the most loved hospitality brand in the world.

Fernandez: Given your success, and that of others from the Thiel fellowship, do you think more aspiring founders should look beyond a college education as their path to entrepreneurship?

Agarwal: I look at this differently. I always tell people that I believe that thy should not let school/university come in the way of their education.

They should keep learning, and the source of their education doesn't matter.

Fernandez: OYO Hotels & Homes is undoubtedly an expert in hospitality. In what ways do you think founders can be more hospitable or empathetic toward their users or customers?

Agarwal: Broadly, we operate in the service sector and hospitality industry, more specifically where one needs to constantly evolve to meet changing consumer demands. Offering a great customer experience at a large scale is the core focus for all of us at OYO.

I think regardless of the size of the company and the management team, founders need to be field-oriented, as in be in regular touch with the frontline staff and customers. Most of my growth has come from surrounding myself with the right kind of people while making sure that I am very field oriented. I still spend the majority of my time learning from people on the ground because I think that essentially makes an entrepreneur's value proposition unique.

Fernandez: What advice do you have for founders in Asia who want to build a successful global tech company like OYO Hotels & Homes?

Agarwal: While one is in the process of coming up with a truly innovative solution, it is essential to keep an open mind. One should accept failure, and be willing to learn, unlearn, and relearn again. We have always believed that an overnight success story is backed by at least five years of dedicated hard work and perseverance. Often, it is not the most complex solution, but the most creative one that can help solve a problem. The importance of innovation cannot be overstated. For any business, and startups in particular, it is vital to inculcate the spirit of curiosity and lateral thinking to succeed in the long run.

At times, we tend to get carried away by what we think are good ideas, but in reality, they may not serve the customer's purpose in any way. It is crucial that we understand the customers' requirements and direct our efforts toward providing the best possible solution for their requirements.

Also, I think perseverance is an irreplaceable trait. There is always light at the end of the tunnel. Way too many people give up early without realizing that impactful or big things take time. It's important to keep putting in the effort.

Shao-Ning Huang

Co-founder and Deputy CEO, JobsCentral

In 2000, **Shao-Ning Huang** *co-founded JobsCentral with Der Shing Lim (whom she married in year 3 of the business) in Singapore. The two met at the University of Michigan where she studied business and he studied electrical engineering. In the United States, they encountered Monster and thought that Singapore needed a similar job portal solution.*

Unlike most startups today, the couple bootstrapped their entire 11-year journey. After pooling together US $13,200, the co-founders raised another $145,000 from their families. The investment paid off handsomely. In 2011, CareerBuilder contacted the co-founders, which by then had eight million page views a month and processed 150,000 job applications from a user base of 700,000 job seekers.

After four months of negotiation, the team exited JobsCentral to CareerBuilder for what was rumored to be one of the highest exits in Singapore at the time. The couple remains active in Singapore's tech ecosystem, this time as investors at the helm of the angel community, with AngelCentral.

© Ezra Ferraz, Gracy Fernandez 2020
E. Ferraz and G. Fernandez, *Asian Founders at Work*,
https://doi.org/10.1007/978-1-4842-5162-1_8

Gracy Fernandez: Since the story of JobsCentral is framed by your partnership with your husband, we ought to begin with your personal history. Can you share the story of how you met in college?

Shao-Ning Huang: Chronologically speaking, we started the business in 1999, together with a few other friends. We tied the knot only in late 2001. Though we were both from Singapore, we actually met at the University of Michigan in Ann Arbor in 1996. He went there to study engineering, and I studied business. We met at the freshmen orientation organized by the Singapore Student Association on campus. We hit it off well and became a couple in sophomore year.

Fernandez: Outside of being a couple, did you work on any projects or jobs together that helped you get a sense of one another's working style long before founding a company together?

Huang: No. Although we were both holding exco positions in the Student Association, we never had the experience of working together.

Fernandez: What formative experiences did you have at IBM that would ultimately help you in building JobsCentral?

Huang: I was hired as the only business control person at the IBM technology group in Singapore, reporting directly to the CFO. Basically, I studied past audit reports to figure out what's going on. I did process reviews and workflows, redesigning stuff to ensure control and governance. I was required to review process across all functions—finance, logistics, procurement, and HR. It quickly exposed me to how businesses are run and the importance of control and governance.

But the "hard lesson" in being the only business control person on site meant that I had no friendly relationships at the office. No one would have lunch with me, as everyone saw me as the "internal police" that could be trouble for them. It was a tough job for a fresh grad, honestly. I learned very quickly how to make small talk and get myself invited to lunch.

After we started up in 1999, even though a two-person team couldn't have much separation of duties, I was very particular about proper documentation, tracking, rules, and guidelines. I came to realize that not many small companies at our stage really cared about such things. But it really helped us when it came to scaling, as we had clear-cut processes mapped out, and we could easily trace all histories and records. I was also quite particular about how we structured our finances and ensuring that proper accounting and audit were done along the way.

Fernandez: Who first came up with the idea of the jobs platform, and how was it pitched to the others?

Huang: Three of the original group of six founders were studying in the United States between 1996 and 1999, which was the time when the Internet was booming in the US. We read daily about Internet successes and instant dot-com millionaires. The hottest stories then were Amazon, Yahoo!, Monster, and eBay. Naturally, when WebFactory was birthed as our company [JobsFactory was a product], we looked at these successful models and tried to see what would be relevant for Singapore. And jobs were something that we could understand very well as new graduates. JobsFactory [later changed to JobsCentral] was launched as a mass job portal, but since we were self-financed, we couldn't really afford mass marketing.

Just when we were struggling to figure out how best to acquire jobseekers, and honestly, on the verge of giving up, I received a postcard invitation from the UM Business School. It was holding a virtual career event for business school alumni. That gave us the idea to convert what we had built by then, to become a virtual campus career fair.

It's worthwhile to note that career guidance and job search services were not provided at Singapore universities then. In fact, only one university catered to internship support. It took us a while to convince our first school partner to work with us, but after that, it was a path of no return. We niched into campus jobs, and consciously moved away from mass market for the next three or four years.

Fernandez: Choosing a name for a startup is crucial to its branding. You toyed with multiple possible names, such as JobsFactory, before arriving at JobsCentral. Can you share the thought processes involved in brainstorming and finally choosing your brand name?

Huang: JobsFactory was the original brand, and was a collective decision by the original six friends who came together for the business. In fact, the company name was WebFactory as we were crazy ambitious, and we thought we could do anything to do with the web. The thinking then was that JobsFactory would be the first product, and we would move on to BookFactory and so on. But "Jobs" kept us very busy for fourteen years.

JobsCentral came about in 2006. It was a conscious decision to create a new brand. By then, we were already well known in the Singapore market as the campus career specialist covering first jobs for graduates and for scholarships. JobsFactory was synonymous with campus recruitment in the minds of our HR clients. As such, it was not an ideal brand to use for a mass market job portal that targets the PMET experienced white-collar professionals. It was very obvious we needed a second brand.

But it was definitely a decision that our staff did not easily accept. By then, we had a team of close to 30 people; we divided the team and resources to build the second business, which was to become a new core. We spent a few months explaining and convincing our staff of the necessity for this move, even though there was a possibility that the new service could cannibalize our campus services in coming years.

Fernandez: I'm sure you already had a very strong dynamic as a co-founding team who were also partners. What was your relationship like with your other co-founders?

Huang: Of the original six co-founders, only two of us converted to full-time when we launched in April of 2000. We returned the funding to some of those who did not come on board. The two of us persisted and learned to sell very fast! We sold hard to get cash flow, and with the launch of our first campus career fair in mid-2001, we closed our first official financial year with approximately $250,000 top line revenue. After that, we went on to bring on board our CTO, Eric, in 2002 and our CMO, Michelle, in 2003.

We had a sales co-founder who came on board in 2002, but she left around 2007 and bought out her shares.

Der Shing, Michelle, Eric and I worked together for 11-12 years. We had our ups and downs, and we fought at times, especially during the early years. The most beautiful thing between us is the near complete faith that no matter what Der Shing or I managed to sell, Eric and Michelle would make sure the product was delivered and on time! We had limited resources at the start, so we had to do everything in the cheapest possible way. They always could manage to do it. While we had our respective functional roles, when it came to crunch times, everyone would roll up their sleeves and help. I remember all of us sitting with our event team at the back of the site office folding flyers the night before the fair. And I remember our silliness in the stretch limo when the four of us flew to Chicago to visit CareerBuilder's office.

Fernandez: There were already several dozen job platforms in Singapore at the time you founded JobsCentral. Why did you think you could distinguish yours by focusing on recent college graduates?

Huang: We first were validated as a viable business as a campus recruitment specialist, and then used that client base, jobseeker database, and know-how to start a mass market job portal in 2006 onward. By niching as a campus service and partnering with the universities and polytechnics, we had a captive user audience, and did not need to spend huge chunks of money for marketing. And being the first mover in this campus space, we gained traction very fast. We signed exclusive partnerships with all tertiary institutes in Singapore by the end of 2002 and turned profitable by year end 2001.

Fernandez: What were the biggest challenges as your dynamic shifted from being just partners to business partners, and how did you overcome them?

Huang: The initial challenges were more in terms of decision making, and who should do what [functions]. We quickly learned to play to each other's strengths, so he headed up system and engineering, while I did testing, customer support, finance, and admin. But this was work reserved for after six p.m. Our day jobs were both sales. We were out seeing customers all the time. As we had no external funding, we were very clear that if we couldn't sell, we would not survive.

The real challenges came when we had kids. Our first boy was born in 2002, and the second one in 2003. We planned a lot on business front, but not so much on the family front. We are lucky that our families were behind us and really helped to look after the boys when they came along. We wouldn't be able to focus on work so much if not for the help from our parents. Also, 2004 was extremely stressful due to the SARS outbreak in Southeast Asia. The economy came to a standstill, and really put a brake on our growth. Almost all the MNCs held back their management trainee hiring. And we were not even able to meet customers. SARS was highly contagious, so most companies stopped holding external meetings.

We fought a lot during those years, of course. But one thing that was quite miraculous was that we never thought about parting ways. We tried many things to avoid conflict, like not talking about work after we got home, but those things never worked. We talked work all the time, to the extent that our boys identified with our company even when they were just two or three years old. I think we were clear that we needed to provide for the boys. We really did our best to make sure the business worked.

While it's hard for two alphas to work together, in hindsight, I realize it was actually an extreme luxury that I enjoyed for many years. I know my partner never had second thoughts about me or our family, and me him. I only realized how invaluable this was when I started another business with another partner after we exited JobsCentral. I had the constant nagging worry that my partner was not dedicated and plotting something against the business, and it turned out I was right.

Fernandez: When there was tension between you and your partner, how did you ensure it did not affect other people on the team?

Huang: We tried to keep our home conflict to ourselves. I don't know if we were successful on this front (I will make it a point to check with my old colleagues in our next gathering!) but we tried very hard to make sure we were professional at the office and did not bring home stuff to the office. We definitely had work-related conflicts, too. So at home we tried our best to keep those issues away from the kids. So our car really was our personal board room. Out of the car, we tried to be all smiley!

Fernandez: How did you manage to convince schools to partner with JobsCentral, rather than turn to any of the other job platforms already on the market?

Huang: I remember there were three bidders for the university to choose from. One was Monster. The other was a software firm. The third was us. We were the least experienced and had the least backing. I would like to believe it was our sincerity and commitment to excellent service, but truth be told, it was because we offered our services for free. We took a big gamble with our business model. While the career e-fair would be held in the school's name, we did not charge the school partner at all. In return, we got to keep all the advertising revenue from the participating employers. It was a matter of the number of employers we could bring onboard—sell to. The school partner's job was to ensure the event was marketed to all graduating class and alumni. We committed to bring in good, brand-name employers and jobs relevant to degree holders. We each bore our respective costs. It was a win-win partnership that worked for many years.

Fernandez: As you were a digital startup first, were there any challenges in selling offline exhibition space to these employers?

Huang: Interestingly, no. In fact, we saw very quickly that we had to be a multi-channel career search and information platform. Our second channel was print. We went into the career magazine publication in 2003 and did that brilliantly. Career exhibitions were our third channel. Selling was not difficult because there were print and exhibition budgets. The challenge was in our internal operations. We had to learn editing, designing, printing [for the magazine], and then exhibition management work [for the fairs].

Fernandez: You initially tried several business models, like headhunting and placement. Can you share the story behind these aborted business models, and how you eventually came to be a jobs portal?

Huang: We were a job portal at the core. Headhunting and placement services were experiments to help us extract more revenue from our jobseeker databases. Neither worked out—not because of the model, but more due to our personalities and preferences for simple and efficient business models. Placement and headhunting are pretty much "relationship" businesses. A lot of effort is needed to build relationships with both the customers and the candidates, with no guarantee of outcome. In addition, both segments suffer from bad collection problems. Not to mention, within just the SG market, there were easily more than twelve hundred headhunter and placement firms. It was extremely crowded with low or no barriers to entry. Within a few months of experiments, we quickly learned to double down in the blue ocean and left the red for good.

Fernandez: You achieved ramen profitability—or a break-even point—about eighteen months after your founding. Did this milestone come sooner or later than you initially expected, and why?

Huang: Looking at the current tech scene, breaking even in eighteen months is unheard of, but back then, I would have wanted it sooner. We launched in April 2000, the month when NASDAQ crashed, and the Internet went bust. We had no funding. If we didn't break even, we couldn't survive. I would have preferred it to be sooner.

Fernandez: You've mentioned that one of your lowest points was having to negotiate the buyout of one of your former partners. Can you share this story?

Huang: We had the unspoken understanding that we would have only working partners. So when one of the partners decided to take a one-year sabbatical for personal reasons, we were upset, but we agreed, with the understanding that she would be back with the team at the end of the year. This happened when we had just launched JobsCentral in 2006. We were profitable but not stable yet. It was crucial that all hands stayed on deck. But when she asked to extend the sabbatical at the end of that for another year, I personally felt very betrayed. I can't speak for the other partners, but I was very emotional and upset, as I felt cheated and betrayed by a close comrade.

We made a business decision to buy her out, but she was unwilling to sell, as she was also equally emotionally attached to the business. And it's double complicated because we did not have a shareholder agreement to provide a framework for such situations. It was a very emotional and hard thing to do. But I'm happy to say that, in the end, we managed to work out a fair offer and we are still friends.

Fernandez: How do you think founders can more proactively prepare for these type of situations with their co-founders to better deal with them when they do arise?

Huang: Talk about all that could go wrong before you start, and what you each would do to resolve those differences, and have all the decisions documented. Most crucially, if you have to split, know how you would split and what would be done to ensure that the business could continue. Do the scenario planning and have the relevant action plans mapped out, with mutual understandings and everyone signed off. So the shareholder agreement is a must and especially the deadlock clause/management. The idea is to make sure that you make the rational business decisions now, instead of later when the parties could be clouded by emotions. Think of it as signing a prenuptial agreement before you get married.

Fernandez: In 2004, JobStreet tried to acquire you. Founders all over the world, of course, dream about this moment. Can you share the story of how you turned them down, and why?

Huang: The whole episode with JobStreet was a very big learning experience for me, personally. I learned a lot from Mark in the few months that I spent with him. But at the end of the day, it was a mathematical decision. They gave a valuation offer that was just fifty percent more than our annual sales that year, so it was a number that we could not accept.

Fernandez: You first expanded overseas to Malaysia in 2009. What were the challenges of replicating your job portal in your first foreign market, and how did you address them?

Huang: The first of the challenges was finding the right local partner. We started with the premise that we wanted to partner a local business that was already either in the HR space or the advertising space. It took us a whole year of search and exploration to find the right JV partner. After that, it was trying to drive internal alignment between the two businesses, recruiting the right management team to run a brand-new business, how to make use of existing resources to help the new business grow without compromising the growth of existing businesses, and so forth.

Even though Malaysia and Singapore are similar culturally, it was a steep learning curve because our business practices and expectations are very different. To address these cultural and practice challenges, Der Shing and I traveled monthly to meet, train, and review with the whole team there. It was demanding and very taxing, especially since I just had my third baby in 2008, but it was necessary. Later, this experience proved very useful when we opened our joint venture in Indonesia.

Fernandez: So many startups, even in the job space, choose to go it alone when expanding internationally rather than partnering with another company via a joint venture. Why did you feel it was necessary to put up a JV to navigate the business landscape of other markets?

Huang: For the job space, we had to deal with both HR and jobseekers. We believed it was crucial that we spoke the local cultural language in our operations and marketing outreach. Our ideal JV partner would be an existing business already either in the recruitment or advertising space so they would already know the local practices, or what the HR/jobseekers are like, and ideally have existing assets (databases, customer list) that we could tap into. Setting up shop directly without local partners was our plan B, if we were not able to find a like-minded JV partner within the target time frame.

Fernandez: Can you share an example of how your JV partners helped you better navigate the local landscape in a way that wouldn't have been possible for you and your team to do alone?

Huang: Technically, anything could be learned, but with a local partner, the learning curve is greatly shortened. For one, our partners spoke Bahasa and that greatly helped in dealing with the government agencies. Governments are usually the biggest employer in the respective economies. Getting their contracts as a foreign pure play usually would take much more time. Also, when it came to hiring and firing, the local GM who knows the local practices and insights—not just the published legal guidelines—probably saved us a lot of headaches.

Fernandez: Both you and your husband have a background in sales. How did you try to grow as product developers? Which product changes, features, or developments are you most proud of that you stewarded?

Huang: We were self-taught sales people. He was trained as an electronic engineer while I was trained in business and finance. However, I think most of what we know was pretty much learned on the job.

When we started in early 2000, the concept of product teams for websites was new. We basically designed everything from scratch, based on market needs, common sense, and iteration from successes and failures. I think what really helped was our constant contact with clients. We were basically "translators" of client requirements for our tech team. And because we were detail oriented and used to go strictly by request frequencies—or data-based decision making, we pretty much designed our systems based on customer feedback and requests.

What I am most proud of in the product design process is the mindset I acquired. It's "common sense" now to say that we have to listen to customers. We learned it the hard and expensive way during our early days. The very first version of our portal was designed on idealism and pure imagination—what we thought HR wanted. We were so wrong.

Our first version—in addition to full job-posting and application-processing tools—had applicants tracking job ad usage and e-invoicing capabilities. Only after we launched and started talking to HR users locally, we were shocked to learn that many HR teams in Singapore had to share their computers! Yes, we didn't talk, and we didn't survey any of our target customers during the design phase! What a joke!

The next humbling lesson… while many HR were curious about this new way to recruit and impressed with what we had built, we spent easily the next few months visiting customers to teach them how to log in, how to post jobs, and how to receive applications in their inboxes. This taught me a precious lesson: do not over build. Many features are good to have but end up being white elephants. We improvise to drive efficiencies and address pain points. Do not over assume the pain points.

Fernandez: While it's important to listen to users, the converse of that principle is that sometimes they may not know what they really need. This dovetails with the idea that people at the turn of the twentieth century would have asked for faster horses rather than cars when forced. Did you ever conceptualize features based on intuition that your users did end up needing?

Huang: I would think that it was the rollout of our mobile app in 2009. We were the first job portal to do that because we saw the sales of smartphones increasing and how we were using mobile phones more and more for both personal and business life. We started with a job alert push system to help users stay on top of new opportunities, and then one-click applications that did not need desktop access.

Fernandez: In addition to learning how to become product developers, how did you learn product marketing?

Huang: Later, as we expanded, we caught on to two main trends before our competitors. First, was the use of Facebook marketing to get users. This allowed us to get jobseekers rapidly. Second, as previously mentioned, was the development of our mobile app once it was clear that the iPhone was a game changer.

Fernandez: Can you share the story of how CareerBuilder acquired you? Why did you choose to finally go with them, especially after rebuffing the earlier attempt of JobStreet to acquire you?

Huang: Between 2003 and 2009, there were three to four investment and acquisition interests from media firms both locally and overseas, and also one PE firm. Nothing materialized, as there was no meeting of the minds most of the time. But those were good learning episodes that helped us realize what was important to us. Also, we were very cash-flow positive and profitable, and were able to fund our own overseas explorations. In fact, we used our own cash reserves to invest in other classified plays from 2009 to 2011. Those helped Der Shing and I learn to evaluate other businesses and served as the foundation for our angel investing careers now.

After the last negotiation fell through in 2008 with a UK firm, we set a local IPO as our liquidity goal. So when CareerBuilder called in mid-2010, it was a big surprise, and we approached the negotiation with a rather indifferent attitude. We met up with the Asia Pacific President who flew in a few weeks after that. We took those meetings purely as learning meetings, and we were not expecting much. Then we were invited to visit the headquarters in Chicago, and we met with the CEO and the full management team. It probably helped that we were educated in the Midwest, and we had a common language in terms of job board technologies, sales team management, the NCAA, football, deep dish pizza, and so on. They very soon gave us a term sheet, and we negotiated a little, and decided to work together after they gave an offer that all four of our partners could not say no to.

Fernandez: What happened after the acquisition? To what extent did you both remain involved at the newly acquired entity, and in what capacity?

Huang: The first year, post-acquisition was pretty much business as usual. Other than financial reporting system changes, we were just trying to learn from the US teams and what good or bad things we could adopt or avoid for our growth here. The major struggle started in year two, where we had to integrate the core technologies. By then, our CTO had decided to leave. Der Shing's scope was transitioning to own the Southeast Asian expansion plan, while I had to shoulder the whole Singapore P&L and launch new product to Singapore and Malaysian markets. It was stressful then. We were always working together as a team, supporting each other in the boardroom and the bedroom. But with this role change, he had to travel a lot, and I was basically responsible for close to eighty percent of CareerBuilder's AsiaPac revenue.

Fernandez: When did you finally decide to leave post-acquisition, and what were your immediate plans?

Huang: I was very depressed between 2012 and 2013. I went to work every day as usual, but I felt a big part of me was missing. I took a sabbatical in the second half of 2013 to attend classes at Harvard. After I came back to Singapore, I realized that I had never learned a crucial corporate survival skill—managing up.

After being a business owner for 10 odd years, I knew how to manage my co-founders, different functional teams, internal or even cross-border teams, business partners, etc. But I never learned how to manage UP, and how to navigate office politics. Long story short, I got so stressed fighting for resources and issues with the Chicago office that I had no idea what I signed up for. I was under so much stress that I did not realizes that I was not putting on weight (I was pregnant with my 4th kid then). All the years of market share and competitor fighting did not prepare me for such "in-fighting." When I finally caught on to the signal that my body was giving me, I decided to throw in the towel. I figured that my health was the most important thing. By then, my other co-founders were also in the last month of their notice to the company. I did not have any plans after leaving. I thought I would just chill and spend more time with my kids. I was pretty sure I would do some other businesses after a while.

Fernandez: Post-acquisition, how did you try to focus more on the personal relationship with your partner that you had to focus less on by necessity while building the business?

Huang: It's still a work in progress today. When we were running the business together, we were aligned without needing to say too much. Which meant that we did not communicate much as a couple about our life goals and intentions. We thought we understood each other, as we were on the same boat and sailing in the same direction. But after we stopped, our conflicts really grew and only then did we realize that we were on the same boat but for very different reasons. Now that we are not on the boat anymore, we have to figure out what we are about as a couple, and as a family.

Right after we stopped working, my mother-in-law was diagnosed with cancer and she deteriorated very quickly. It really hit us how fragile life is and how random, too. My husband's outlook changed a lot after his mother's passing.

Over the last two years, we went through a lot of re-discovery, and new "forming and storming" in our relationship as a couple. We learned and relearned a lot about each other. I know I am very lucky to have him. We have learned new insights about me that I am not proud of, but he is willing to work with me to become better. I think we just started our "performing" phase.

Fernandez: Can you share more about your current work as an angel investor? It's particularly interesting that you turned to venture capital since you bootstrapped JobsCentral the entire way. In what ways are you trying to provide the capital and know-how that you yourself wish you had back when you were starting and scaling the business?

Huang: Our angel investing work was not intentional. We started seeing a lot of startups in 2015 because we had a lot of time on our hands. Our older boys were all in school and I, as an Asian mom, did not like the idea of traveling and leaving my boys behind. So we were "grounded" during non-holiday months.

We allocated some of our sales proceeds for private equity plays and in earlier stage venture funds. And as we met with more and more startups, we decided we were relevant for them—founder mindset and been-there-done-that experience sharing could really help to shorten the learning curves—and some of them were interesting investment opportunities. We did not intend to be professional angels or even venture investors. We both founded other startups and tried out different work before we realized that we seem to be getting quite good at it. Most probably due to our open and frank feedback and advice to founders, our "deal flow" grew simply by word of mouth.

By the end of 2017, we realized that we had a "following" of both startup founders and investors who were curious/keen on angel investing. We realized that we are good "translators" for the two groups. With minimal efforts, our casual pitch events helped 14 companies raise US \$2.6M in 2017. So in 2018, I decided to form an angel group, called AngelCentral. The intention is to support more investors and for them to be smart angels, so that our Southeast Asia ecosystems grow.

The times are quite different now vs then. I won't go into the "wrong" trends and behaviors I have observed in this space. I believe that if we could help more angels invest smartly and better, the startups will gain, and our ecosystem will flourish. There was a fair bit of not-so-good early investment practices that were unfair to early founders. But angels are really a good potential source for what founders need in their early days: first dollar of investment, first sales referral, and first employee. We just need to help them discover each other and have fair and better ways to connect them.

Fernandez: What unconventional advice do you have for founders who want to build a successful startup like yours?

Huang: Keep the revenue model simple, especially if you have limited resources in the first few years. Give your model a fair amount of time to run before deciding if it's working or you need to pivot. I see many founders nowadays experimenting with two or three revenue models together and never giving fair time for the market to react and respond.

Achmad Zaky

Founder and CEO, Bukalapak

Indonesia has four unicorns—the most in any market in Southeast Asia. The first three are Traveloka, Tokopedia, and Gojek. The fourth and latest unicorn, Bukalapak, was founded by **Achmad Zaky** *in 2010, with Nugroho Herucahyono and Fajrin Rasyid.*

Zaky studied informatics engineering at Bandung Institute of Technology (ITB), during which time he earned a two-month scholarship to Oregon State University and also represented ITB at a Harvard University national model United Nations event.

During college, Zaky poured his competition winnings into failed business ventures, including a noodle company, but that did not stall him and he eventually started Bukalapak. Within a year of its founding, the e-commerce platform had more than 10,000 merchants.

As a unicorn, Bukalapak is an industry-defining giant in Indonesia. There are now four million merchants on the platform, who collectively process more than two million transactions per day, which amounts to an annualized run rate with a gross merchandise value of US $5 billion. In 2019, Bukalapak started its regional expansion with launches in Singapore, Malaysia, Brunei, Hong Kong, and Taiwan.

Gracy Fernandez: Your first business was a noodle shop business. What lessons did you learn there that would eventually be helpful to you as a tech entrepreneur?

E. Ferraz and G. Fernandez, *Asian Founders at Work,*
https://doi.org/10.1007/978-1-4842-5162-1_9

Achmad Zaky: Selling noodles started my journey of being an entrepreneur. I think if there is anything worth learning, it's how to react to failure. I lost quite a sum of money at that time, and I was broken-hearted that my first business failed, but it was the catalyst for everything that I am today. I am grateful for that failure, because it was the best thing that ever happened to me. Failure led me to be more meticulous in preparing my next exploration.

Fernandez: An important part of any failure is analyzing what occurred, so you can take a different course of action in the future. That said, why do you think your first business, your noodle business, failed?

Zaky: I think the primary cause was that the place was not built with the aid of meticulous planning. It existed only because we had the eagerness and the hunger to experiment, but we didn't realize that planning is an essential part of everything.

Fernandez: What problem did you want to solve when you founded Bukalapak?

Zaky: Building software has always been the greatest passion of mine. I went back to my hometown in Central Java for a while after I graduated. I saw lots of people in my hometown that has small businesses that were still making the same profit they made ten or fifteen years back. I was thinking about how I could build something that would help them grow their businesses. That was the problem that I was trying to solve, and it is the same motivation for me today.

Fernandez: Why did you initially only see Bukalapak as a side business or a portfolio company of Suitmedia, and not a potential stand-alone company?

Zaky: We were not sure Bukalapak could get big fast. On the other hand, we needed a cash cow so Bukalapak could run very efficiently although not generate revenue. The idea was that we would sell Bukalapak as our success story when we sold our service to the companies. Bukalapak was popular enough at that time. And it worked. But after one or two years, we realized that Bukalapak could be really big. After that, almost all of Suitmedia's top management moved to Bukalapak, and we created these two separate entities to run independently. We separated the office, too. I sold most of my shares in Suitmedia to the management there.

Fernandez: How did you pitch Bukalapak to your college friends? Why did you choose to seek them out as co-founders?

Zaky: My initial thought was it was a big mission, and there was no way I could do everything all by myself. I met with Nugroho, who is now the CTO at Bukalapak, my long-time friend from high school, and I told him about my vision in building Bukalapak. About how we could help millions of people grow their business. He was fascinated by this. He was really obsessed about constructing software that could be used by millions of people. That was where we sort of just "clicked."

I met Fajrin, now the president of Bukalapak, after we made the move to Jakarta. We were still small at that time, and Fajrin was working for BCG. I showed him how we might be able to bring change to optimize our economy sector by growing SMEs exponentially through software, and he finally bought it, too. Both of them are great friends of mine, so it took us no time to eventually have the same goals for Bukalapak.

Fernandez: What were the biggest challenges in building a C2C marketplace in Bukalapak while you were bootstrapping for more than a year?

Zaky: The biggest challenge for us was to convince ourselves that Bukalapak could be big in the future. There were times when we really focused on getting money for projects, but Bukalapak was like our little baby. I guess we just couldn't let go, even though it was tough building it.

Fernandez: Why did you try to sustain Bukalapak through side projects rather than try to raise venture capital immediately?

Zaky: It was more of a mindset to want everything to be done by us. And there were fewer VCs nine years ago than there are today. I'm not sure how many VCs there are today in Indonesia, but there weren't many back then. We also sought to minimize risk by funding it through side projects. If push came to shove, we didn't want to owe anybody anything.

Fernandez: In hindsight, what do you see as the advantages and disadvantages of this approach—sustaining through side ventures—over raising VC money as soon as you start?

Zaky: The most important advantage for us was that we were used to work with high limitations due to budget constraints and we really pushed ourselves to find another solution. I wouldn't say that raising VC money sooner would have its disadvantages, because it was more of the circumstances that made us go into that direction.

Fernandez: How did you initially try to differentiate Bukalapak from other existing C2C marketplaces available in Indonesia, from either local or international competitors?

Zaky: Bukalapak started getting traction in the bicycle community. There was bicycle trend boom in 2010 and 2011. We were coming at the right place and the right community. I brought a lot of sellers from those bicycle communities. From there, the snowball effect was slow but sure as it was happening together with the growing trend of bicycle hype. Even though we didn't do anything, everyone in this specific bicycle community kept talking about Bukalapak. The hype was so big, even people who couldn't ride a bicycle, bought one. So more and more people learned about Bukalapak.

We replicated this model by conquering other categories in the community, like cameras, gadgets, gemstones, motorcycles, cars, music, and so forth. Our spirit and core has always been the community. We can say that we're pretty close to our sellers. It's like a big family.

Fernandez: How did you do your initial market education efforts for Bukalapak for the sellers and buyers at the bottom of the pyramid, who may have never had any previous experience with e-commerce, and in some cases, even the Internet?

Zaky: I've done this part at the very basic level. It's as simple as meeting the street sellers face to face. The best way of educating them was talking and doing a run through of the apps directly. From that experience, I learned that they need a lot of convincing, and meeting them directly was the best choice. I did that for a year on the street every single day and managed to acquire more than ten thousand sellers with that method.

Fernandez: When you spoke to these merchants face-to-face, what were their most common concerns or objections, and how did you address these?

Zaky: Operating the applications. Mobile phone booms in Indonesia I think in the past five or six years and when we started all of these, people don't have the best understanding towards mobile apps. Technology literacy is still a problem here in Indonesia, and that's why we developed different and simpler app for our merchants.

Fernandez: You previously mentioned that you choose Batavia Incubator because of their deep understanding of e-commerce. What did they understand about Indonesian e-commerce that other venture capital firms or institutional investors did not get?

Zaky: Batavia Incubator formed a really special bond with us. At that time in 2011, to have someone that believed in our vision that we can be bigger than any other startups in Indonesia was more than anything. They knew how the e-commerce market in Japan evolved. The partner, Takeshi Ebihara, used to run a tech company in Japan. At our level, where we were only two to five people, his experience really mattered. Moreover, I guess more than the understanding of the business landscape, we chose them because they paid us a great deal of trust, which was priceless and crucial at that time.

Fernandez: After fundraising from Batavia, you decided to step down as the managing director of Suitmedia. Even if you were no longer involved in the day-to-day operations of Suitmedia, did you leverage your ownership of Suitmedia to help grow Bukalapak in any way?

Zaky: No leverage. I gave most of my ownership in Suitmedia to my partner who chose to run Suitmedia. Everyone could really focus on the venture where they have their vested interest. At that time, I really believed that Bukalapak could get even bigger.

Fernandez: Many founders will have to make similar decisions as the one you made between Suitmedia and Bukalapak. What is your advice on how founders can make better decisions when deciding between startup or business opportunities?

Zaky: I believed in the vision of Bukalapak, and I think all of the founders should put their belief in the vision of what they are trying to build. We believed that Bukalapak's emergence could really support MSMEs throughout Indonesia, and so it happened.

Fernandez: What problems or challenges did you more clearly recognize at Bukalapak when you started working on it full-time, and how did you address them?

Zaky: Team building. I started to scale the team. We had trials and errors in hiring. We hired some, but we also fired a lot. I was not an HR expert and e-commerce stuff was really new for many people at that time. Xinuc, my co-founder and CTO, also believed that we needed to hire a higher grade of engineers compared to Suitmedia. We knew that building software for a company and for consumers was different. So, our standard of hiring was a bit higher. We started to contact our friends who were really good at coding. We convinced them that Bukalapak would change millions of small businesses. Meanwhile, we kept hiring and the company kept growing. This made talent in the market notice Bukalapak more and more. They saw that Bukalapak had a good reputation. We kept raising the bar year after year. We raised more money and made bigger milestones.

Fernandez: One of the distinguishing features that helped you grow was your escrow feature. What were the operational or technical challenges of developing and scaling this feature, and how did you overcome them?

Zaky: The biggest challenge was getting people used to it. Most people used direct contact and transfer. They said it was simpler and more convenient. In reality, it was more complicated and dangerous. You needed to contact the seller directly via SMS—there was no WhatsApp at that time. Sometimes sellers did not reply to your message, which was not convenient at all. People always think a new thing is complicated because they have never tried it. Moreover, using direct contact can be dangerous because sellers just don't ship the product. I had that experience. It was pretty common in e-commerce before the escrow system.

Fernandez: How did you then convince people that escrow was the safer and more convenient option over direct contact and transfer? Or was the switch to escrow all forced adoption?

Zaky: Escrow was in fact the safest option for people to do online shopping. There were a lot of fraud cases back then with direct contact and transfer method, so people automatically switched to escrow. The liability of other methods than escrow that convinced people to switch, back then.

Fernandez: In 2012, one of your European competitors started flooding the market with generous subsidies, and you thought it could be the end of Bukalapak. Can you share one example where you creatively competed with them during this time rather than engaging in a subsidy or price war?

Zaky: We never believed subsidies or price wars were a sustainable business model. I think this belief came due to the fact that we have less money than others. One day I found an insane fact that one of our competitors bid a Google Search as high as ten thousand IDR per click. That was way higher than us. We bid around two hundred IDR at that time. Fifty times lower than them. The other competitors started increasing their bids, too. We chose to withdraw from the campaign and switched to organic SEO because we couldn't afford the budget to bid with them.

So we invested a lot in SEO.

We also tried to find a new way to grow. We knew that if we did not grow, we would die. There was the largest forum in the country, called Kaskus. We built a sharing feature where our sellers could share their products instantly with Kaskus. We scrapped the Kaskus website to access our sellers' accounts, because Kaskus did not provide API. We quickly grew organically from this growth hack, and it was free. But, after one year of phenomenal organic growth, Kaskus blocked us because they thought we were their competitor. Kaskus also had a very strong buy-and-sell feature.

Fernandez: Did you leverage traditional media to help you compete with your international competitor?

Zaky: We also found new way of growth on TV. We did not have a luxury production budget for TV. It was very expensive. My team proposed to create a low-budget TV ad starring me as the main actor, so the company wouldn't have to pay any celebrity fees. It would be shown only during Harbolnas, which is three days. Harbolnas is a version of Cyber Monday in Indonesia. In the ad, I apologized to companies' management if their staff was not productive during these particular days due to the many promos from Bukalapak. It went viral. It was a very successful short campaign. After that, we grew even more.

Fernandez: When did you feel you had finally surpassed or defeated this international competitor, and why?

Zaky: I don't think we ever think of ourselves to have surpassed or defeated any competitor. Essentially, we see every player as co-opetition. While we do compete, we are all also working towards the same goal which is providing solutions to our users, directing potential buyers to merchants, and enhancing Indonesia's digital penetration and financial inclusion. Indonesia is a large country—there surely is enough space available for multiple players.

Fernandez: What do you think allowed you to scale so quickly that you became Indonesia's only fourth unicorn?

Zaky: I think the model and the timing was just right. The C2C platform works very well in developing countries like Indonesia. We have many small sellers. We also have many consumers who are looking for cheap products online. Indonesia is the fourth largest consumer in the world.

We were also lucky because of the timing. We are pioneers in this space. In 2010 to 2014, the e-commerce marketplace was not so common. Not a lot of people believed in this model. They thought an Internet business was bullshit, especially an e-commerce marketplace, because they could not see it.

But we always improved the system and the sellers. More and more people trusted the model. In 2015, mobile was booming in the country. The Internet users grew fast because of mobile penetration. My mom also bought a smartphone.

I met the Gojek founders in 2015, when they asked for us to invest. Gojek was a very small startup at that time. We definitely rejected them because we did not believe how a Gojek motorcycle taxi driver could use a smartphone. By 2016, Gojek was growing like crazy. We might have been wrong in this case. Because people use Gojek and Grab, more people were believing in online commerce or transactions. More and more people began coming to Bukalapak, too.

Fernandez: Even if you may have passed on the initial opportunity to invest in Gojek, did you end up collaborating with them later on for Bukalapak?

Zaky: Gojek and Grab are our logistic partners. Their services benefitted our users and most Indonesians e-commerce, particularly when addressing hyper-urban demand.

Fernandez: One of your biggest competitors is Tokopedia. How do you maintain a culture of innovation in order to stay ahead of well-backed competitors like Tokopedia?

Zaky: I can confidently say that Tokopedia is our friend. They never attacked us. We grew together in different segments. We focused more on male categories. For them, because they have a lot of money, they can focus on broad categories. I think the more focus, the better. That's how we stay ahead of the others. We really focused on our strength.

Fernandez: When did you choose to diversify into fintech and streaming products? What were the challenges of dealing with this more diversified product portfolio?

Zaky: New business will only account for five to ten percent of company activities. We still focus on the core of our products, which is marketplace. But when a new business is growing, we invest more and put more attention to it. We work like venture capital inside the company. Culturally, everyone in the company can try anything that they think may make the company bigger.

First, start with a free idea. If your idea is almost free—because any idea needs a bit of effort to execute, don't think too much, just do it. Then, if your idea needs a budget—for example, 100 million IDR, present your ideas to us. If the idea makes sense, and we can see the potential, we might give you the money. It's like an angel fund, and so on until funding of series A, B, and so forth. If the metrics don't look so good, we will kill it. That is pretty much how we work.

Fernandez: How does this system work in practice? Do these employees who pitch an idea become equity shareholders in the new venture? Share more with us about how it works, as it's a rather unique model.

Zaky: No, we want everyone to work as a team for the unified benefit of Bukalapak. Some key leaders are rewarded through ESOP

Fernandez: What's been your most successful subsidiary to emerge from your internal VC?

Zaky: To say this correctly, it is not an internal VC but rather more about thinking like a VC inside the company. What I was saying, is that we encourage all of the people in the company to come up with an idea. I think one of the examples that came up from this model was BukaGlobal. The idea's actually emerged from one of our teams, and it was soon realized into a product and still going on until today.

Fernandez: Indonesia is often a big enough market on its own for startups to scale nationally. Despite this fact, why do you think it's important for Indonesian startups to expand regionally, and when do you plan to do so for Bukalapak?

Zaky: Our strategy has always been to strengthen our presence in the market. That's why we think the Mitra Bukalapak program will optimize our significance in society Mitra Bukalapak is a program in which we partner with mom-and-pop shops all over Indonesia to help them grow their businesses so they can provide digital product service—air time, electricity, water, insurance, etc.—to their customers. We also try to help them replenish their grocery supply with same-day delivery service. Currently, we have more than 25 million kiosks and agents combined and more than four million sellers throughout Indonesia. We are currently the biggest digital economy in the region, and we need to position ourselves as such. We've recently done some international expansion with BukaGlobal, in which you can purchase and sell within Southeast Asia. BukaGlobal is the latest initiative from Bukalapak that was launched in May of 2019 to enable all customers in Singapore, Malaysia, Hong Kong, Brunei Darussalam, and Taiwan to connect with more than four million sellers in the Bukalapak platform.

Fernandez: What are the next major trends in e-commerce, in both Indonesia and Southeast Asia as a whole?

Zaky: I can't say much about major trends. People can be wrong in predicting something, like I did with Gojek.

Fernandez: What unconventional advice do you have for founders in Southeast Asia who want to build a business as successful as Bukalapak?

Zaky: The worst thing that happens to you might be the best thing, and the best thing that happens to you might be the worst thing!

Patrick Grove

Co-founder, iflix

In 2014, **Patrick Grove** *co-founded iflix, a video-on-demand subscription service headquartered in Malaysia, with backing from Catcha Group, the digital venture group that he founded in 1999.*

Grove had a broader goal for both sides of iflix's marketplace: to combat piracy, the most common way people in emerging markets access entertainment, and to provide fans with great international and local content through one convenient platform.

Now boasting a monthly base of 19 million users across Asia, iflix may be on its way toward an IPO. Amazingly enough, iflix would not be Grove's first IPO; he has already taken five companies public.

Gracy Fernandez: You founded the Catcha Group back in 1999, and it's grown to be one of the leading investors in the digital sector, especially within the ASEAN. A few of the notable investments in Catcha's portfolio include the iProperty Group, owner and operator of Asia's number-one network of property websites, and iCar Asia, the ASEAN's largest network of automobile sites. What made you venture into the video-on-demand industry?

Patrick Grove: I think many who venture into a new industry first see a problem they want to fix. In our case, my co-founder Mark Britt and I observed the proliferation of video-on-demand in North America and Europe, powered by the Internet, that hadn't yet made its way to Asia.

© Ezra Ferraz, Gracy Fernandez 2020
E. Ferraz and G. Fernandez, *Asian Founders at Work,*
https://doi.org/10.1007/978-1-4842-5162-1_10

While the West had access to major Hollywood shows and movies, people closer to home were much more likely to buy a pirated DVD in order to be part of the global conversation. We figured everyone deserved to be entertained, especially markets that, from a Western perspective, were often overlooked.

The chance to turn that around by delivering a service that simply didn't exist at the time, and tap into the multibillion-dollar piracy industry, were compelling.

Fernandez: In 2015, iflix launched operations in Malaysia and the Philippines after it received $30 million in funding from Catcha and the Philippine Long Distance Telephone Company [PLDT], the largest integrated telecommunications company in the country. Can you share a bit on how you designed the company and developed the product to stand out from other existing video-on-demand providers?

Grove: At the time, many of the markets we launched in shared a common set of challenges—things that people in the West may take for granted. For example, not everyone in our markets had a credit card, so we were challenged by ways to collect payment.

We partnered with, and got support from, each market's telecommunication giants. iflix was then bundled in telco deals for the benefit of customers, and the telcos had a value-add to attract new customers and keep existing customers. In this way, iflix could collect subscriptions directly from the telcos, instead of individual users. It was an incredible opportunity to reach large audiences very quickly.

Fernandez: Telcos are potentially a high-impact channel for many tech companies in Asia. Can you go deeper into how you successfully struck deals with local telcos?

Grove: Our experience running businesses in Asia taught us that channel partnerships were a quick way to build awareness and momentum. As a result, telco partnerships became a great go-to-market strategy very early on. Telcos wanted to include iflix as a value-added service for their customers, and we were able to leverage their established networks.

Fernandez: Were there any other ways you tried to set iflix apart?

Grove: The price point of iflix was also a major differentiator. iflix was priced between two and three US dollars per month, roughly the price of a single pirated DVD. For the same cost, we offered our customers an unlimited library of premium content. We've since introduced a free tier to make the product even more accessible.

Fernandez: Even if this makes sense mathematically, did iflix have to engage in any level of market education to convince people to move away from the legacy solution of piracy? What did this market education involve?

Grove: The ultimate draw was amazing content that would delight audiences. A month-long free trial of iflix was just the beginning of transitioning users from piracy to our platform. When we launched the free service, there was an initial challenge with communicating to our audiences that the free service wasn't a limited-time offer and that there was no catch.

For example, iflix's first original drama series in Malaysia, which we made available for free, was pirated. It didn't make sense to us. Why wouldn't they just watch the HD stream directly on iflix? The challenge rested with us to try harder to educate our audiences that free meant free.

Fernandez: Have you seen this thesis come true? Has the availability of iflix reduced piracy in the markets you are available in?

Grove: The popularity of steaming and the growth of iflix's user base is a great sign that people are adopting alternatives to piracy, but piracy, by its nature, is tough to track. It's no longer just DVDs and illegal torrents. It's also jailbroken, open source media players that play a part.

Fernandez: One thing that's noteworthy about iflix is that it was founded through a wealth of experience. You've already led four startups to IPO during the time you were conceptualizing iflix. You have five now. How did this affect the way you built iflix?

Grove: If there's one thing that my previous experience in leading tech companies to IPO has taught me, it's perseverance. What we were trying to do across emerging markets with iflix was not as straightforward as it may have been in the West, but we were conditioned by experience to push through the challenges—and the naysayers—to finally get to yes, whether it was in relation to investors, government bodies, or partners.

Fernandez: Can you share a story about what taught you how to persevere—even in a space as challenging as video-on-demand?

Grove: Fundraising may be the most obvious example. For iProperty, we were told "no" 74 times before getting our first "yes." Had we given up, we would not have built the largest real estate portal in Southeast Asia and achieved one of the largest exits in that ecosystem. For iflix, we were told "no" 115 times. Yes, we keep track. As an entrepreneur, the grind is part of the process, and in my opinion, too many entrepreneurs quit too soon.

Fernandez: Every great company has had its humble beginnings. How did you go about obtaining the first batch of content available on iflix? Can you tell us how the acquisition process worked?

Grove: Thankfully, iflix had powerful supporters from the very beginning. Rick Hess, another co-founder, saw the opportunity from day one. He just so happened to be one of Hollywood's most powerful executives. He was able to make introductions and call meetings on iflix's behalf to get the company off the ground, which led to some groundbreaking partnerships with Hollywood's major studios.

With Rick's support and the studios' endorsement, we established an advisory board comprised of Hollywood and global entertainment heavyweights for strategic input into iflix's operations, content, licensing, production, distribution, tech, and content marketing.

Fernandez: If these heavyweights were able to do the heavy lifting once you got them on board, what were the challenges of recruiting them onto your team in the first place? How did you pitch the iflix vision? Did they have any concerns about your model, and how did you convince them otherwise?

Grove: Members of our advisory board could see the industry tailwinds with the success of streaming services in North America, Europe, and China. They got on board because they could see that Southeast Asia's emerging markets were an untapped opportunity.

Fernandez: Even if you were already a veteran serial entrepreneur, iflix still surely had challenges when you were starting out. What were these challenges, and how did you overcome them?

Grove: One of our biggest challenges was building strong local teams. Unlike international players, we didn't have a global headquarters that controlled multiple markets, so when we started to expand and offer our service across Asia, the challenge was to scale our teams just as quickly. We were passionate about building local teams and engaging local experts to build each business from the ground up. After all, who knows a local market better than those that live and work there?

We played to our strengths and put together dynamic teams who understood the level of disruption that we were trying to achieve. With that shared vision, the teams came together like puzzle pieces.

Fernandez: Can you go deeper into your model for local hiring? When you say that you engaged local experts, were these consultants, freelancers, or agencies, or your first native HR hire, and why did you choose this option?

Grove: We looked for smart, passionate people who could navigate their local ecosystems, who understood the rules, regulations, and protocols—legal and cultural. Speaking the local language was crucial, too.

Fernandez: What did the iflix product look like at its first launch? What needed to be changed or added to this initial version?

Grove: From day one, iflix offered customers a massive library of unlimited local, regional, and international shows and movies that users could stream on any Internet-connected device. We rushed to get the service out so that people could enjoy it.

Very soon after, we realized that mobile broadband availability and costs would limit consumers, even if our service didn't, so we introduced the ability to download and watch offline, which was a game changer. It's still one of the product's most popular features.

Fernandez: Similar to Facebook and Internet.org, have you done anything off-product to either increase the availability of mobile broadband in your target markets or dramatically lower the cost for consumers, and thus increase the iflix user base?

Grove: Our close working relationships with telcos allowed us to advocate on our customers' behalf. We had success with the introduction of iflix-only data bundles and concessions that enabled our users to stream more.

Fernandez: At the time of iflix's launch, many people in Asia probably already subscribed to other international or local video-on-demand platforms. What was the most challenging part about acquiring users in this competitive landscape, and how did you do it?

Grove: Truth be told, they weren't. Pirating content was still the number-one way most people watched the latest programs. Netflix was not yet available in our territories, so our first challenge was actually education. Not many people knew, or trusted, video-on-demand services.

When other players entered the game, it was a matter of offering a premium product at an affordable price point to serve the best content. We paid very close attention to what people wanted to watch and made data-informed decisions to strategically acquire, develop, and create more local content.

Fernandez: Based on your data, were there any surprising trends in the type of content your market preferred, and did this change your content acquisition or creation strategy in any way?

Grove: When we launched, Western models suggested that Hollywood content would work well in Asia, so we acquired a huge library of content from Hollywood. Over time, we were able to see trends in our data that suggested our audiences had a bigger appetite for stories, formats, and talent that came from closer to home. The more local content we acquired to test that hypothesis, the more it rang true, resulting in a significant pivot in our content creation and acquisition strategy.

Fernandez: I'm sure you've tried several different strategies or growth hacks to drive user growth, especially in iflix's early history. Which was one of your most successful, and why do you think this was the case?

Grove: We may have been a little naive to think that a monthly subscription to thousands of hours of top content that cost the same as a single pirated DVD would be enough to change people's piracy habits. We've learned it's a generational shift, and that will require a bit more time. Taking cues from Spotify, iflix introduced a free tier in 2018, which was one of our most successful strategies in driving growth. There was no trial period, no hidden costs, and no tricks. That tier was supported by ads, which was something users were okay with.

Fernandez: In what ways did you change or iterate the iflix product or its content offerings based on user feedback?

Grove: We listened to feedback and we looked at data, too. Our customers were clear when they said they wanted more local content—local stars telling local stories in local languages.

Our priority shifted from Western content to acquiring, and then producing, incredible local programs and movies that showcased the talent in the region. For example, we negotiated to have local movies on iflix that came straight from cinema. Owners loved the chance to extend the traditional theatrical run of their shows, and iflix became a destination for anyone who missed the theater experience.

When we introduced iflix Originals in 2017, we made educated guesses about what would work best, and it worked out really well. For example, one of our most successful Originals was a serialized spin-off from a major blockbuster in Indonesia called *Magic Hour*. We took advantage, knowing that audiences were already immersed in the storyline and vested in the characters.

Fernandez: Another thing that makes iflix special is that it promotes local shows and movies. The company makes a point of featuring more than just popular international content. What are some of the challenges of producing and promoting original local content?

Grove: iflix's local original content underpins the company's commitment to localization and supporting homegrown talent. The aim is to create impactful, locally relevant content that has a familiar appeal, while raising the bar on local, free-to-air TV.

We see iflix as a platform to create a positive difference in the production ecosystem. We love the chance to support the growing creative community for the benefit of our audiences.

Fernandez: You lead many efforts to support the growth of the creative community, which may one day provide iflix with great localized content. What are the biggest challenges of these community-building efforts?

Grove: It takes time to produce content—anywhere between six to eighteen months for a single movie or series, so the output for originals is yet to meet demand. The industry itself is growing, so the pool of talent may not be as established as it is in, say, the US or India. We're proud to play a part in the evolution though. By supporting the creative industry, providing a platform, and urging the transition away from piracy, we want to make a lasting impact.

Fernandez: Part of how iflix markets local content is by getting celebrity advertisers, such as Kris Aquino, for the Philippines. Why and when did you decide to adopt this strategy?

Grove: iflix's collaborations with celebrities have been integral in raising awareness about the service since we first launched. Their reach and influence was a massive asset in getting our message out to the public, and their endorsement built confidence in our product. Our young, social-media-savvy viewers were well connected to celebrity culture through the likes of Instagram, Twitter, and Facebook, and our alignment with the region's biggest names in entertainment paved the way for quick adoption and promotion of iflix and the content tentpoles that we offer.

Celebrity partners were also instrumental to our understanding of local entertainment ecosystems, with trusted insights into what audiences preferred.

Fernandez: Regarding the international video-on-demand [VOD] platform, some have questioned the inherent sustainability of a model based heavily around original content, especially with more players popping up. How are you tackling this challenge?

Grove: As we focus on local content, our economics is inherently different from most major international VOD platforms. At the end of the day, we believe that if we focus on delivering value to our consumers, we will build a great business.

Fernandez: iflix is now operating in twenty-five countries across Asia, the Middle East, and Africa. What was scaling into these countries like, and what were the changes that you had to incorporate into your strategy in order to better suit each market? Can you share a story from these expansions that particularly stands out?

Grove: iflix is now operating in twenty-two countries across Asia, the Middle East, and North Africa.

Every expansion includes its own set of unique circumstances, but the iflix team is incredibly crafty when thinking outside the box is required. One incredible story, which still leaves me in awe to this the day, was an incident that happened in Indonesia in iflix's early days.

In order to launch on time in Indonesia, our studio partner's volume of content had to be ingested into our system. Our server, however, was in Thailand, and the Thai Internet infrastructure was not built for transferring terabytes of information in a short period of time. It was a huge roadblock, and we were running out of time. So we loaded up hard drives in Jakarta and bought a plane ticket to Bangkok!

That "whatever it takes" attitude continues to ooze out of the iflix team and makes me incredibly proud of the lengths we go to deliver.

Fernandez: Are there specific restrictions on content in some areas? How do you address these cultural sensitivities?

Grove: Some of the territories we operate in are more conservative than others. There are religious and cultural considerations that have to be taken into account. Since we're led by local teams in each market, we're aware of and cater to these requirements proactively. We censor to local standards, where necessary. We curate our libraries in the same way. Most of our decisions are based on what the data shows that our customers want to watch.

Fernandez: What makes iflix so different from other streaming services is that it really caters more to emerging markets than to established powers in the West. Why did you decide to target these audiences? What are the differences between their contexts and those in the United States or the United Kingdom, and how did these affect the way you run and grow iflix?

Grove: Let's start with the obvious. People in the West are more used to paying for content. They have ways in which they can pay for such services. They're spoiled for choice when it comes to what's available to them, and there is infrastructure to support access to services similar to iflix.

We started with the basic belief that everyone has a right to be entertained, even in parts of the world where delivering that entertainment isn't as straightforward. For some of the people in our markets, that means never owning a regular TV or subscribing to cable, using a mobile device on a pre-paid plan, or paying for services on a daily basis with vouchers from convenience stores. To some people in our markets, ten dollars per month is an exorbitant amount of money to pay and a large portion of their disposable income. We had to be sensitive to those limitations and work around them.

Fernandez: From a pricing perspective, can you share any creative ways you've made entertainment more accessible to this wider base of people?

Grove: From the outset, iflix's service was priced well below our competition. But we went further in 2018 by launching a free tier to completely eliminate cost as a barrier.

Fernandez: iflix has successfully grown its presence around the region, so much that it is considered Netflix's biggest competitor. In which countries have you displaced this American entertainment company as the number-one provider? When did this happen, and why do you think it happened?

Grove: We think we're in good company, but we don't see Netflix as a competitor. Our challenge is to make amazing entertainment available to the mass market, and that means eradicating piracy. Netflix is a complement to what we are trying to do, and they've done a good job educating audiences in this part of the world about what video-on-demand services are.

Fernandez: What goals do you have for iflix in the coming years? Do they include to IPO, like some of the other companies you have led?

Grove: The goal at the end of the day is to build a product and a service we can be proud of, and I think we're well on our way. An IPO would be another fantastic milestone.

Fernandez: What unconventional advice would you give to budding founders in Asia who aspire to found businesses as successful as iflix?

Grove: I'd say schedule time to journal. I've learned that it's great to have an idea, but it's even better to have a plan. Although it's important to ask yourself, "What do I want to achieve?", it's even more important to ask yourself, "How will I achieve that?", and then set time aside to make a plan.

Fernandez: Some aspiring founders may scoff at the idea of reflecting and journaling. Can you share how journaling has helped you grow iflix, or your previous ventures?

Grove: I distinctly remember sitting in a Starbucks some years ago and scribbling "How can I make $100 million in twelve months?" It took time, and several sessions of jotting down plans and ideas, but the process went a long way in organizing my thoughts and putting together a plan to make that a reality. By writing down a goal, no matter how big or audacious, it's possible to work backwards, incrementally, to devise a plan. When a plan is broken up into smaller steps, it becomes manageable and achievable, whether that goal is professional or personal, physical or emotional.

Chitpol Mungprom

CEO and Founder, Zanroo

Chitpol Mungprom *founded Zanroo with Udomsak Donkhampai in Bangkok, Thailand, in 2013. As a marketing technology company, Zanroo began by offering a social listening platform. Zanroo later created Arun, which allows companies to track their return on investment across owned media, earned media, and paid media. The company is currently active in 15 countries and employs more than 160 people. The company is expected to become the first unicorn from Thailand and a world leader in marketing tech.*

Ezra Ferraz: What were you doing in your career and life prior to founding Zanroo? Did you have a background in marketing?

Chitpol Mungprom: In the early days, I thought I could become a pop singer, and I had a few businesses such as selling authentic leather goods and running a food catering service. I graduated with a degree in engineering but ended up very exposed to social media, trying to build my business persona.

Ferraz: By the time you founded Zanroo in 2013, social listening was already one of the most crowded spaces in software. Why did you choose this field over another you could have entered in marketing technology?

© Ezra Ferraz, Gracy Fernandez 2020
E. Ferraz and G. Fernandez, *Asian Founders at Work*,
https://doi.org/10.1007/978-1-4842-5162-1_11

Mungprom: At the time, social listening was still new in Thailand. There were some companies trying to use foreign software, but they were not designed to understand Thai. They were optimized for English and other western languages, where there is spacing. When someone says, "I love you," for example, you know exactly what it means.

In Thai, on the other hand, there is no spacing. The words are put together—imagine "iloveyou"—so it becomes a technical problem. With no spacing, how can you identify each word? And if you cannot identify each word, how do you know what the whole idea is referring to? And if you cannot tell what the whole idea is, how do you know it's positive or negative for your customers? The solution we made parses the sentence first, before identifying each word.

Ferraz: Did you discover this problem from using foreign social listening software?

Mungprom: We had actually started three websites for e-commerce, and then a portal that tracked trends people were talking about in Thailand, all in real time. But the e-commerce websites were not making any money from advertising. And the portal was not making any money either. Then I realized that we have a lot of data from our portal. How can I convert this data into income, especially since our server costs are so high? Our data would be relevant to enterprises, so we decided to focus on social listening. In our first month as a marketing technology company, we made one million Thai baht [THB].

Ferraz: What did Zanroo's minimum viable product [MVP] look like?

Mungprom: It was very simple. If you were the customer—let's say a banking company—we could use Zanroo to learn what people were saying about you on social media platforms like Facebook, Instagram, YouTube, or even local forums. We didn't have any dashboards, we didn't have any analytics, and we didn't have any premium features. We just sold companies on the premise of getting market information in real time.

Ferraz: In several interviews, you mentioned that you got your first few customers by calling the numbers of companies you saw on billboards. Can you tell me a little bit more about that story?

Mungprom: After I invited Ome [Udomsak Donkhampai] to join, I felt a lot of pressure. He was the champion of the Microsoft Imagine Cup in France, so he had come from a good job with a high salary. Since I had to shoulder his salary and his friend's salary, who was also a developer, we were going to die if I could not find any money. At the time, I did not know anything about funding, so we would have to get it from customers.

If I saw any brand that I did not know but I believed could be my customer, I just listed it down on a notepad. Everywhere I went—from walking through a department store to, yes, even driving down the highway—I wrote down the company's name and its telephone number. On a single day, it could be hundreds of companies. I would cold-call each one of them.

Ferraz: Once you had a meeting, how did you pitch Zanroo, given that social listening was relatively new?

Mungprom: I explained it in their terms. If the prospective client was a gym, I would tell them that it would be good to know who wants to exercise on a given day. Let's say there are a thousand interested gym-goers. If you know who they are, where they are, what they want, and why they want what they want, you can talk to them easily on social media. You can say, "Why don't you come in to my gym today?"

Ferraz: What could you tell this gym about their space in general?

Mungprom: We could tell them what other gyms are doing on social media. The campaigns that they are running. The influencers that they are using. From this competitive intelligence, we can help our client learn what works and what doesn't work in acquiring the right customers through the right content.

Ferraz: How would you charge a company like this gym?

Mungprom: We price on the number of keywords and the volume of data each brings. If they choose to listen for the keyword cycling, for example, the cost would be cheaper, since it's so specific. If they choose the word exercise, on the other hand, we would have a lot more data coming in, so we would have to charge the company more.

Ferraz: As your early customers began to use Zanroo, what kind of feedback did you get from them, and how did you change your MVP based on what they said?

Mungprom: The very first client said, "Oh, Chitpol, it looks like your product is not finished." So, I said, "Yes, it's not finished because we just started. What I can deliver to you is my commitment that whatever we agree on today, I will deliver everything to you. If I am not able to deliver everything to you, you don't need to pay us."

Ferraz: What feature did you need to deliver for them?

Mungprom: It's a bit complex, but we made it so that each company can have a hierarchy of keywords. This made it easier for our software to understand the nuances of the information coming through.

I always list the features that clients ask for.

Ferraz: After earning one million THB in your first month, did you still cold-call potential customers?

Mungprom: You have to understand the pressure was always back and forth between me and my partner. If there were not enough clients, the pressure was on me. If there were enough clients, the pressure was on my partner to deliver the feature we committed to. The problem is that in order to deliver, he needs more people—not just programmers, but also accountants, customer service representatives, and messengers. The pressure then swings back to me. I had to find more customers to generate more revenue so that we could hire these people. So, during our first year, I focused on sales one hundred percent. That was a lot of cold-calling.

Ferraz: Though many different companies could benefit from social listening, did you take steps to focus your cold-calling?

Mungprom: My target customers were companies in industries that have high involvement on social media. For example, before you buy a car, you access the manufacturer's website, read reviews you find on Google, check the comments on Facebook or Twitter. So, my first customers were in automotive, real estate, and banking.

Ferraz: Since you were so focused on selling to these customers, what strategies did you pick up?

Mungprom: Because my clients mostly work five days a week between eight a.m. and six p.m., I segmented my time. On Monday, I had to make up to several hundred cold calls—enough so that on Tuesday, Wednesday, Thursday, and Friday, I would have between four and seven meetings. This was my KPI [key performance indicator].

Ferraz: How often did you meet your KPIs?

Mungprom: Most of the time. If not, I would just make more calls. [laughs].

Ferraz: What advice do you have for founders on getting better at sales, so, like you, they can rely less on venture capital, at least at the start?

Mungprom: I think this is all about mindset. Some startup founders work hard to convince their prototype only to investors but I feel it is much better to focus your energy on selling it to customers for the best value. In return, investors will be interested.

Ferraz: After founding Zanroo in 2013, you bootstrapped until 2017. Why did you choose to grow organically for four years without the aid of venture capital?

Mungprom: Because we have a vision. From day one, we wanted to expand Zanroo to ten countries, and we believed that earning money from customers was more sustainable than borrowing it from a bank or raising it from investors. I saw many of my friends fundraise and then not know how to scale on their own.

In short, we wanted to grow by ourselves and find our own way. During our first five years, many investors from China, Japan, the United Kingdom, and Thailand approached us to invest, but we still refused. We felt that we could grow up to ten countries with our own team.

Ferraz: What were the challenges of trying to grow entirely through your own revenue?

Mungprom: The problem is that customers always want long credit terms, and some companies still pay late. But we of course, cannot pay the salaries of our staff late. If our staff expects salary to come out on the twentieth day of the month, but they get paid the thirtieth, the delay has a big emotional impact on how they feel about working for our company.

Ferraz: How did you manage to pay your employees on time?

Mungprom: First, I made more cold calls. More new clients means more money and less risk. Second, we worked with external legal to draft better contracts that require clients to pay an additional charge for late payments.

Ferraz: When did you decide to look for new clients beyond Thailand?

Mungprom: Most startups wait until they become strong in their home country before even thinking of expanding to other countries. I wanted to prove that we could make it outside of Thailand.

As I was twenty-one at the time, I was not well-traveled. I did not have any friends who were foreigners. My former boss, who was Malaysian, was the only foreigner I knew. I called him and told him the story of Zanroo. Even though he had his own trading company, I asked him to close it down—importing and exporting was hard to scale—and join me instead. Together, we quickly scaled Zanroo in Malaysia after I earned one million THB, and then we went on to Singapore and Indonesia.

Ferraz: What were the challenges of doing business across so many different markets in Southeast Asia?

Mungprom: The business cultures are very different. Here in Thailand, we drink a lot. But in Malaysia, they do not drink. They only drink Milo [a chocolate drink]. We needed to understand the local culture in order to deliver the best service. To do so, we worked with local partners we could trust, or we hired the best local people we could find.

Ferraz: What did you look for when hiring?

Mungprom: To hire and retain good people at the operational level, we looked at three things: twenty percent was their background, thirty percent was the interview and examination process, and the last fifty percent was how they performed during the onboarding process.

For potential leaders, we focus more on attitude. Attitude is abstract, of course. My definition of attitude is the ability to recognize and solve problems, to think on your feet, and to talk to people.

Ferraz: Some of your hires served as consultants for your clients. Why did you feel compelled to offer these consulting services in addition to your social listening?

Mungprom: Some countries—such as Vietnam, Myanmar, Cambodia, and Malaysia—are not mature markets. They do not know how to use social listening software, or they don't have enough manpower. If they do have enough manpower, they tend not to have experience with social listening software. So, I saw consulting services as another opportunity to help them.

At the basic level, we need to convince them on the benefits of social listening. They may have never done social listening, so why should they start now? We try to explain it to them in terms of the impact on their brand. Once they understand these benefits, we ask them whether they want to do the social listening themselves, or whether they want us to handle it. Most are willing to pay more for the consulting services because they don't have the know-how or they don't have the manpower, and they believe in us.

After we sign the contract, we send a team to train them on how to use the software, listen for particular keywords, and generate reports.

We do this for businesses in almost every country.

Ferraz: What did you learn as you expanded regionally?

Mungprom: Once we scaled to five or six countries, we faced a lot of international competition in some markets, such as Singapore. Yet even though we had more competition, we still managed to go toe-to-toe with the very best. That made me question my original plans. Why stop at ten countries? Why can't Zanroo become a truly global company?

Ferraz: During the four-year period you bootstrapped, Zanroo recorded between 200 and 400 percent year-on-year revenue. What kind of growth did you feel you needed to see in order to expand beyond Asia and into the rest of the world?

Mungprom: After some reflection, I realized we would not globally scale our social listening tool. Our competitors have been on the world market for too long. They already have many clients, and they have good relationships with them. There was no point in fighting with them on the global market.

This thought was scary. I had grown Zanroo to a team of 160 people. They have families, they have expenses to pay for, like their cars or condominiums, and they have high hopes for the company. It was no longer enough to find more clients or even expand to ten countries. We had to create a product that could scale the world.

Ferraz: You landed in social listening after trying to build e-commerce and portal businesses. How did you discover your second product?

Mungprom: I traveled the globe in search of our next big idea and spoke to founders from all over the world. I went to the United States. I went to the European Union. I went to China. I went to Hong Kong. In order to deliver something the world wanted, I needed to understand digital marketing better than anyone else. That's how we came up with Arun.

Ferraz: How does Arun differ from social listening?

Mungprom: In the media world, we have paid media, owned media, and earned media. Our social listening helps clients keep track of earned media anywhere on the Internet. What are people saying about your brand—positive or negative—in real time? If I talk about a company in an online forum, that is earned media.

Like our original platform, Arun monitors earned media, but it also combines paid media and owned media. Owned media is media you own: your website, your Facebook page, your Twitter and Instagram accounts. Paid media is media you must spend to get. For example, if you pay Google AdWords to have your company advertised on their search results, that's paid media. Display ads and influencer marketing also fall into this category.

By tracking all forms of a company's media, we can measure the return on investment [ROI]. As of now, they do not know how or where they earn. It's almost like traditional marketing. You spend a lot on above-the-line marketing, like television, radio, and print ads, but no one can really track the ROI across these channels. You just don't know. Now that people have largely moved to online marketing, we can measure their ROI through Arun.

When we did our market research, we learned that many companies have tried to integrate paid media, owned media, and earned media, but no one has really succeeded. That's why when we participated in a marketing conference in San Francisco, we claimed that we were the first in the world to offer this kind of service.

Ferraz: What kind of response did you get in San Francisco?

Mungprom: Very positive. We were able to gain a lot of feedback from customers at the conference, and representatives from twenty different companies wanted Arun as soon as they could. That really validated our hypothesis. Arun fulfills a need for companies around the world.

Ferraz: You decided in 2017—after several years of turning away investors—to finally raise a series A. What prompted this decision?

Mungprom: I started thinking about what we would need if I wanted Zanroo to go global instead of being in only ten countries. I determined we would need three things. First, to scale the world, we would need much more money than we currently had or could eventually gain through bootstrapping. Second, I did not have any connections in the United States, the European Union, or even China. If I got the right investors, they could introduce us to strategic partners in those markets. Lastly, I needed a larger team to create a product that could address a basic need of every customer in the world. These new hires would be in technology, marketing, and sales.

Ferraz: Now that Zanroo is active in fifteen markets, what is your next goal for the coming year?

Mungprom: While we're operating in fifteen countries, most of these are for social listening. Over the next two and a half years, we want to scale Arun to more countries.

Ferraz: Based on this current growth trajectory, Zanroo is expected to be the first unicorn to emerge out of Thailand. What does this milestone mean to you?

Mungprom: It's a measure of how many people we can help. If we scale to forty countries and become a unicorn, we will help our customers and their business communities by delivering them a product they find useful. We will also help our internal stakeholders, such as our partners, our staff, and their families. We will make their lives better. That's why we have to scale to more countries, earn more revenue, and deliver more features.

Ferraz: How close do you feel you are to reaching the unicorn valuation that would be a huge achievement for both Zanroo and Thailand?

Mungprom: It is going to be a tough ride—not just scaling the revenue, but building a sustainable growth with a balanced customer, product and Talent strategy. Zanroo cannot be doing only social listening to achieve that. We will dive deep into our core technologies to uncover what we can possibly disrupt.

Ferraz: Many people frequently overlook Thailand as a tech ecosystem. Why should more founders consider building businesses there? Why should we be bullish on Thailand's tech ecosystem?

Mungprom: As Thais, we are creative, passionate, and hardworking people. We excel in our passions but we were a little shy in the past to deal with foreigners. But now, the young generation of Thais are internet-savvy and eager to connect to the world. In fact, a lot of us are into computer engineering.

Ferraz: What advice do you have for entrepreneurs in Asia who would be eager just to reach the scale that Zanroo enjoys today?

Mungprom: You need to set a realistic goal. It can be short term or long term. After you determine your goal—your why—you need to identify how you will get there and what you will need to get there. You may need to have the right product. You may need the right finances. You may need the right people. But the biggest thing you need to have is the ability to connect the dots—which combination of these factors will take you to your goal.

Lastly, I think most people forget the when, which is more important than even the why. Too many founders say they want to get acquired, or IPO, or be a unicorn, but they don't set a target date. We need to know exactly what to do to achieve our goal by a set time, and it has to be something realistic. It's important not to lie to ourselves. Most entrepreneurs only believe in themselves, and that's important, but you need to get everyone else—your partners, your customers, your advisors—on board with your plans. If they also believe you can achieve your goal according to your timeline, then you will.

Mohan Belani

Co-founder and CEO, e27

In 2007, e27 started as a community group among passionate tech and startup enthusiasts who wanted to build the Internet ecosystem in Singapore. e27 was so named as a result of a white paper written by Paul Graham on investing in companies where founders were 27 years old or younger. The "e" stands for entrepreneurs.

In 2012, **Mohan Belani** *and Thaddeus Koh decided to run e27 as a proper media startup serving the regional tech ecosystem. The goal was to provide a platform to empower founders to build and grow their companies, with media as a start. As an online publication, e27 aims to provide this generation of entrepreneurs with the news and knowledge they need to successfully start and scale their business. e27 covers news from Southeast Asia as well as emerging markets across Asia Pacific.*

One of e27's key differentiators is its focus on community. Founders, investors, and other stakeholders can contribute content for editorial review after making a profile on e27. While other publications have guest contributions on the side, e27 may be one of the few that makes growing this community content channel a core focus of their content strategy.

© Ezra Ferraz, Gracy Fernandez 2020
E. Ferraz and G. Fernandez, *Asian Founders at Work*,
https://doi.org/10.1007/978-1-4842-5162-1_12

In addition to its flagship publication, e27 also organizes Echelon Asia Summit, the largest tech and startup conference in the region, gathering over 15,000 attendees from across region. e27 also runs the regional Echelon TOP100 program, gathering 100 of the most promising startups from across APAC. e27 has raised over US $2 million in funding from strategic institutional and angel investors.

Gracy Fernandez: What were the benefits of studying business in the heart of Silicon Valley at Stanford University?

Mohan Belani: Stanford provided a strong theoretical foundation to what was happening in Silicon Valley. The business cases that we studied were from companies that were literally in our backyards. Some of our lecturers were previously entrepreneurs or running companies while teaching, so the knowledge shared came from real-world experiences, and not just theoretical concepts. It was also refreshing to meet students from different backgrounds—tech, business, sciences—coming together to learn about business and building companies. Stanford is truly a melting pot of ideas and innovation.

Fernandez: What was your first exposure to the startup and tech ecosystem while at Stanford University?

Belani: I was studying part-time at Stanford as part of the National University of Singapore Overseas College Program, a one-year program in Silicon Valley, while working full-time at a startup company. The company was called Kriyari and renamed to iStorez a few years later. It was started by a serial entrepreneur, Anand Jagannathan. I was employee number one. I was very lucky to be given the opportunity to work with such an esteemed entrepreneur. It was a phenomenal experience, as I was exposed to many different aspects of a startup, from marketing to attending board meetings, to participating in trade shows. My evenings and weekends were spent attending various tech events and discussing ideas with friends—not to mention some pretty amazing road trips. One of the most valuable experiences that I had was volunteering at events.

Fernandez: What kind of events?

Belani: Startup events, mostly. Although there was one event that I really wanted to attend when I was still an intern, that was going to be held in New York. So I tried to ask my boss if he needed an extra hand for his visit there, he said no, since airline tickets were expensive. So I did the next best step: I asked the event organizers if they needed volunteers, and told them I really want to learn from the people who were attending. Fortunately, they said yes. What was really surprising was when I got there, the organizer just gave me a VIP pass, and said: 'Hey, just go and have a good time.' I ended up reaching out to 30 contacts who I connected with my boss. He was very happy with what happened that he reimbursed my expenses and even gave me a raise. From that time on, I imbibed the mantra that there are many different ways to solve a problem, and you should not always accept no and give up. It is important to try and it is important to ask. You just have to see if it works.

Little did I know that my volunteer experience will help me further into my career. It allowed me to meet a lot of people and get a better idea of how to build a community. It is while volunteering that I got a better idea of the ins and outs of running tech events.

Fernandez: Why did you decide to found e27 as a community site?

Belani: e27 was founded by a group of people—more than twenty of us—in 2007 as a community for people keen on startups and building the tech ecosystem. The goal was for people to come together, discuss ideas, and potentially found a startup. It was never intended to be a real startup or business. All of us were in it for community reasons. Some of our early e27 founders included the founders of MoneySmart, Zopim, PointStar, and MindFi, all of them are really amazing startups today. Through our community activities, we were able to meet a lot of like-minded individuals and some of the early pioneers of the Singapore startup ecosystem. We were also able to work with the Singapore government and forward-thinking corporations and organizations to help build the tech ecosystem locally.

Fernandez: In hindsight, what do you think were the advantages—as well as disadvantages—of having started e27 as a community site rather than an explicit startup?

Belani: I don't think there were specific disadvantages, it just so happened that's how we started—as a community. We were a group of friends who believed in one purpose which was to help the startup community to flourish and grow. That purpose helped us to do anything and everything under the sun to learn and grow. We learned about pitching, we learned what investors wanted, we learned the ins and outs of the startup community, which eventually became beneficial for the success of e27 and to our personal growth as well. It was not our core focus at that point to make money. We saw this as a means to something else—our own startups. In fact, that's exactly what happened to me because I ended up leaving for almost two years to work on a gaming company, Gokil Games.

Fernandez: What made you leave e27 to found Gokil Games?

Belani: I left e27 in 2010, when it was more of a tech community. Just like the other co-founders of e27 that started their own companies, I was inspired to do the same. My interest was in social gaming, and it stemmed from an early interest in gaming. I've always been interested in the gaming industry. I had the opportunity to start a company with someone who was well known in the social gaming industry in the US. I decided to take on this challenge and start a new company focusing on building mobile social games for the Southeast Asia market.

Building Gokil Games was a rewarding and challenging experience that taught me how to manage product teams remotely and better understand how social gaming mechanics work. This experience also allowed me to work with engineers and designers, to build a product. It was very different from the content- and events-related work I had done at e27. I used to code when I was younger and really enjoyed building things. This brought out that side of me.

Fernandez: As you were running Gokil Games, what made you feel that e27 had the greater potential, so much so that you would eventually decide to return to it?

Belani: To some extent, e27 was always at the back of my mind. There is a lot of fulfillment in working with founders and seeing their startups grow. That is something I definitely missed when running Gokil Games. Gokil Games was rewarding in its own way. We had a good team of engineers and designers, and it was fun coming up with design ideas and features. However, there came a turning point when I was fundraising for Gokil Games. I questioned how much I enjoyed doing what I was doing. While it was fun, there was very little purpose in the company.

At the end of the day, I was working on a product that was not really needed or making a difference in people's lives. I am a purpose-driven individual, and Gokil Games did not fit well with my core values. I kept in touch with one of the investors interested in what I was doing, and chatted with him about e27. I also sat down with Thaddeus to see if he was keen to work together on it. We decided to focus one hundred percent of our efforts in building e27. We had enough money for about six months, which we felt was a good timeline for us to try things out to see if we could make this work. That decision led us to where we are today.

Fernandez: How much had e27 changed during your hiatus? And what issues or challenges did you immediately set out to fix?

Belani: The team that was involved in e27 then had done an amazing job with the limited resources that they had. I was fortunate to be able to build upon their work and bring it forward. When I took over, I had the task of figuring out what e27 stood for, what are our core values were, and what our mission was. It was important for us to focus and concentrate our efforts on the most meaningful activities, while keeping the company afloat. As I took over, we were trying to do many different amazing things, but I believed that focus was important for us to truly succeed. Some of the ideas we looked at included how to better cover the ecosystem with our media platform, events we could do, potential products we could build (Jobs, Database, Investor platform), and markets and regions we could localize into.

Fernandez: What made you realize that the potential for e27 was much larger than a community site and could serve the broader Asian tech ecosystem?

Belani: To be honest, it took us a while to get to that state, because the tech ecosystem needed some time to mature. My co-founder, Thaddeus Koh Jit Siong, and I decided to put our heads together in late 2011 to give e27 a shot at becoming a "real" startup. The startup ecosystem was starting to get more serious around that time. The government was heavily supporting it, and there was an influx of global investors coming in. We were also starting to see some good ideas solving real problems. We knew that startups would be the organizations that would solve the big problems in Southeast Asia, not corporations or governments. And hence, we wanted to do anything we could to support the growth of the startup ecosystem. Our initial belief was that startups can make the world a better place, and this is something we still believe in today.

Fernandez: In previous interviews, you mentioned that your dad was against you starting e27. Why were you certain that you wanted to start the company despite your parents' wishes?

Belani: Unfortunately, this is not true and has been positioned incorrectly. My parents, especially my dad, have always been one-hundred-percent supportive of e27 and what I do. At no point in time did they ask me to stop e27 or do something different. They have been supportive of me at many stages in life, from the types of schools I wanted to go to—polytechnic instead of junior college—to the interests I wanted to pursue. They just wanted to make sure that I was fully aware of what I was trying to do and ready for the challenges involved in building companies, as opposed to something more stable like having a job.

My dad was a businessman himself and worked very hard to support a large family at a very young age. He started out in sales and opened up an electronics store, subsequently branching into jewelry and tailoring. He was astute in realizing what his customers wanted. Unlike me, he had to start a business to help the family, and not to solve a problem he was passionate about. For him, starting up was a challenging experience that took his time away from family and a balanced lifestyle. His hope was for me to not have a challenging life like him, but instead to have a good education and a more holistic life—something he could not afford to have. He probably did not realize this, but I spent time at his shop observing him and learning what it was like running a business, and I am sure that played a part in me wanting to build e27. As they saying goes, the apple does not fall far from the tree.

Fernandez: As e27 grew its readership, what did you try to do consciously differentiate from the coverage of other tech-focused publications in Asia and abroad?

Belani: I always believed that we had to focus on what was most important to us and our users. While we are aware of the fact that we have competitors, and they are working hard to be better than us, we also did not want to get distracted by what competitors are doing and to always be reacting to them. We had not raised much funding, and our team was very small, so we were also careful to not stretch ourselves too thin and try to do everything. Our focus on our users made us realize early on that articles and content should not be our only focus, and hence, in 2014, we launched the startup database and the jobs sites. This was something heavily requested by our customers, and if we had simply followed what our competitors were doing, we would not have realized these opportunities.

Fernandez: Many founders do stretch themselves too thin in the interest of trying to seize every opportunity.

Belani: Definitely. Even today, we have to turn down many opportunities and ideas on what we should do as a company. I think that is one of the biggest challenges in the life of a founder. Founders should be open minded to listen to ideas and feedback, but they have to internalize them and see what makes sense from users. Founders cannot shut themselves off from feedback and ideas. Once the internalization is done, then comes the focus and execution. What has helped us immensely is imbibing John Doerr's "OKR" system, which stands for "objectives" and "key results". It says you have to have goals every quarter. So every time you have an opportunity that comes up, you have to ask yourself: Does this help me achieve my goal? If it's a distraction to your goal then it's an easy no. I always have a list that I look at every quarter to revisit past ideas and see if they are relevant to where we are now. An idea might not be relevant today, but might be very relevant three months from now.

Fernandez: How do you balance the need for views with the need to provide helpful content to Asia's founders, investors, and other ecosystem players? These are two goals that can sometimes be at odds with one another.

Belani: We believe that if you do the right thing, the traffic will come. It was important for us to build the right culture in the content team from the start, such that the team worked on stories that the ecosystem needed to know about, and not just stories that get traffic. It is very easy to fall into the traffic trap, and we are cautious not to do so. We believe in providing the best pos-sible coverage of the ecosystem, and in order to get there, the writers need to be flexible in covering different types of stories—startups, investors, and government-related matters. Traffic is just one measure of success, and we did not want to get overly caught in gunning for traffic. We also did not want to have a culture in the content team where writers only wrote stories that would potentially do well traffic wise.

Fernandez: If traffic was only one measure of an article's success—and at times, a superficial one at that—how did you measure the success of a par-ticular piece of content?

Belani: I've come to realize that the success of any piece of content cannot be based on website traffic alone. It may sound corny but for me success is when we see an article from us that engages the community. It may not always translate to views, but it may translate into valuable, constructive discussions.

In particular, I feel how effective our content is when we get feedback from the founders themselves and when they share how our work has helped them.

But I know it wasn't always the case. In our early years, I had an experience when a friend of mine wouldn't even send our team any copies of his press releases, saying he doesn't appreciate our writing. It was constructive and helped us do better in coverage.

Now we get more story pitches than what we can handle. So the constructive feedback has definitely helped e27 grow.

Fernandez: When did you decide to start your flagship event series, Echelon? It is almost like running a startup within a startup.

Belani: The very first Echelon—it was called e27 Echelon—was organized in October 2009. It was a one-day community event that we put together to host the founders of Techstars. We published an article to announce the event.[1]

We organized it with the intention of it being a one-time event. We were approached by a government agency—Infocomm Development Authority—to host it, since they were hosting the Techstars founders. We brought together speakers from some of the popular startups then—SocialWok, HungryGoWhere, iTwin—and had a few companies pitch. There really were not many to choose from then. It had just over one hundred people, and we were quite happy with how the event went. Little did we realize that the moment it was over, the first question everyone asked was, "When's the next one?".

From there, we very quickly moved forward to get Echelon 2010 going. That is the first time we set our sights for it to be a regional event with a conference, exhibition, and pitching element.[2] It was the community and our users that drove the growth of Echelon.

Fernandez: Though the event was enjoyed by the community, you certainly had the highest possible standards, as someone who had a background in events. What did you realize you could do better based on your first Echelon?

---

[1] https://e27.co/techstars-founders-david-cohen-andrew-hyde-speaking-at-e27-echelon/
[2] https://techcrunch.com/2010/06/08/geeksonaplane-at-echelon-2010-in-singapore-an-overview-of-south-east-asias-web-scene/

Belani: Our team has zero background in events. We knew how to bring people together, but we had virtually no experience running a conference and exhibition. Everything was trial and error for us. I still remember carrying cocktail tables for the exhibition and laying wires for the Internet access. A lot of the team members stayed until late at night to pack the goodie bags. It was hard work but a lot of fun.

The first Echelon was simple: we gathered different members of the startup community and let them connect and pitch to potential collaborators and investors. It was an intimate, productive gathering. I knew while organizing the event that it was going to be a simple so I had no regrets about it. If anything, it just allowed us to think of the importance of such events and why we have to keep on doing them. We always made sure that in the next year we'll have a better slate of speakers, or we'll have talks that will be relevant to the community. It's always about sending the best content forward.

Fernandez: What are the challenges of running a company that is equally online and offline, like e27? How have you overcome it?

Belani: We are still continually evolving and learning how to do this better. In the earlier days, we were definitely more events-focused, which was quite clear in terms of the number of events we did versus the number of articles we published. The structure of the teams and overall culture of the company was very events-centric.

Along the way, we realized that in order to execute our mission more effectively, we needed to spend more effort on the online parts of e27. This required a cultural shift—training and some changes in our teams—to execute.

In today's e27, we believe that it is important for all team members to wear an online and an offline hat. Hence, content team members are actively involved in the organization of Echelon, and Echelon team members create content on e27. I believe that it's important to integrate the offline and online activities to deliver one holistic experience.

Culture building requires time and constant reinforcement of expectations from everyone. Culture is about how you do things as an organization and not about free lunches. And that takes time, so it's important for founders to be patient. We are still working on building and evolving our culture.

Fernandez: How do you recruit journalists for e27 who are not just great writers, but truly concerned with the welfare of the tech ecosystem in Asia in order to be aligned with the company's mission?

Belani: I believe that it is important that everyone align with the mission and the core values of the company. We repeat our mission and the core values during every town hall that we run. We refer to it during our discussions, and at times, we reflect on our mission to decide what we should and should not do.

Our number-one core value is "respect the ecosystem." It is there for a very good reason. In the past, we had some bad actors who behaved like they were above the ecosystem and believed the ecosystem would not be where it was without them. This included writing articles that were detrimental to the ecosystem or behaving like their work was above everyone else. This definitely caused a lot of damage internally to the morale of the teams and was a wakeup call for us to drive hard on what our mission and core values are.

I am always cognizant of the fact that e27 would not exist if not for an amazing startup ecosystem. This is something I constantly emphasize to the team. I remind them that we should feel blessed to be given the opportunity to work with the ecosystem, and this is something that should never be taken for granted.

We don't want to be a media company that rains on the parade of startups. We want to be a champion for the ecosystem, and play a positive role by giving them constructive feedback.

Fernandez: What are the challenges of being both a startup and an organization that covers startups? How do you address this?

Belani: I believe a major challenge that we have is balancing the need to make money with the desire to serve the ecosystem. While we do need to generate revenue to sustain our activities, we also need to be mindful that startups do not have that much money to spend.

We need to make sure that the programs we make are affordable and effective. We are also cognizant that startups do not just pay with money, but with time. Founders are typically fighting to execute as much as they can within a short runway. If our activities involve too much time, or they don't provide enough value based on the amount of time invested, then founders will not want to participate.

We are outcome- and impact-driven. We believe in providing results to the startups and not just goodwill.

All of this has to balance with our own personal growth and ambitions as a company.

Fernandez: Can you explain in more detail how this challenge plays out—the need to balance revenue generation with the need to serve startups, who don't have much to spend—in terms of pricing your offline and online products?

Belani: It is important for us to deliver sustainable value to companies. For example, Echelon is a valuable platform. However, it is not possible to create such a platform too many times in a year.

We diversify our work and efforts and do more sustainable activities. Diversifying means working with other players in the startup ecosystem, not just startups, to generate revenue. An example is working with corporations on their innovation programs or with governments on market access activities. The revenue generated from these activities could be used to subsidize the work we do for startups.

In terms of sustainability, it is important that our work be scalable and impactful. This would mostly be via our online site e27.co. One of our efforts was to launch our contributor program. This gave founders a voice and avenue to grow their thought leadership efforts, while making it free for them. We in turn monetize via corporations and governments that want to advertise on e27.

Fernandez: What do you feel is e27's greatest achievement to date, and why?

Belani: I would not peg our achievement to one specific event or product but more to our culture and desire to support the ecosystem. Throughout the years, we had many ups and downs, and while it was tempting to give up, we stuck to our guns and focused on delivering on our mission. I believe my team's relentless and selfless desire to be better at executing our mission is our strongest achievement, and this is something we will continue to work on in the years to come. For example, team members are always on the lookout for how to help startups in our network, even if they or e27 do not benefit directly from it. This is mainly through introductions to investors/founders and supporting the ecosystem in intangible manners.

Fernandez: What is on the roadmap for e27?

Belani: Our mission drives our roadmap and activities, and our goal is to figure more ways to execute our mission. We believe that e27 as an organization needs to be less events driven, due to the time and space limitations with events. We believe that we can impact more entrepreneurs and startups by having more scalable ways to execute our mission. We are working on ideas on our online platforms that help entrepreneurs build and grow their companies. We would like e27 to be more of a self-serve platform for founders to achieve their goals. This would include tools that allow them to share more updates on their companies, reach out to investors, and match-make with customers.

Fernandez: What unconventional advice do you have for Asia's founders who want to build a platform as iconic as e27?

Belani: e27 still has a long way to go. If I were to share just a couple of things that really helped us get to where we are, first, I would advise founders to work on a mission that they are genuinely passionate about. When the going gets tough, it will be the mission that drives the company forward and holds the team together.

Second, do not keep to yourselves when building your company. Build a network of founders whom you can share your problems with. Always realize that every problem you are facing, other founders have faced too. No problem is unique to you. By tapping the wisdom of other founders, you will get interesting insights on how to tackle your own problems.

Zeeshan Ali Khan

CEO and Co-founder, Zameen.com

Zeeshan Ali Khan *built and launched his first batch of online portals with his brother Imran Ali Khan's help to much fanfare in the UK. Following up on this success, he expanded his operations to Canada, Australia, and the US, before relocating to his Pakistani homeland.*

Back then, in 2003, the digital landscape in the country had yet to realize its true potential. Fast-forward 12 years, after Khan first introduced Zameen.com to the local web-scape, and Pakistan now boasts a whopping 56 million internet users spread across the length and breadth of its political territory!

Zameen.com is one of the companies at the forefront of the country's evolving Internet culture. Named after the Urdu word for "land" (which "Zameen" is a neat transliteration), Zameen.com brought thousands of the country's denizens one step closer to achieving the Pakistani dream: owning a patch of land to build a home.

By incorporating an impressive slate of modern technological tools, Khan and his team at Zameen gradually revolutionized the real estate industry in the country; streamlining the way people buy, sell, and rent property.

Ezra Ferraz: What inspired you to launch Zameen.com back in 2006?

© Ezra Ferraz, Gracy Fernandez 2020
E. Ferraz and G. Fernandez, *Asian Founders at Work*,
https://doi.org/10.1007/978-1-4842-5162-1_13

Zeeshan Ali Khan: Well, to set the record straight, 2006 wasn't exactly the year when our Zameen.com journey began. The company's founding—or at least its ideation—goes back a little further.

Back in 2002 to 2003, the developed world witnessed a major IT boom. At the time, I had newly graduated as a Chemical Engineer from Imperial College London, while my younger brother, Imran Ali Khan, was fresh out of Oxford University.

In retrospect, and based on my own assessment during the period, the potential that the IT sector held was something that I didn't think anyone should have ignored. Based on this observation, it didn't take long for me to start investing in stocks and taking a serious look at IT as something that I could be doing for a long time to come.

These developments, by way of original motivation, coincided with my need to do something for myself. And so the moment I graduated, I found my mind literally bursting with ideas that I wanted to execute; all of which revolved around proposing digital solutions for existing problems. Of course, there was pressure from my family and friends to secure a job and just get on with life. Starting a business did not seem like a good idea to any of them.

Over the next couple of months, I worked on various different portals with Imran. He worked at Deloitte, while I focused on our ventures full-time. But it wasn't long before he quit his job to work with me.

Our e-commerce portals took off in the UK, and then we replicated their success in Canada, the US, and Australia. Some of our portals earned us millions, while others didn't do as well. These experiences taught us a lot, and just a few years down the line, we began to look at Pakistan—our home country.

We visited Pakistan regularly between 2003 and 2004, and it was clear that the digital landscape here was non-existent. The infrastructure required simply did not exist for something like Zameen.com to take off. But what we did find was an innate urge within the people to own property. Simply put, it is the "Pakistani Dream" for locals to possess it; with many people, in fact, saving all their lives to do this and build their own homes. The word zameen is basically Urdu for land, and so it wasn't surprising that it resonated strongly with our audiences owing to this very reason.

We understood the need for Zameen.com in the market, but knew that it would be a very long-term project. This is the reason why despite the portal kicking off in 2006, it was allowed to grow organically until 2011 to 2012.

In 2003 to 2004, when we conducted the first round of market research for the project, we discovered that around 7.5 million Pakistanis were using the internet. When we launched the portal, this number stood somewhere around 10 million, and by the time we began looking for funding, this number had jumped to 17 million. Now in early 2018, close to 56 million people in the country use the internet—and as internet penetration has grown, the number of solutions that people are willing to trust this medium with has also grown! Back in the day, people didn't do much on the web. These days, however, Pakistanis of all stripes even buy their groceries and medicines online through mobile apps!

Ferraz: How did people in Pakistan find homes to rent or buy at the time, and how did you plan on developing Zameen.com to be an improvement over these solutions?

Ali Khan: The property market had a very different landscape before Zameen.com arrived on the scene. The portal literally revolutionized how property buying, selling, and renting was done—but we achieved this feat by taking existing methods and introducing a more process-oriented, data-driven, and tech-savvy approach to the equation.

Simply put, we brought a major chunk of the property market under one, digital roof, along with the complete process of finding the right property unit—be it a plot, apartment, or home.

The lengthy answer to this question, however, is two-fold: Zameen.com has deeply impacted how consumers look for and acquire property, just as it has influenced how agencies and developers operate in the market.

One side of the equation has to do with the consumers. Now if I talk about the consumer-end, I can tell you that back in the day, finding the right property was a long and tedious affair, filled with trust issues, uncertainties, and often false promises.

If someone wanted to purchase a house, they would need to find an agent they could trust. For this end, they would normally resort to their personal network to locate a professional. So, if they wanted property in an area where they only knew a few people, the process could become problematic. Honestly, I can't even begin to explain what challenges investing in a different city brought about. Pakistani property, as such, is different when you look at different regions in the country. So, someone from, let's say Lahore, wouldn't be able to easily navigate Karachi's real estate marketplace. Lahore measures land in marlas and kanals, while Karachi is all about square feet and square yards.

Moreover, an average consumer was hardly informed on all these issues—knowing next to nothing about the prevailing market trends, and not understanding how the market operated in different parts of the same cities, let alone the pricing and other nuances across various areas.

The second part of the equation concerns the agents. Typically, agents had to wait for people to come to them with their property requests, and finding renters and buyers took longer. In some cases, this also led them to pushing mismatched real estate to the wrong consumers.

What Zameen.com did was that it removed all the ambiguity surrounding property transactions and created a more connected platform. We enabled people, in general, to put up listings for properties that were up for sale or rent.

How did this help agents? Well, they no longer had to look for multiple clients; the clients themselves found them through the listings.

And how did this benefit consumers? They didn't have to wait for a friend of a friend to find them an agent with the right property options to offer. Instead, they had a wide variety of listings on their fingertips to go through on the website.

As Zameen.com grew, we added features that helped people make better property decisions. The Zameen Index, for instance, is data-driven, and it gives you insights on how the market is performing in the country. Also, it allows you to break down results based on the city that you need information on. It contains historic data that goes back almost a decade, so it helps people not only see recent trends, but also how the market has evolved over the years.

For ease of use, the website also comes in an Urdu version, and you can even do instant size conversions if you are trying to secure property in a city that has measuring metrics that you're not fully acquainted with. There are a lot of these things [website features], both big and small, that I could talk about. Zameen.com is also the first internet portal to have developed a location database and mapped out entire cities. Before this, there was no location hierarchy.

However, we don't just focus on dealing with local demand—we have also tried to address the overseas Pakistani market, which currently makes up 30% of our traffic.

For overseas Pakistanis, the situation—prior to Zameen.com's advent—was quite difficult, because they had no reliable source of information. The website apprises them of a catalogue of all the property types that are on offer, alongside detailed analyses of market trends and insights so they can make informed decisions.

What's key here is to understand that we more or less developed a virtuous cycle which further facilitated the growth of the business. If we had quality leads, we were going to get more traffic; if we had more traffic, we were going to give more business to agents; and if agents had more business, they would be pushed to introduce even better leads.

In a way, you can say that Zameen.com is basically an evolution of the older processes through which property buying and selling was carried out in the country. We have made everything cleaner, more efficient—and put it together in one easily accessible space.

Ferraz: What's interesting about Zameen.com's founding story is that it was not only a startup, but also a family business in a way. Can you share your working history with your brother leading up to Zameen.com, particularly with regard to Bayut.com? What other businesses did you two work on together, and what was your relationship like?

Ali Khan: Well, I've already gone into some detail about the work that Imran and I did together before Zameen.com. I think that, this being a family business, is what has made it worthwhile and easier to manage. Who else would you go into business with if not someone you can trust completely?

I've always said that when family is involved, there is no need to separate the personal from the professional. Imran and I stuck together mostly because we're practically twins—with only an 11-month gap between my birth and his. We did our A-levels together, went to university at more or less the same time, and when the time came for me to start something, Imran had my back!

Our brother Haider Ali Khan joined us when we ventured into the UAE market, before which he had been working in the US for more than a decade. He is the primary figure behind Bayut.com's success. Haider has an engineering background and his prowess in all things tech has helped take Bayut.com to new heights. In fact, the website just recently achieved a big milestone, and is now one of the fastest websites in the world. Through the Bayut.com platform, we also managed to enter the Saudi market recently, with Bayut.sa's launch.

In terms of real estate, Zameen.com was our first online portal; followed by Bayut.com in 2008 and Bproperty in 2016. Following their creation, we managed to push them to leading positions in the markets that they currently operate in.

Ferraz: What do you reckon were the advantages and challenges of working with your brother, and how did they manifest themselves as you went about building Zameen.com?

Ali Khan: Honestly, working with Imran is not something that I would call a "challenge." We are essentially stronger together and run this business like a combined venture in the truest sense. And it's not just about the three of us—our entire families live, breathe, and dream these portals.

Both me and Imran have lived together for so long—sharing the same room, doing the same summer jobs, and what not—that we sort of function on the same frequency now. However, what's most important about our relationship is that both as brothers as well as co-founders, we have always kept our ears open to feedback. There are ideas that I have, and then there are ideas that Haider and Imran have—and they don't always have to be the same. The key thing is to be able to hear and understand this messaging.

It's easy for the three of us to work together because we don't have to second-guess in trusting one another. Because of this reason, we have a lot of room and liberty to focus on our strategies and plans.

I think the challenges have always been external in our equation; never from within. And because we have been facing them together, we have been able to tackle them head-on and find solutions faster. This is particularly true in the case of Zameen.com, and generally for all the other portals that I have worked on. I never held a corporate job; I had an internship for a few months, after which I got ready to invest myself entirely into filling the gaps that I saw in the market. Imran was my pillar of support during this period; he would spend a whole day working and then return home to help me with my startups. Passion drove me to go for the big kill, but it was family that fuelled the fire.

Ferraz: What was the tech ecosystem in Pakistan like at the time, and what resources or networks did you tap into as you built Zameen.com [i.e. co-working spaces, accelerator programs, local investors, etc.]?

Ali Khan: When we began working in Pakistan, I can honestly say that there wasn't much that we could rely on in terms of a cohesive tech ecosystem. That's not to say that there wasn't any talent here—if anything, the situation was quite the opposite. But the sad reality was that the talent that the industry had to offer was not being used to serve the country it was in.

The tech ecosystem was more of an outsourcing effort back in the day. Pakistanis did not use digital solutions to solve everyday problems, so what you saw was a lot of developers in the market catering to the orders received from the developed world. The apps, portals, tools, etc., being created to serve someone outside Pakistan.

While this situation is changing, a lot of our outsourcing effort is still geared towards the outside world.

When we entered the Pakistani marketplace, we wanted to create bespoke solutions that made sense to its consumers. And we have followed this client-ended orientation as a matter of policy; no matter what region or country we operate in. Furthermore, this is also the reason why our solutions do not fall under a one-size-fits-all paradigm—so something that we're doing in Bayut.com may not work for Zameen.com, and the things we have created for Bproperty may not work for Bayut.com, and vice versa.

If anything, I believe that we have been an important part of a revolution of sorts that changed the trajectory of our local tech ecosystem. We have developed and executed tech within the company to manage our processes, our teams, and so on. Over the course of the last five years, Pakistan has witnessed a significant jump in the number of companies willing to work locally; rather than only acting as outsourcing outlets.

We never really looked for local investment for our portals, but we were part of a few collaborations with local universities geared towards finding and hiring good people. Our focus had been on recruiting people and working on them within the company to change their way of thinking.

Zameen.com maintains a culture of open-floor offices; we don't have a closed-door structure. The whole team works as an amalgam: you will see someone from tech going over to someone from content, just as easily as you will see someone from sales heading over to design with ideas. What we've noticed with this working arrangement is that it gels the teams together—causing efficiency to go up, our vision coming together better, and our people getting to know and helping each other. In all these respects, we function like one, big family. Now, there still aren't many open-floor spaces in Pakistan, and I find this observation concerning.

Over the last few years, I am proud to say that we have developed leaders in our offices. Zameen.com—or, indeed, any of our portals—is not a place where people can come and do something typical; we believe in breaking the mold and ignoring the status quo, and Team Zameen was built through the efforts of people who cherish the same ideals.

Ferraz: Though I'm sure you drew a lot from your experience of building Bayut.com, how did you conduct the requisite market research to learn more about the nuances of Pakistan's real estate market?

Ali Khan: Zameen.com predates Bayut.com by a couple of years, but I think it's safe to say that since both the portals operate in such widely different markets, neither one has influenced the other to any noticeable degree.

With Zameen.com, because it was primed towards our home country, we had some idea of how the market worked. But what we didn't want to do was to venture into it with just empty assumptions. When we visited the field in 2003 to 2004, we conducted surveys and focus-group studies to see whether the market was ready for the platform. Based on our findings, we realized quickly that this was not so—because the infrastructure, simply, was not there.

Despite this constraint, we did not want to leave this gap unattended for someone else to lay claim—so we decided to launch Zameen.com in 2006 and allowed it grow organically. In the next four to five years, the website had gained considerable traction from overseas Pakistanis, although locally it proceeded at a slower pace.

As internet penetration in the country grew, people's propensity towards finding online solutions to their problems also registered an increase. During this time, we continued to scan the market to substantiate the strength and size of the demand for online solutions.

Since the website had grown organically, we also had a lot of telling data to play around with. So when we decided to monetize the portal in 2012 and find investments, we did it backed by our accurate surveys and ground analyses; along with all the other data that the portal had acquired over the period.

Our data helped us see that even within Pakistan, there would always be a variation in how we addressed different cities. There was a difference, for instance, in how the rural and urban cities were operating; but beyond that, and even between the metropolises we were active in, we saw a huge disparity in market operations and practices. It was on the basis of all this information, then, that we were able to create lasting strategies.

Zameen.com continues to be a website which offers exclusive, authentic data and insights on the property market. And in order to maintain its unique market prestige, we need to constantly keep our data updated, and then compile it so that we can keep updating our strategies.

Emerging markets have their own evolutionary processes, so it's important to grow with them and stay a step ahead. The only way you can do this is with updated data and market analyses.

Ferraz: I'm sure you must have had some assumptions about how the market would react to Zameen.com, based on your experiences with Bayut.com. What surprised you the most about how the Pakistani market adapted itself to using the new platform?

Ali Khan: When you plan, organize, calculate, and measure, then there are very few surprises that you need to fare with in between. I can honestly tell you that in the last ten years, nothing has really surprised us—because we anticipate everything.

All our ventures and portals are different, but the one thing that binds them together is in the way we use data. I've always said that you cannot build businesses on assumptions. This is why you need to conduct your research and fact-gathering operations long before you consider taking any steps towards your actually launching your venture.

We built Zameen.com after taking a deep look into what the market needed, and pivoting, controlling, and changing our strategies based on the feedback we received. For example, when it turned out that the bulk of agents in Pakistan would not check their emails because of their total lack of affinity in working with digital tools, we changed our process to sending them text messages instead.

But we only did this after failing to connect multiple times. We had to understand the market inside out before we began pitching solutions for it. It makes no sense to me when people try to follow their gut instinct" to success—which is actually hinged on a lot of premeditation and field research.

You can have the best idea in the world, but if you do not understand the ground reality of the market that you are trying to enter, then you will fail—and that is why so many businesses simply fall apart despite their being built on the bedrock of a lot of creative thinking.

In terms of our experience in running our portals, all three of our websites, Bayut.com, Bproperty, and Zameen.com, are exceedingly different from each other. Each of these has different models that they follow. Bproperty functions on a hybrid model, Zameen.com focuses on a mix of classifieds and transactions, and Bayut.com is your quintessential property portal. It was market research that helped us understand that our success in Zameen.com would not fetch us the same results in the case Bayut.com. Similarly, it facilitated us towards the realization that a solution intended for Bayut.com would not work for Bproperty.

Ferraz: What was the biggest challenge of growing Zameen.com in its first year of operations, and how did this compare to what you experienced in Bayut's case?

Ali Khan: With respect to Zameen.com, I'd say the first operations began when we completed our investment round. The challenge for us then was to figure out how to go from a freemium to a premium model so that we could start generating revenue.

We also needed to build up a strong sales force with a key focus on KPIs, ARPA, etc.

Even more important, we needed to educate agencies on the value of a lead, for which we had to build numerous client touch points. You have to understand that Zameen.com emerged in a nascent marketplace, where the issues of a lack of regulation, unavailability of land data, and a lot of general public mistrust made for a difficult situation to begin with. And on top of this, we had to contend with agents who didn't even use email accounts, as mentioned; because of which they needed to be sensitized to what the website could offer to them in terms of revenue and profit.

During the first few years, we weren't just generating leads, but also handling their affairs as far as lead management is concerned. We developed internal tech to track them and then worked towards creating processes through which each lead could be matured into a sale. Then we had to teach our affiliated agencies how this could be managed and help them execute deals.

I believe that market adaptation comes about sooner rather than later when you have worked out your strategies properly. While there was a lot of education that went into, and continues to go into, helping agents understand how using our products amounted to being a good idea, I should state that having clearly defined goals and strategies helped us a lot.

Apart from this, I think it was also about the people who were working with us. Bayut.com operates in a market that follows a model which has been adopted in most developed countries. So, the portal's workforce also conforms closely to this reality and executes tasks accordingly.

At Zameen.com, we had to source people who could go from being typical tech guys to full-fledged product developers. There work was not only restricted to developing something, but also about living the experience (on a deeper level of understanding). The local tech scene, in contrast, has always been more aligned with people developing for experiences that they might never otherwise relate to.

Now resolving this disconnect was a challenge—but at Zameen, I'm glad to say that we didn't fare too badly off! Right now, we develop, we hand over, we find bugs, and we redevelop. Seeing our applications in practice is very important, and doing so helps my team understand what needs to be done—and what can be managed better.

Ferraz: One of Zameen.com's values states that "certified professionals make everything easier for all involved." How did you develop the platform to cater to real estate professionals, and what changes did you make based on their feedback?

Ali Khan: When we developed the platform, we had to give a lot of branding space to agencies. This is somewhat part of the local culture as well—both agencies and developers are interested in better visibility for the services they want to provide, and branding figures as a key part of this equation.

Going forward, we had to customize the portal to cater to the branding requirements that arose from our users' end. But even with this arrangement, we knew we had a good opportunity within our grasp. With each new branding option, we began to educate agents with regard to how it could influence a lead and bring them quality clients.

Agencies also had to be taught that handling a lead on time is much more important than branding. Over time, we have shown them how attending to a hot property or a super-hot property [Zameen's lingo for highly sought-after real estate] correlates directly with instant profits. Both of these were features that we included in the website to deal with the need for branding, and to focus our approach towards acquiring quality leads.

Another thing that I think is pretty important in terms of the agencies we choose to work with is our Trusted Agency tag. We built a process to verify agencies through multiple checks. The market, as such, suffered from a serious trust deficit when we first penetrated it, and this attempt at labelling formed our effort to sort out quality agencies for our users' benefit. It further helped matters when many agencies actively began working to improve themselves to get tagged.

Back in 2018, we introduced our Zameen Affiliates Network. This network consists of agents certified to sell inventory in the projects we own or exclusively sell and market, and offers an impressive schedule of commissions. Through a series of Business Connect events held annually across the country, we empower these agents to utilize the technology we've developed and earn formidable cuts. The response to these events, so far, has been quite encouraging, and we are looking forward to expanding our efforts on this front.

The portal has gone through many changes over the years. When we see the need for something, we make it happen. The website's continually evolving design interface itself is testament to this fact. Our data showed us that a progression was needed, and we made this disruption happen.

Ferraz: Throughout Zameen.com's history, which side of the platform did you find harder to grow—the professionals, or the users' end? How did you address this challenge?

Ali Khan: This goes hand in hand, I would say. If you work well with professionals and help them create quality leads, the users tend to come naturally. And if you ensure that the professionals on the website stick to strict standards, your users become happy. When users are content, the traffic figures increase on their own.

However, it's not always possible to focus on just one aspect, and then hope for the other to improve on its own. Over the years, the needs of our agencies have largely informed us how to tweak the portal to better cater to our users. And the needs of our users have had a significant role to play in how we asked agencies to manage their leads.

For instance, on Zameen.com, we introduced the Verified Listing feature. This indicates that a listing so inscribed will only bear authentic pictures of a property option, giving people a chance to see what the unit they're interested in buying or renting actually looks like. This makes life significantly easier for users because then they know that what they're seeing is what they will get; resulting in a significantly larger pool of quality [eager to convert] leads for agents.

Verified Listings, as such, constitutes only one example of the controls which we have added to ensure that professionals get to address leads in a proper manner. If someone begins to throw in fake properties, then users will definitely get annoyed and traffic will fall. However, if a user knows that what they're looking at is a quality listing, then they will be able to make property decisions much quicker.

Both sides are an integral part of our business, and without one, the other cannot survive. It's the basic demand and supply element more or less upon which our operations are hinged. In our case, when you ensure that both are streamlined, you get better results.

When we started out, managing both of these aspects was hard; but as time has gone by, things have gotten easier.

Ferraz: Did you leverage any synergies with Bayut, in particular, and the EMPG mother group, in general, to accelerate the growth of Zameen.com?

Ali Khan: EMPG, as such, has been geared towards creating a diverse set of solutions that work in different markets for some time now—based on the understanding that there is no one standardized approach that suits all. But while we can't exactly leverage all of what Bayut.com is doing in Dubai, the Ajman market is different and has a lot more in common with the Pakistani market.

However, when it comes to Pakistan and the rest of the UAE, there are some things that we can harness to our advantage. In the start, we did not leverage these synergies at all, to be honest. But over the last few years, we have started to do so, because there are a lot of overseas Pakistanis in the UAE, and a good number of locals living here who want to invest in the UAE. On a related note, I should tell that we have been able to use data from the UAE to improve our events targeting overseas Pakistanis, for instance.

In terms of tech, there are things that Bayut.com is doing that are years ahead of where Zameen.com is at the moment. This puts us in a good position because we have a solid roadmap of where we want to see the portal progress to in Pakistan in the coming future.

Ferraz: In 2012, what prompted you to bring Gilles Blanchard on board as an angel investor and chairman?

Ali Khan: Gilles was our first investor and came on board in 2012—as you rightly stated. He is the founder of SeLoger.com, France's largest property portal. He had originally pitched his company with the idea of coming to Pakistan and taking Zameen.com head-on. However, the other owners saw the country as a risky prospect and expressed their reservations.

Gilles, instead, sought us out and came on board as our angel investor. He did this because he could see the potential that the Pakistani market had to offer—in terms of bigger opportunities than the saturated and highly competitive developed markets in Europe had in store.

Gilles brings with him a reservoir of knowledge. He has worked in multiple countries, focusing largely on property verticals.

Typically, investors do a good amount of data analysis before they make a decision on where and what to invest in. Gilles picked us after a number of thorough and probing sessions like these—being entirely compatible with our own approach. Zameen.com turned out to be a perfect fit for him from an investment point of view.

We have a lot in common too, as our stories are similar in places. For instance, Gilles started working on SeLoger.com more or less the same way we did. The company started as a very small setup, while Zameen.com took flight from our bedroom office.

Now we were not actively seeking investments around the period when we found Gilles. We were focused more on growing our reach organically, but we obviously had plans to go big too. I think that things happen at the right time—when Gilles started looking for us, the number of internet users was slowly growing. Once we agreed to a partnership, there's been no looking back.

Ferraz: In 2014, what prompted you to raise venture capital, and why did you choose the two VC firms that you did?

Ali Khan: After Gilles came on board and we began to monetize the business, we put into motion a lot of our plans and strategies that we had been waiting for some time to implement. Each time you execute a plan or strategy that does well, your next step will always be to find more funding so that you can grow further.

First of all, you need to raise capital to build your business—with your business plan telling you the amount of investment that is needed. So every time we needed more funding, we reached out to investors who were likely to show interest in our business plans.

Now, our growth metrics were always either in sync with our plans or ahead of them. They were largely the reason that we found the two VC firms that eventually ended up coming on board with non-controlling interests.

I think getting an investor is much like getting married; one should always put a lot of thought and research into the process. We always had very clearly defined goals for the future, and we knew exactly what we needed to do to grow the business. This orientation is also what defined our rationale for pitching to investors.

The generation of Pakistani investors before this one wanted to put money into a business but did not want to suffer any losses. Today's investors, on the other hand, are much more realistic with regard to the patience needed to see any noticeable revenue growth. We know that we need to have enough funding in place to make sure that our key metrics and sales continue to see growth, and KPIs get met.

And I would like to add for entrepreneurs that they should not give up too soon. These are long-term businesses and nothing happens overnight. The speed of growth is different for an emerging market because of its unique dynamics. When attempting to set up shop here, you will need more resources, you will have to work against broken and missing regulatory structures, and you will need to invest more in terms of understanding the market—but it will all be worth it at the end.

Ferraz: Zameen.com has two notable content plays—its property magazine, and its real estate price index. Can you share the thinking behind these two different initiatives, and how they have helped the company so far?

Ali Khan: The Zameen Index is Pakistan's first real estate price index—and it was created through a collaboration with a leading Pakistani university. A lot of research went into its development, so that it could provide accurate results for people interested in looking into market trends and insights. We had to develop a sophisticated algorithm to ensure that the trends that the index depicted were the real deal.

Why did we create this? We had so much data at our disposal that not using it to empower our seemed like a disservice. Every listing that we have on the website, even today, is checked manually. No one else has such a large pool of real estate-related information.

In addition, most things we do have a user-centric intent; and the index is no different. With it, we hoped to equip people with more information so that they could make informed property decisions. Not only veterans, but also first-time real estate investors. This is where the index truly shines its brightest.

The Zameen.com Magazine is Pakistan's first property magazine, and it has recently begun to talk a little bit about home and lifestyle-related themes as well. The magazine has a news section, some pages reserved for projects and developments, market insights, and expert interview/opinion pieces that shed light on upcoming market conditions. So if you're looking for something that can give you a ball-by-ball update on the market every month, then the publication can definitely equip you with some good reading material to tune to.

Our motivation behind starting the magazine was to tap into the areas that we were missing out on digitally. Print, to its credit, is still huge in Pakistan. We knew that we had to keep key market players interested and the magazine was how we did it.

We also realized that there existed a disconnect between agencies, developers, and the users that they served. For instance, back in the day, unless you were from a specific neighborhood, you would not know about the agents that operate there. So we thought: what better way to fill in the gap than to produce content that can help highlight projects and developments for the users that they are made for.

Although both of these tools were created keeping end-users in mind, they go a long way in helping agents and developers too. Since we work directly with agents, the magazine's insights get supplemented with important details about the ground realities that we obtain from their advice and interviews. It's a bifurcated street—content is primarily produced for users, but agencies/developers get their push as well.

Ferraz: What are Zameen.com's most recent developments accrued over the last year, and how have they helped your users?

Ali Khan: Zameen is more or less in a constant state of evolution. We are always looking into feedback from our clients and customers to see what we can make better and how.

For instance, after organizing events around the country, we realized that one was needed abroad. People are able to gauge whether they want to invest or not much faster when they can directly interact with the developers and agents behind a project. That is the reason why, in the last year, the number of Expos that we conducted went up locally, with events organized in Lahore, Islamabad, Karachi, and Multan. This is also the reason why we launched the Pakistan Property Show by Zameen.com in Dubai in 2017.

The show was an expression of our commitment towards catering to our overseas audience. Around 30% of the website's traffic is made up of Pakistanis resident abroad, and our data indicated that an event of this nature was needed. So we thought, why not take the country's property options to them?

The first edition of the show broke records in terms of footfall. The exhibitors who took their projects to Dubai with us ran out of business cards within the first few hours of its opening. Now, we're all set for the event's third edition in December, which will be bigger than ever.

So, wherever we see a need, we try to fill the gap with a solution; be it digital or otherwise. In terms of just the tech side of things, the website itself has become faster than ever before. Its new interface comes with a fresh look and feel, and it has been changed based on the feedback received from both our clients and our customers.

We have added new features to ensure that there is absolutely no chance of there being any spam content on the site. This not only helps just the visitors or customers that load it, but also the clients who we work with directly. It is with these details, the very small ones, that we are able to ensure quality for anyone that uses the Zameen website or app.

Apart from this, we introduced the site's Video Properties section. Our own media associates go and create the footage that is to be used in these videos. We even have drones out to get the most accurate, holistic [relief] view of the properties that concern us. Zameen.com also maintains the largest repository of city maps in its archives—seeing as it quite literally mapped them all out.

If you decide to move to a new city or locality, it helps to have some prior knowledge about it. This is where our Area Guides section can help, as it includes comprehensive information about the facilities, security arrangements, and independent histories of different real estate zones spread all over the country.

By 2018, we felt that we have gathered enough data and experience over the years to create our very own project development arm. This is how Zameen Developments came into being, and today, the company already has a couple of projects underway—with some nearing completion—such as Zameen Opal, Zameen Ace Mall, and a few others.

This year, we also executed our third successful TVC featuring our brand ambassador, Fawad Khan. Like with our previous two TVCs, this ad also premiered on national television to a massive audience response.

We have also, simultaneously, been working on expanding the Zameen Affiliates Network—having enrolled a total of 7,000 affiliates to the company's fold, till date. To facilitate their inventory-selling pursuits, we created a portal called Propforce which helps them to manage leads and keep their data organized.

Ferraz: What are EMPG's plans going forward, and how does Zameen.com figure into them? Does the group ever plan to unite all its portals under a single mother brand, similar to what Naspers has done with OLX?

Ali Khan: We work with highly localized models, because we believe in being more local than global. So, in keeping with our extremely user-centric philosophy, and with EMPG serving as the mother ship, the group's individual portals are going to keep the markets they operate in happy for the foreseeable future.

The reason we cannot come under a single brand banner is because we're offering bespoke solutions—a business orientation that will never change. And these are emerging markets, which come with their own set of challenges and opportunities. As I've said before, there's no one-size-fits-all philosophy at play here—because it simply wouldn't work.

So I don't think a rebranding strategy would make sense for us. We will, however, constantly keep evaluating expansion opportunities into other markets, as we have in the last few years.

Going forward, EMPG will be doing big things in emerging markets, but it will do so in a way that is specialized for each transactional space that it goes into.

When considering the growth of Zameen.com, I think there's still a lot that we need to accomplish. We have grown from a purely classifieds model to a sales and marketing model, and our evolution was informed by the needs that the market presented to us.

We will keep stoking this progress further while we remain within the confines of the real estate vertical, so that we can continue to focus and build up our revenues and increase our user base.

Right now, Zameen.com works with close to 15,000 agencies in Pakistan—a significant share that no other local company can claim to stand shoulder-to-shoulder with. But my goal isn't just these big numbers, I want to be able to work with every single agency in the country. I want people from urban cities to consider us their only real estate choice available, but I also want people from our far-flung areas to find solutions to their realty problems through our platform.

Ferraz: As a Pakistani tech company, what do you hope Zameen.com can show or demonstrate about the local tech ecosystem?

Ali Khan: Pakistan has so much to offer. Our local tech ecosystem has been creating a versatile range of solutions for the entire world for some time now. We have people building apps to address all manner of problems—and these solutions are working for developed countries. When Zameen.com came onto the scene, we wanted to take all this local talent and harness its potential to create locally relevant solutions.

So what Zameen.com has done, in effect, is to go a step further and develop exclusively for the local market. Our solutions zero down on what the customer is looking for, and then ensure that the resolution is delivered. We started off with just a web portal, but today, we have expanded into apps, an Urdu website, transactions, the Index, Zameen Forum, Zameen Trends, and so much more.

But Zameen.com's in-house tech advancements don't just go as far as the products we make for our consumers and clients are concerned. We create a lot of tools and apps to manage our teams and internal workflow. So where other people use external portals to track, measure and improve on their work, Zameen.com resorts to the use of its own original utilities.

So, from the content team to the sales force, and from our operations to the techies themselves, everything is measurable. This doesn't just help give us an edge over our competition, it also helps us deliver stronger performances as well as keep our Zameen family happy.

Ferraz: What unconventional piece of advice do you have for entrepreneurs in Asia that you have not heard given before?

Ali Khan: I think I'll focus on Pakistan for this one because Asia is huge and diverse, and one thing that would work in one place won't work elsewhere.

My key advice would be to not just go along with your instinct. Over 80-90% businesses are based on instinct, but the vast majority of them never take flight.

Sizing your market and opportunity is very important. People go into businesses without realizing the market potential and realities that they are playing with.

Ask yourself some heavy questions, such as: Will my idea get absorbed into the market? What is my target audience? What does it feel about the idea? Does the market offer a conducive environment for my idea to take root and grow?

Only take a leap of faith on an idea that will work based on your research; not on one that simply sounds great.

Akiko Naka

CEO and Founder, Wantedly

In 2010, **Akiko Naka** *founded Wantedly in Tokyo, Japan. Originally conceived as a question-and-answer site similar to Quora, Naka eventually pivoted Wantedly into a social recruiting site built around casual office visits.*

Job seekers could meet HR representatives at the office for a chat, and if there was mutual interest, proceed to a more formal interview. The experience was designed to find the kind of culture-fit employees who not only perform better, but stay longer.

Naka taught herself to code to build the original version of Wantedly. The platform is now active in Hong Kong and Singapore, and counts over two-and-a-half-million users in Japan alone.

Ezra Ferraz: Prior to founding Wantedly, you were a growth coordinator at Facebook Japan, and before that, you were in equity sales at Goldman Sachs. What were the formative experiences at these industries that inspired you to create a social recruiting network?

Akiko Naka: When I joined Facebook, I was surprised to see how the social-network was changing society and impacting the world. Before Facebook came to Japan, we had a dominant social networking service called Mixi. It was totally anonymous, so people would use nicknames, which made Mixi a very different user experience compared to Facebook.

© Ezra Ferraz, Gracy Fernandez 2020
E. Ferraz and G. Fernandez, *Asian Founders at Work*,
https://doi.org/10.1007/978-1-4842-5162-1_14

Facebook turned the Japanese Internet scene into something more intimate and trustworthy because people started using their own names and showing their profile pictures. It changed the atmosphere, and I was very pleased by how it was creating a positive impact. I thought I wanted to build something like that.

Ferraz: How did this change that you noticed—that people were no longer afraid to be off the anonymous online world—inspire you to build Wantedly?

Naka: In early days, Japanese users would use photos of cats or anime characters for their profile pictures. Because of the efforts of the Facebook Japan team, users gradually decided to use their real photos and their real names.

I wanted to leverage that idea of using real connections and identities to make an impact on the world. That was the very simple idea I had when I started.

Ferraz: Were you surrounded by other people in Japan who were also pursuing startup ideas? The stereotype is that Japanese culture may be more risk averse, especially toward high-risk ideas like startups.

Naka: Yes, I often encounter that stereotype, especially when I'm outside of Japan. Compared to other countries like the US and China, the Japanese are much more risk averse. We only have a few unicorns. But over the past few generations, younger Japanese are starting to take more risks and start their own companies.

Ferraz: What was the tech and startup ecosystem in Japan like at the time?

Naka: There is a healthy startup ecosystem in Japan. I think one of the most important factors of the ecosystem is angel investors. Because of the few startup booms in the past, there are number of prominent angel investors in Tokyo who founded their own companies and then took them public or sold them to other companies. I personally believe wisdom is much more important than mere money when it comes to running a startup. So with that wisdom given by the angels through mentorships, there are more successful startups and I see more serial entrepreneurs.

One of the biggest obstacles to Japanese startups is the language barrier that prevents them from expanding beyond borders while the domestic market is shrinking. Japan is a big market, but ruling only this market is not enough to compete against tech giants from overseas.

Ferraz: On a more personal note, did any friends, family, or colleagues discourage you from leaving your safe and lucrative career to pursue a tech startup? What were their concerns, and how did you address them?

Naka: I told my mother that I was thinking about quitting, and she said, "Don't you plan on working at least five years?" and I thought that was a reasonable reaction for someone of her age. But I left anyway. It required a lot of courage.

Ferraz: Can you take me into a snapshot of your first hundred days in forming Wantedly? Did you create an MVP? What did it look like? How did you actually begin the company?

Naka: After I started Wantedly, I just had this idea of building a product that incorporates real identity social networks and sociographs. But I was still experimenting with the idea.

While I was doing that, I had so many inquiries from my connections back from Facebook who wanted me to help them run their social media marketing campaigns. I was one of the very few experts back then, as it was a very new phase. I unexpectedly fell into helping out people and became so busy that I couldn't work on my own project for a few months. So to answer your question, I made no progress in the first 100 days.

Then I realized I should focus on building a product. I was afraid of losing old connections, but I decided to focus on my project. I had a friend, an engineer, who was working for another company full-time, but he was helping me out part-time after work. We worked together late at night. I was doing design and he was building the server side.

The first idea was more like the Q&A website, Quora. I really liked the concept, so I built a prototype for a few months. It consisted of two types of users: people asking questions and people answering questions.

Later, I decided to show it to my ex-colleagues back at Facebook and my friends. The feedback was that it was vague. It's hard for people to know what kind of questions they should ask, so I thought I should narrow the topic down to a particular area, which is "people." The idea was that people could use their connections to find somebody they are looking for.

For example, someone is looking for a tutor for their sister. That person can ask their friends or the friends of their friends, "Hey, my sister is looking for a tutor. Can you recommend anyone?" That kind of concept was the first pivot that we made. In the beginning, Wantedly was not only for jobs, but more of a "finding people" platform.

Ferraz: Did this "finding people" purpose shift after you launched?

Naka: It stayed that way for a while. After we completed building the first version of the Q&A website, my engineer friend got so busy at his job that he could no longer help me. That was a big issue because improving the product fast is more important than the launch itself.

So I decided to teach myself how to code. I knew how to code basic HTML, and I studied some Java in the past. I picked up a book and self-taught Ruby on Rails.

When I was able to code by myself, I found my inner peace for the first time as I no longer had to sit and wait for the progress that my friend was making. Instead, I just had to work hard and keep coding. If you can code by yourself, you know how hard it is to make changes, which helps you to grown mutual respect between engineers.

I knew an editor at TechCrunch, so I went and pitched him my idea. "I built this new product. Would you be interested in featuring me?" One day, he did. That created the first traction.

I also had a viral feature—when people signed up for Wantedly, some users would share on their walls that they had joined Wantedly. I think the article and the viral feature boosted the launch.

Ferraz: During this start, which was the harder side of the marketplace to grow? Was it the companies looking for people to hire, or was it the job applicants?

Naka: I focused on acquiring companies first. Wantedly works like Kickstarter in a way, so the most important thing is content to attract users. Contents means job postings.

I was friends with some of the prominent startups back then, so I went to see them. I asked, "Would you like to put job postings on my platform?" Three companies said yes. Those companies were very popular so they didn't have to post on any other third-party platforms for recruiting, so it was very exclusive that they had postings on Wantedly.

Ferraz: Was this concept very new in Japan, the idea of visiting offices that you would want to apply to? How did you get job seekers to buy into this idea?

Naka: Initial users were mostly early adopters, so those forward-thinking users blessed the concept of office visits and the idea was accepted naturally. On the other hand, it was much harder to convince companies, because the concept was very new. I would say nine out of ten HR people that I met said, "No, that's not going to work. We are very busy. We don't have time to spare to just meet and have coffee." I faced so many rejections at the beginning. Gradually, because of those three launch partners, those really cool companies, more companies decided to onboard. Because of the content, we also saw a growth in users.

Ferraz: Were they getting good leads from the meetups with the jobseekers?

Naka: Normally, it takes about three to six months because of the hiring process. So we were not sure whether the concept would work in the first few months, but gradually we started to see the success. So yes, our clients were able to make great hires.

Ferraz: Did you give any guidelines to your client companies to prevent it from just being a normal interview? Did you keep it open to however they wanted to run their visits?

Naka: In the early days, I knew all of my customers directly, so I made sure that they followed the way we wanted them to do it. We were trying hard to encourage and educate them so they could provide great meet-and-greet experiences.

I wanted users to experience the perfect office visit experience. We were okay to let go some of the clients who were not willing to accommodate the visit experience. I was trying to create this new process and experience.

Ferraz: Can you walk me through the process of a visit? So, I would contact one of these companies, they would invite me in for a visit, and then what would it be like from there?

Naka: You tap on the "Want to Visit" button, and then a notification will go to the company, they will check your profile, and if they are interested in you, you will get a message on our iOS or Android app, or website. It's like Messenger or WhatsApp. The company will ask you, "Do you want to come and visit the office?", then schedule the date you visit, Very simple.

The first visit should be very casual. You tell them about yourself, and the company will do the same. If you're mutually interested, the company will ask you, "Would you like to proceed to the official interview process?" That's when you might have to send in a CV.

So the first visiting experience is like window-shopping. You don't necessarily have to be fully determined to change your job. You can just explore new opportunities. In a way, it's like meeting potential employers without head-hunter arrangements.

Ferraz: What was the appeal or the advantages of having a casual chat before initiating the formal interview process?

Naka: There are advantages for both parties.

For users, they are able to get a real sense of how the company is operated, what the culture is like, and what kind of people are working.Traditionally, the only way to know the company was just to hear from the interviewer. That's very limited and biased information users can get which might lead to mis-match.

For companies, you get a chance to meet great talents. If your company is unknown, normally it's really hard even just to get applications. But by using Wantedly, companies can at least get access to so-called "warm leads" and be able to pitch your dream, and nurture the interest of the candidates.

Ferraz: You had been bootstrapping to grow Wantedly until you raised US $4.5 million from angel investors; but even then, the startup is still mostly funded out of your own pocket. What were the reasons that drove you to choose to bootstrap versus raising money very early on?

Naka: I think my background influenced that decision. I used to work in the finance industry at Goldman Sachs. I used to sell equities so I had a basic knowledge of how venture capital works, and I didn't want to be fully controlled by investors who have a relatively short time frame.

When you raise money from VCs, you have a timeframe set because the VC has their own deadline to make returns for their LPs [limited partners]. Sometimes, they push too hard so you have to give up what you really want to build. They might decide which direction you're heading in. Of course, there is an upside to having that pressure.

The bottom line is, I really enjoy building things. That hasn't changed throughout my life. One of the reasons why I started Wantedly is that I always enjoy building things that impact society in a positive way. My first priority is to keep control, so I was careful in choosing who to get money from. I raised a small amount of money from angel investors, and a few corporates as I went. Mostly, I raised from people who are experienced in building their companies from scratch, so they would mentor me. I learned so many things from their anecdotes.

Ferraz: Can you share an example of something you learned from one of your mentors that helped directly with building Wantedly?

Naka: The things I learned from my mentors were mostly things not written such as how to face difficult situations with handling under-performing employees, or employees causing harm to the organization.

Ferraz: Because you were bootstrapping for a while and you didn't want to have the pressure of investors immediately wanting a return, how did you use that freedom to create or to explore different, exciting features or business directions with Wantedly?

Naka: Our new concept of the office visit experience was unique. So being able to take time to educate the market and focus on improving our products allowed us to build the solid foundation of the growth that we stand upon today. If we rushed too fast to go after revenue, I don't think we could fully establish this office visit experience.

Also, having a user-focused culture instead of a focus on revenue allowed us to nurture this great engineering culture we have today. Our approach is that we focus on users, create great products that serve them well, and then the revenue follows.

Ferraz: As you started to hire all of these engineers and product managers, did you hire them through Wantedly?

Naka: Yes, most of our hires were through Wantedly or through mutual friends and introductions. Our CTO came in through Wantedly as well. He used to work for Goldman Sachs. He graduated from the University of Tokyo—a top university in Japan. He had a major in computer science, he went to grad school, and he joined Goldman Sachs. He was one of the youngest VPs, but then one day, he came to our office for a visit. He wasn't really serious about changing his job in the beginning, but after the visit, he started to consider it. Eventually, he convinced his wife and joined the team. He later became our CTO and is a crucial part of the company.

Ferraz: How did it work for the company visits at Wantedly? Did you personally handle all of them, and in any certain way?

Naka: In the early stages, yes, I was meeting everyone who visited our small office, and told them about what we were doing, about our vision and culture. Well, that's the point of using Wantedly. Mingle with office visitors, and share your passion and vision so they might consider applying to your company.

Ferraz: As you started to grow the client side and expand beyond colleagues you already knew, how did you get more big-name clients, like Sony and Dentsu, to list on your platform?

Naka: Most of those large clients came as inbound inquiries. As I mentioned earlier, if we had raised money from VCs, they probably would have pushed us to build a sales team in the earlier stages. If we had a stronger sales team, they would grab large corporate clients. We didn't do that. We tried to focus on the user experience, and that eventually made our customers happy, so they started to talk about us in the HR community, and so we grew through word of mouth. Eventually, large names noticed us and were interested in us. We still get a lot of inquiries from large companies these days, but most of them are inbound leads.

Ferraz: To facilitate the organic word of mouth, do you have other inbound efforts—for example, content marketing oriented toward educating Southeast Asian job applicants around the concept of social recruiting and company visits?

Naka: Yes, we had regular marketing efforts like blogs, twitter, and Facebook pages. We also had owned media. But I don't think those efforts are the core reason for organic word-of-mouth. I think the most effective measure we took was the formation of the SaaS model sales team. We barely had a sales team in early days, and we had only three sales in the first three to four years. As we grew bigger, we got more structured. The SaaS model sales team consisted of Marketing, Lead Nurturing, Inside Sales, and Customer Success. For new clients, inside sales provides a thirty-minute free session to hear problems they have, and explain how to use Wantedly. Clients would come to our office, or we did the meetings online.

Our customer success team gets in touch with clients regularly and helps them make the most out of Wantedly.

Ferraz: When prospective clients come in to Wantedly, what are their most common concerns? You mentioned earlier that time could possibly be one of their concerns—that these visits eat up too much time. What were their other concerns, and how did you address them?

Naka: Most of the companies are concerned about time, but as they realize that the hires they make through Wantedly tend to stay longer at the company, the investment they make is not bad. It's better than chasing after candidates who turn over quickly.

Some of the companies aren't comfortable adopting the office visit style because they're so used to their old-way of recruiting. They go through résumés, select, and then interview. The majority of the companies have to learn the new approach. Price-wise, we are very affordable, so that's not a problem.

Ferraz: Once you're able to successfully convince them to onboard with Wantedly, how do you ensure their success as a client and that they're able to hire the right people for their companies?

Naka: In the early days, most of our clients were startups. Startups usually have people with a high digital literacy, so they know how to use Facebook and social media. They were successful in using Wantedly on their own. They didn't need much support. Now, as we have a growing number of diverse customers—I'm talking about over 30,000—we have lots of small companies who are in small cities. Some of those CEOs are older and they don't even know what Facebook is.

For those people, we have built a customer success team. The customer success team gets in touch with those clients continuously and provides support. If there are needs or features that they are not sure how to use, the customer success team will support them. We have metrics to measure how successfully these customers use Wantedly and meet the talent.

Ferraz: Some older clients may not even have Facebook. What is the most frequent challenge that they have? Is it that they don't know what types of attractive content to post or how to engage with prospective job applicants? What is the biggest problem that they need assistance with?

Naka: Creating a job posting is the biggest challenge. Here I'm talking about "Wantedly-Style" job postings, not the traditional job descriptions. They don't know the most attractive tagline or title to use for their posting, and people have very shabby photos. We have an option to help those people with writing and taking photos.

Ferraz: Your customer success team is oriented toward content production and helping produce attractive content for job seekers?

Naka: The metrics we track change over time, but right now, one of the metrics that the team is focused on is the percentage of clients who are successfully posting high-quality job content.

Ferraz: Airbnb grew as a company once they were able to help their users post more attractive photos of their listings. In Wantedly's case, how much of a difference will attractive photos of the office and the people make in terms of getting inquiries?

Naka: We learned the idea of hiring photographers to increase the quality of contents from Airbnb too. We had a program for about a year or two in which we would send photographers for free to take photos. The traction of posts changes dramatically when you have a really attractive photo. The percentage of people who apply for the opportunity is much higher now. It's about the photos and the title.

Ferraz: The goal of every founder is to make their office space attractive so they can get applicants. What have you found to be most true for job applicants? Are these photos of the office space itself, of people interacting, or of office events? Which is usually the biggest selling in terms of the multimedia?

Naka: Photos, interaction, events setups—every element is indispensable. But I think the photo should be the most important, because that comes first. If your postings are not attractive, you don't even get the chance to meet the users.

It's important to have photos of people working at the company because it conveys the atmosphere of your workplace. We have strict standards for these photos. We try to manage our photo posting quality as Apple does. Apple has strict standards for their App Store. We review all of the postings every day, and if there is a posting that doesn't meet our standards, customers need to fix it before they can publish.

Ferraz: You mentioned that a lot of clients early on were startups. Have you had success stories where a company was able to scale largely through the talent they were able to get through Wantedly?

Naka: There's this one startup called Retty. Retty is like Yelp in Japan. That company was able to hire their CFO through Wantedly, and about half of their employees were hired entirely through Wantedly. I'm confident to say that we're really boosting the startup ecosystem in terms of helping those startups to have access to talent. Every startup has a Wantedly page in Japan.

Ferraz: When you find that all of these companies are recruiting through Wantedly, is it for a certain type of position? What are the trends that you've seen on what types of positions people are recruiting for through Wantedly?

Naka: In the early days, it was mostly engineers, designers—people who are involved in building products—but these days, we are seeing more diverse positions, such as sales, back office, and so on. There are companies that managed to hire dog-trimmers, doctors, or even chefs.

Ferraz: How are you encouraging the diversity in job postings? Are you taking any steps to actively encourage moving beyond the initial pool of designers and developers?

Naka: It's spontaneous. The thing is, on Wantedly, you can post as much as you want. It's not as if you pay for posting. It's limitless. In general, most of our clients create postings for all of their openings, and that creates diversity, so we don't need to push to diversify the job postings.

Ferraz: In March of 2015, you expanded into Indonesia with a foreign-language version of the service. Of all the countries in Southeast Asia and East Asia, why did you choose Indonesia as your first foreign market?

Naka: Indonesia was the fastest growing country in Asia in terms of population. Back in 2012, I went on a tour of Asia.

I was by myself, and I asked my friends who worked for VC to introduce me to prominent startups. Back then, I was able to meet CEOs of now large companies when they were just starting out—companies like Traveloka and Tokopedia. I could feel the energy of the city, where those startups grew quickly.

Ferraz: What were the challenges of making your first foreign-language version of the site? Did you have to localize it in any other way besides the language?

Naka: We are a two-sided platform to match users and companies, but we always start from the company side. So it's crucial for us to have a local team that reaches out to the customers, has sales meetings, and explains how to use Wantedly. It's not that clients sign up organically and start using it. Each region has its own local culture and business customs, so we have to localize the way we operate.

A challenge product-wise was localization of the user interface. The original version of Wantedly was built in Japanese, so we had to translate all the text on the platform.

Ferraz: You're now present in over fifteen countries, and you've recently started Wantedly Hong Kong. How different has it been to operate Wantedly as an international company vs just a company in Japan? What are the challenges of running a global tech company now?

Naka: I think the physical distance was the biggest obstacle for our team to overcome. It's important for people to fly into each other's offices as often as we can to communicate. Another thing is accessibility to information.

Most of the Japanese startups, including us, operate in Japanese, and all of the documents are in Japanese. I think it's important to have a centralized information database in English so that members from other countries have easy access to it.

Ferraz: As the CEO and founder, how did you overcome the physical distance? Are you flying to all of your regional offices constantly? What is your day-to-day like in terms of overcoming this challenge?

Naka: In the early days, I tried to visit offices as often as I could—perhaps once a quarter. Most of the time, if there's a conference, that's more convenient, so I can attend the event and visit teams at the same time. It's also important to have the country managers come to Tokyo once in a while.

Ferraz: I imagine that it's a challenge for most founders in Asia to fly from country to country. On a personal level, I imagine that can get physically taxing. How do you preserve your energy and your sanity when traveling from country to country?

Naka: I was younger back then [laugh]. Now I don't travel as much as I used to because we have a strong international team, and the manager does the trips. In terms of sustaining my energy, in general, I try to stay healthy, I don't drink much. I sleep well. I prioritize sleep over everything, and I exercise once a week. Your health is the foundation of your work.

Ferraz: You've already scaled to a lot of countries in Asia, but you've mentioned in other interviews that you also want to scale into Western countries like the United States and the United Kingdom. What do you think are the greatest challenges in achieving this goal? Who are the competitors in the West that you would have to face, for example?

Naka: I'm not sure when I said that, but I said that many years ago [laughs]. In terms of competitors, there is no other service like Wantedly in the United States or the United Kingdom. I think we are unique, and this concept of visiting companies is not easily accepted by recruiters because it's so counter-intuitive.

In North America, where abundant funding is available, and there are many entrepreneurs seeking opportunity, execution is more important than having an idea. Your idea will be copied, or even get improved by competitors. So once you are determined to enter the US, you need funding. Having a deep understanding of users is another important factor. What are the pain points of the users? I think the same goes for the UK. I mean, it's the same everywhere, but North America is the most competitive, so I wouldn't easily think about going.

Ferraz: HR departments at companies have limited budgets. How do you pitch the virtues of Wantedly vs indirect competitors, other job platforms, and so forth?

Naka: Wantedly adopts the freemium-model, so customers don't have to secure a budget upfront. Customers will be happy to pay once they see the initial traction using our platform. Our strategy is to focus on users, then make users happy, so there will be lots of happy testimonials, which will be far more convincing than any other types of sales pitches.

Ferraz: What has the response to social recruiting been like around the world? Have you received more interesting or surprising responses from some of your other markets?

Naka: Outside of Japan, we are facing a lot of setbacks and rejections. But that was the case in Japan as well in early days. I think, in general, people don't like to change their old habits that they formed over the years. It will take some time to introduce a new way—such as letting them invite people to their offices to have a casual chat.

It's always hard in the beginning, but once I heard about the success cases, I knew Wantedly worked. The people you hire through Wantedly are more loyal to the company. You have good chemistry going around, so I think it's a "time will tell" situation.

Ferraz: You mentioned that you wanted Wantedly to have a great engineering culture. Now that you're a much larger organization, how are you taking steps to preserve the engineering culture that you started with?

Naka: One is purpose. Engineers are in demand everywhere in the world, so they can easily find jobs with good pay. In that sense, engineers tend to seek something else besides money. They not only look at salary, but want to feel that they are working for a greater good, or feel they are part of something bigger than themselves. They consider causes and missions.

Also, ownership is very important. I think at some companies, product managers decide everything and tell the engineers what to build, but at our company, we encourage engineers to take initiative. So, their job is not to build something. Their job is to solve problems. For example, if one of the engineers has a mission to grow the number of monthly active users by three percent, that engineer can take any measure and not be limited to only engineering. That engineer can reach out to PR or work with another department to hit the target. We treat our engineers as more than engineers, so I think that has made our engineering culture unique and competitive.

Ferraz: Can you give an example when a Wantedly engineer was tasked to solve a problem and they used non-engineering means to try to solve it?

Naka: One of our engineers—he's been with us for three or four years—he's now leading a project to make a blog function at Wantedly, so companies can write blogs about their culture. The KPI for the lead engineer is page views until the end of the quarter. To meet that target, he was not only building the product, but he has also hired content writers to come up with interesting content. He reached out to influencers to ask them to write posts on the platform. He had meetings with PR managers to set up a press announcement for new shipments. Normally, engineers wouldn't do that. They leave things to the product managers or the director, and they just code. That's an example.

Ferraz: Have you found that engineers like to stretch themselves in other business directions when you give them accountability and ownership?

Naka: Yes, we do. We have been accelerating the hiring of engineers, so as the number grows, we see more diverse types of engineers. There are types of engineers who just want to code, but at the same time, there's a certain percentage of engineers who are into entrepreneurship and who want to lead projects. Not only do they want to be an engineer, but they also want to solve the problem with means other than coding.

Ferraz: You have a front-row seat to the growth of Japan's tech ecosystem, as you can see from the volume of hiring from product-centric companies as well as Wantedly's own growth. How has the ecosystem grown in the past few years?

Naka: It definitely has grown a lot. I think there have been three big startup booms in the past, in the Internet sector. The first one was at the same timing as the dot-com bubble in the US, when companies like CyberAgent and Rakuten were founded. The second wave was mid-2000, led by social game companies. I think social games like Zinga were big in the US back then, too. Companies like DeNA and GREE became popular at the time. The last wave was from 2010, lasting until now. It was led by the rise of smartphones, and social media that totally changed the landscape of the Internet scene in Japan.

As every cycle passes by, there is more wisdom accumulated in the ecosystem, that is native to the Japan market, and more angel investors became active, who play important roles.

Even in the current cycle, the ecosystem has grown much bigger. When I started my business back in 2012, raising a few million USD would have made a big headline, but that's nothing today. Right now, you can raise 50 million USD without going public, so the role that VC is playing has grown big, too. Previously, the only way to get funding was to get loans from banks, or to go public.

Ferraz: What will it take for the startup and tech ecosystem in Japan to be even stronger?

Naka: We need to play by different rules. When you look at the US and China ecosystems, the size of the addressable market is far bigger, whereas the Japan market size is shrinking fast as the population declines. There is no way to compete against those strong ecosystems by just doing the same thing. Japan is known for a strong manufacturing industry, so I think there might be a chance that Japan can become the center of innovation for robotics. I already see many AI startups collaborating with established Japanese manufacturers like Toyota and Kubota.

Ferraz: What is your vision now for Wantedly?

Naka: We have around two and a half million monthly active users in Japan, which doesn't sound like much, but when you think about it, it's a job platform for building a career, so the number is not that bad. It's not like an e-commerce website or a gaming app. Still, we consider ourselves as not that big. We are hoping to grow five times larger—so, up to ten million monthly active users. I think that's going to make a big impact. Our mission is to make a world where work drives passion. We want to reach ten million users within Japan, but we also want to serve users in other regions as well. Hopefully, we will have the same amount of monthly active users outside of Japan.

Ferraz: If you had to give one piece of advice to entrepreneurs in Asia, what would it be?

Naka: You have to find what you really love. The problem you want to solve. You shouldn't be building a startup just to make money, because running a startup can be so hard that you might give up easily if you don't love what you are doing. You see it all over the news—people launching products or raising money, but it's harder than it looks. Success stories are shared on the media, but not many failures are shared, which are the majority.

So first you have to find what you love to do. Something you can do without getting paid, and that you keep thinking about 24/7—even on the weekends. If you are willing to pay to get involved in the project, that's a really good sign.

Ferraz: In addition to that sort of macro-level advice of finding something that you're truly passionate about, do you have any more hands-on advice? For example, if you're a non-technical founder, it's wise to learn how to code so you can have a greater sense of your product.

Naka: You have to be obsessed about your product. You don't need a vision or a dream in the beginning. Maybe you are the only one who is excited about the idea, and people around you may not take it seriously, or may even think it's crazy; but the bottom line is that you need to be insanely obsessed with it. It's all about product. Being good at pitching or networking will not get you anywhere. You have to be really good at building the product. Scalable and impactful startups all revolve around product.

I think it's good to have a coding skillset because, at the end of the day, if you can code on your own, you can keep pivoting and find the right market fit. Startups rarely get the first product right and usually have 99% failures. Even services like Twitter, Slack, and Instagram are the by-product of main service. So it's crucial to keep pivoting the first product until you find the right market fit.

Building a good product also means focusing on users. I know everyone says that, but it's really true. When I was starting the company, I was so obsessed with "user first" that I seriously thought about turning my company's name into the UserFirst Company. Lots of people compare startups to a war between competitors. In the beginning it's not about competing. It's about serving your users. As long as you are making your users happy, your business will flourish. Media likes to talk about competition and to use an analogy such as war between this and that—but it's all about users.

Ron Hose

Co-founder and CEO, Coins.ph

*In 2014, **Ron Hose** co-founded Coins.ph with Runar Petursson. Coins.ph began as a cryptocurrency marketplace, although the co-founders knew that they wanted to pursue the larger opportunity in creating a digital wallet of choice in the Philippines. Hose had the necessary expertise to build this product, having graduated from Cornell University with a master's degree in computer science and serving as the co-founder and CTO of TokBox, which was acquired by Telefonica Digital in 2012.*

Once Coins.ph focused on its digital wallet, its user base grew exponentially, eventually reaching five million customers by 2018. In 2019, ride-hailing platform and super-app Gojek, which had been thwarted from entering the Philippines by government regulators, bought Coins.ph in a deal valued at US$95 million.

Ezra Ferraz: After experiencing success as an entrepreneur in the United States, what beckoned you to the Philippines rather than building another business there or choosing to go somewhere else?

Ron Hose: I've always been purpose driven. One reason I decided to come here is because I wanted to create something big that can tackle bigger problems and that has a significant impact on people's lives.

Each country has its own strengths and opportunity profiles. I felt that, across the board, the Philippines is good in all sectors. It has a large enough market domestically, but it is also a good base for a company in that region. It has a fast-growing economy, and GDP has steadily grown for the last couple of years.

© Ezra Ferraz, Gracy Fernandez 2020
E. Ferraz and G. Fernandez, *Asian Founders at Work*,
https://doi.org/10.1007/978-1-4842-5162-1_15

In general, despite a lot of infrastructure design-wise, we had a lot of challenges, such as low Internet penetration. I think there's still a lot of value to unlock in this market. For me, this lack of irregular infrastructure is a sign of opportunity. People here are tech savvy, but at the same time, there are a lot of improvements that can be made for everyday life with technology. There's still a lack of access to basic necessities like healthcare, education, financial services, and commerce. And technology, in my experience, can help connect Filipinos to these services. I felt that if I were to spend five to ten years of my life building a business, I wanted to do it somewhere that I really felt at home. The culture and people of the Philippines made me feel at home from day one. This made me want to stay.

Ferraz: When did you first hear about Bitcoin, and what did you think of it? How did you go about purchasing your first Bitcoin?

Hose: The first time I heard about it was 2010, so it was very early on. I was in Silicon Valley and worked for a short period in venture capital. It was interesting, so I thought I should buy some, and then I got distracted, and I forgot about it. That usually happens when you're in a venture capital firm. So it was off my radar for a while, then my co-founder Runar, bought me a bitcoin for my birthday. I held onto it, I think, for a couple of years, then it eventually got absorbed into the company.

Ferraz: What's your first impression about Bitcoin?

Hose: I think back when we started Coins, which was in 2013, a lot of people were really looking at it as a speculative instrument. We realized there was a quick revenue potential with trading. I was not excited by that, basically because I was looking to create long-term value through the business.

I took some time off at the end of 2013, and I started thinking about the different options that might go hand in hand with it, and that was when I realized the impact that blockchain would have on financial services, and that really connected with my mission of building a business that had positive social impact. When I came out here, that was really when the vision for Coins sparked. We're actually not interested in being an end but rather a means to connect individuals to financial services.

We started Coins because we wanted to deliver financial services in a way that was more adept to the needs of the Filipino market. This came about because we saw that eighty percent of Filipinos don't have access to financial services. What struck me was that more Filipinos have Facebook accounts than bank accounts. For me, Facebook's reach demonstrated that the distribution channel for reaching consumers is there, it's just that banks and financial institutions have not figured out how to use it to increase banking penetration reach investment. We set out to be the ones to break the disconnect between banks and consumers.

When I studied more, I learned that the traditional banking models just do not work well for emerging markets. They need to maintain branches, tellers, and armored trucks, which are all very costly. At the same time, they are dealing with consumers that have very low savings rates. Every time a customer walks into a bank, the bank is actually losing money, because the economy is so fundamentally based on cash. The economics doesn't work, and as a result, banks have to turn away most customers that can't hold accounts for them. At the time we started our business, this equation accounted for four out of five households remaining unbanked.

And it is this exact equation that we set out to break.

At a high level, Coins is an access layer to financial services for the bottom of the pyramid—the eighty percent that didn't have access to those services. We set out to be a bridge. What we do is really about lowering the costs of providing financial services. We do that through technology, partnerships, etc., and the more we reduce the costs, the more we can increase our reach to serve lower-income customers that traditionally are not being served by banks. That is the core business model of Coins. We have done this in many ways in terms of tech innovation.

In our sign-up process, you can create your accounts in sixty seconds, whereas banks take longer and have massive CapEx to set up branches. Today, we serve almost ten million customers—all from a 400-square-meter office with 150 employees. We can do that because we partnered with retailers like pawnshops, convenience stores, and banks, so that customers can easily cash in and cash out.

Ferraz: Can you take us into the earlier days of Coins? What was it like when you finally decided to found the company? How did you find your co-founders, and how did you build the product?

Hose: I came into the market with a very high-level idea about the problem I wanted to solve. Emerging markets were experiencing fast economic growth, but most people were still left behind when it came to access to very basic services.

What I saw was that mobile penetration was going to create a bridge, so that you could now offer direct access to these services. I actually met my co-founder, Runar, when I was already in Manila, and then we spent almost a year looking at various business models and trying to figure out where we could do something that creates value. This was in 2013. I figured the research I conducted would help other investors and entrepreneurs looking at the Philippines, so that was also when we wrote a Philippines startup report.

We spent a long time researching different business models. As we were doing this, the thing that kept coming up was that in almost every aspect of business, banking was a friction point, and this had an impact on everyone from consumers to SMBs, and all the way up to big businesses. To send money home, Filipinos had to pay six to seven percent extra. When they wanted to pay bills, they had to get on a jeepney in scorching heat or torrential rain, and then stand in line for an hour at the payment center. With no bank account, consumers and small business owners had no credit history, and so relied on informal "five six" lending, where they had to pay twenty percent monthly interest for a loan to grow their business.

Additionally, businesses here are fundamentally based on cash, and there is not a lot they can sell in a short time. So the two to three days for the money to come up are two to three days wherein funds are audited, as that is the economic cycle. This slows the GDP process, and businesses like sari-sari stores, because they're not with a bank, cannot earn a lot of money or grow beyond that initial scale. Upward mobility is difficult for them, and they have a hard time developing. Basically, everywhere we looked there was a pain point with money, and that's what made for the interest in the opportunity.

Ferraz: So as you set up, what lessons did you take from TokBox and your experience as a venture capitalist that you think applied to the Coins situation here in the Philippines?

Hose: TokBox was really like a mini-MBA for me. The environment and businesses are different, but a lot of the lessons I've learned mainly on entrepreneurship came from there. It made me focus on building the right team. At TokBox, I learned about the economic cycle of markets. We were lucky to raise funding just before the 2008 market crash, and we had investors who supported the company through ups and downs.

With this, I learned the importance of being conservative when everyone is bullish, and to know how to keep things in check when things go up and down. Another thing I learned is to get great investors who can support you through everything that your business goes through. You want people who know when to push back and challenge you, but also when it's time to step back and allow management room to execute.

Ferraz: At what point did you decide to take on the movement to relieve the financial institution problem in the Philippines?

Hose: This was really baked into our vision from day one. Every so often, I go back and look at our early fundraising decks because I like to see how we are doing compared to what we promised investors and how on track I am with my mission and vision. If you look at our seed round fundraising decks from the very beginning, the mission always revolved around financial inclusion.

Ferraz: What were the challenges of building a cryptocurrency platform in the Philippines, and how did you go about addressing them?

Hose: One of the biggest challenges was that we were early in the crypto space. I think we were one of the very first ones who got into providing services on top of blockchain. We had a lot of firsts, which took a lot of trial and error. From a technology perspective, we had to figure out how to build it, what the product should look like, and how to make it consumer-friendly.

The second challenge was regulatory compliance. We needed to understand how the business would be regulated because at the time we started, there wasn't any regulatory framework for cryptocurrencies. There was a lot of work and education. It involved learning about how to fit what we were doing into the right framework to make sure that consumers are protected and the risks were mitigated, and subsequently, with that to be at reach with other industry players. We've invested heavily in measures to assure that every aspect of the business is protected and following the rules.

Ferraz: How do you balance the need for regulation with the need to create a great customer experience?

Hose: We have always been very pro-regulation on this matter because we believe that when it comes to money, the two most important things are consumer protection and crime controls [e.g., money laundering, etc.]. Everyone who participates in this industry keeps the same measures, and we have always invested in these. There is a reason why there is regulation for financial services. We trusted that this is important even, though it added cost and friction for our consumers. If a person goes through us, they have to go through a KYC process. Having regulation ensures that everyone maintains the same standard of service.

Ferraz: Around the time that Coins.ph was rising, there were also several other cryptocurrency companies in the Philippines. When did you realize that there was a much bigger opportunity in mobile money compared to cryptocurrency? How did you set about pursuing this business direction?

Hose: It was from day one. That's the difference between us and the others. We are looked at as a blockchain company, but for me, blockchain was always the means but not the end. We are focused on providing financial access to our customers.

Our customers need to be able to send money to their families, to get a loan if they don't have credit history, to top-up their phones without having to find a sari-sari store, and to pay their bills without the pain of traveling far. So it is always going to be about alleviating pain.

Ferraz: On that note, were there challenges in distinguishing Coins from a crypto company or a blockchain company in terms of your branding to the Filipino public?

Hose: It took a certain amount of education. Especially when the markets were growing really quickly, and all everybody wanted to hear about was Bitcoin. But even at that time, we were out telling customers that they should avoid speculation. We looked at blockchain as a technology, and we stuck to that path. I think that the reason why Coins has been so successful is because when everyone was doubling down when the markets were going up, and all the competitors were coming in as the price was rising, we did the exact opposite. If you look, we actually lowered our exposure to digital currency.

We doubled down on financial services. As a result, our transaction volumes in the digital currency product went up by twenty percent, and then cash transactions went up by eighty percent. As the Bitcoin rally subsided, our numbers kept going up. The moral for that is very simple: when you build a company, there is often a tendency to focus on what makes money. If you're building something that brings value to others, you will have a sustainable business.

Ferraz: Once you went into mobile money, you faced competition that had much larger war chests. How did you compete—and eventually beat—these companies as an agile startup?

Hose: The interesting thing is that it takes an understanding of how the emerging market functioned. The strength of this organization is not just the depth of our balance sheet but that of our relationships. There are two other groups in the market that have wallets and are backed by the largest conglomerates here, wherein their market power is much greater than their capital. To be honest, that definitely kept us up a lot of the time. At the same time, what helped is a lesson learned from Silicon Valley: when it comes to business, it doesn't matter how big or small you are, it matters how fast you run. Building a startup takes risk-taking, agility, and speed. Big companies struggle with this. I guess we were also naive in that way and thought, "Okay, they're big, formidable, and have a lot of resources, but I'm not going to compare myself to them. I'm just going to do my own thing."

We did not carve five million customers away from any of those companies. I would not say we outsmarted them, but that we were able to grow faster because we were small and worked really hard.

Ferraz: What's your edge over companies like GCash and PayMaya, and what is your mindset toward these companies with a bigger budget?

Hose: I recently heard that one of our competitors had $16 million worth of budget for 2018. We used about $10 million of our capital in five years, which meant that we always had to be focused, strategic, and diligent in our efforts. The team knows that this is the culture our company revolves around. Not all wars are won with money. What cannot be replaced is team culture. We were able to hire young and ambitious talent that really cares about what we do. They have worked hard for us and learned a lot. If you ask me, that is one of the things that made us successful.

Ferraz: Since fintech in the Philippines is relatively new, you could not recruit based primarily on domain expertise in the space. What do you look for in potential candidates when hiring?

Hose: In my first company, I had a joint investor, and I remember he had started a small company that was also struggling in finding the best talent. I guess it boiled down to two things. First, we looked for the diamonds in the rough. And really, you only get the raw material in these markets. The talent is here, but not a lot have experience. So we focused on hiring raw talent. A lot were hired directly from college, so we looked at their personal attributes and how passionate they were in what they were doing. Over time, that translated into experience. The will to learn will definitely outpace experience because passion is there. I really enjoy working with and developing that talent. They are very eager to learn. They are smart and humble, which is a really strong combination.

Ferraz: What are the differences between American employees and Filipino employees? How did you successfully navigate these differences as you built Coins.ph?

Hose: Maybe culture in general. We like to think that our company culture is kind of a blend of both. For example, we really focus on performance versus the environment. I think in general if you look at American mind space, it is very individual.

I think the culture of this company and the culture in the Philippines is much more group or community-oriented. We think of how we are working together. It becomes more of the group's success within the team. I think it creates a very positive working environment. The relationships are very strong. It is very much more like a family.

Ferraz: Why did you choose to raise money from Naspers Ventures rather than other VC firms?

Hose: Actually, the leads of the series were Maximum Accelerate, Kickstart, and Wavemaker. I was looking for the investors that would really help us. I found it challenging because many US-based investors might not understand the nuances of the Filipino. They know the nuances of executing the American market.

Each of three investor leads brought something different to the table based on their area of expertise. Kickstart, being a corporate group, brought us local connections. Maximum Accelerate, which was a global fund, brought us direct industry expertise. Wavemaker is based in Singapore but has strong ties in the Philippines and understands the evolution of the business. So each one of them had local growth and technical expertise. That was our triangle for series A.

Naspers actually came in right after that. Every investor you bring in must be strategic. Basically, it is like hiring another person to the team. So, I really took the time to choose the best fit. Every investor brings value.

Ferraz: That's really interesting because I think a lot of young entrepreneurs pitch to whoever is willing to give money, but you were really strategic on how you chose your investors, which I think is awesome advice.

Hose: Yes, that is why I advise you to raise money as early as you can. However, I usually raise a little late. Every time we raise, it is further than our actual break-even. I like going a little late because rather than focus on trying to get the highest possible valuation, we focus on getting the investors that are able to help us.

Ferraz: So in 2018, you reached five million users. I'm sure you used numerous strategies to reach this milestone. Which of these channels surprised you the most and why?

Hose: The people at the bottom of the pyramid spend their earnings on a day-to-day basis, and we thought that the market is not only sensitive to costs. While cost is important, and we work really hard to improve that, what is even more important is service and convenience.

Even the people at the very bottom of the pyramid value their time and convenience. It matters a lot. So we realized our value proposition to people is not in saving money.

If you go on our website today, you will see the main page of the website is about how much time we save people.

Ferraz: If focusing on the value proposition of time in your messaging helped you onboard more customers, which strategy didn't work?

Hose: A lot [laughs]. Ninety percent of what we do. The key lesson is to try many things quickly. Test, learn, and improve. My decision needs to be fifty-one percent accurate. I need to make a lot of decisions. That's how you improve.

We tried a lot of on-the-ground marketing. We are much better at digital. I think we are good at things we can measure and quantify. It is because we can justify exactly what is happening and how consumers are reacting. But even there, we do stuff that fails all the time. The biggest lesson is that in this part of business, you have to roll out ten products to be successful with one.

Ferraz: What's your attitude toward failure?

Hose: I always say that success is about being able to deal with failure. How you work your way out of failure is what makes you successful.

There are so many things that I messed up when I was building this business. So many setbacks. So many times that I said, "Okay, this is it. We're not making it another day." Success is definitely your tolerance for failure and willingness to get up and keep running. That's it. There is no entrepreneur that did not fail a lot of times. We live in this social media world now, where we only see the positive outcomes. All the people are going to hear about is how entrepreneurs and startups exited. They do not know all the blood we shed on the way. There were a lot of nights we did not sleep.

Ferraz: Can you share the story of the Gojek acquisition? How did the idea come up, and why did the deal make sense?

Hose: Last year, we were at a point in which the business was moving very quickly. We were looking at fundraising, and then in the process, we met some Gojek guys.

As the conversation was going, we learned that our ambitions and our values are very similar. We figured that we could do more together. We built up a market here for tech, and we built a really strong team. We think that Gojek has complementary products and complementary technology that can help us scale up a pretty sizeable balance sheet. I guess the math was actually very simple. This is our decision for a business to help us grow and to create a sustainable business. I look at this acquisition as a large fundraiser with a better path and better growth for business—from a CEO execution point of view. My true north is the growth of the business. This is the best possible path.

Ferraz: What is your vision now for Coins.ph?

Hose: It is still the same. There are 100 million people that need to have access to financial resources. The banks are the traditional financial providers, and we help connect the banks to consumers and segments of the market they are not able to reach.

Ferraz: What unconventional advice would you give founders in Asia who want to build a company as successful as Coins.ph?

Hose: If you want to build a business in this market, you really have to understand it in depth. You have to feel the same pain your customers feel every day. As an example, I'm still using a prepaid phone line. I've been living here for almost six years, but I'm still on a prepaid phone line. Why? Because most of our customers are using prepaid phones.

Ferraz: So you're experiencing the same things as them?

Hose: Exactly. I'll never be able to experience every last thing, obviously, but I want to be immersed because it helps me learn what I can do to make my customers' lives and experiences better. In emerging markets, it is really important for you to live in the context of the consumer to really understand and relate to their experience.

Ferraz: What else besides the prepaid phone?

Hose: I minimize my use of banks in general. I do have US bank accounts, and a plastic card, but as much as possible, I try to reduce my reliance on financial services outside of Coins. I use Coins to pay my bills, rent, everything. It's great! And when it's not working great, then that's good too, because I learn about the limitations of our product. And then we figure out what we can do better to address it for our customers.

Ferraz: You told other entrepreneurs to come here. What do you think they would feel when they actually see for themselves that more than 100 million people don't have access to financial services.

Hose: I think the opportunity for using technology to improve people's lives goes beyond financial services. There are opportunities for growth in agriculture, healthcare, commerce, and transportation. The important thing is that you need to experience them. For example, if you're going to build technology for farmers, you need to spend time on the farm. You need to be in the countryside to understand what is driving them.

Living here, I get to know what a *tingi-tingi* [sachet culture] economy is. It is not just about getting a loan from the bank. It's about thinking, "Hey, I need to buy butter. I'm going to buy a quarter of a bar." And someone is actually splitting it. That's a fact. That's a financial product, right? That person is splitting the butter into four. He's basically providing a financial service. Sounds like a food vendor, right? It's not. Every sari-sari store in this country is a financial services provider. So the truth is that everybody has access to financial services. They are just informal or not optimal.

We have to spend some more time to understand all the social economics of their life. "How do I save money? Is there going to be money there when my turn comes?" Those are pains people experience here.

Ferraz: Can you share an example where failure to be field-oriented or user-centric has resulted in products that have failed?

Hose: I'll give an example from Google, my favorite company. About six years ago, Google tried to build a mobile wallet.

They had a lot of capital to do it, but they were not successful. I suspect that one of the reasons is that it is much more difficult to launch a product that is what you *think* your customers need.

We want them to use our wallet because it solves a problem for them. To understand people's pains, you have to live it. That is the answer. I was lucky enough to stay a whole year in the Philippines before I even started my business. I spent a lot of time in the province. I didn't live a very luxurious life. I've been on top of jeepneys.

Ferraz: No way! On top of jeepneys?

Hose: Yeah, and I've slept in the barangay halls. Those experiences shape how we build our product. And the experiences with my team shape it, too, because when we launch something, we always think, "Does this make sense? Does it actually help?"

Zac Cheah

CEO and Co-founder, Pundi X

Zac Cheah founded Pundi X with Pitt Huang in Jakarta, Indonesia, in September 2017. As a financial technology company, Pundi X began by offering a different kind of payment platform through its predecessor—the Pundi-Pundi app, a QR payment system. Pundi X became much more than a traditional payment gateway, as it soon allowed people to experience a borderless payment system with the use of its proprietary products—XPOS, XWallet, and XPASS. The company is currently active in over 30 countries and has shipped more than 5,000 XPOS devices. By 2021, the company aims to ship 100,000 XPOS devices all over the world, transcending borders and cementing its position as a world leader not only in the fintech industry but also in the blockchain technology space as a whole.

Ezra Ferraz: Prior to founding Pundi X, you were working in the browser and mobile gaming industry. What motivated your shift into the cryptocurrency space?

Zac Cheah: It definitely has something to do with my academic history. Since I studied computer security and mobile computing, I am familiar with cryptography, which is a basic feature in computer security. Now, whenever I deal with big clients, security comes up as a huge factor. This eventually led us to create a fintech app in 2016 that is known as the Pundi-Pundi app, the initial foundation that led to what Pundi X is today.

© Ezra Ferraz, Gracy Fernandez 2020
E. Ferraz and G. Fernandez, *Asian Founders at Work*,
https://doi.org/10.1007/978-1-4842-5162-1_16

Ferraz: Can you tell us more about that app called Pundi-Pundi?

Cheah: The Pundi-Pundi app is actually a QR code payment system that is similar to Alipay in China. We created a similar technology and introduced it in Indonesia. Looking back, this was actually the base of what Pundi X is today. Now, we are seen as the new rising provider of point-of-sale POS—devices whereby you can actually use cryptocurrency along with the actual app to buy and sell items. I remember coming into the fintech space to serve a huge need by the Indonesian market. And hopefully, little by little, we are doing just that.

Ferraz: Can you walk us through the current community landscape in Indonesia, and on how they reacted to and supported your startup?

Cheah: It was very simple. Unknown to many, Indonesia has a lot of active cryptocurrency miners [cryptocurrency], and in recent years, the trading market has also been growing a lot. But outside of this, cryptocurrency has hardly had any activity in Indonesia, where a large proportion of the population is still unbanked. What we really want to do is serve the people—like in Indonesia's case, where it hasn't been touched by cryptocurrency. That brings us to how we've tailored our products for today's use. Less than thirty percent of people living in Indonesia have bank accounts. And because of that, we want to make the transactions very physical, very offline, and very convenient. With our technology, people can actually go to convenience stores and pay digitally either through an electronic wallet or through digital currency.

Ferraz: Can you talk about how you planned and executed your public token sale? It is, of course, one of the biggest in Asia.

Cheah: Well, to be frank, I think we were just very lucky that it received the traction it did. We did our due diligence beforehand, but it is still surreal that we were able to raise thirty-five million dollars in just ninety minutes. I think it was received well because people were able to understand and get behind our mission very easily; that is, to push for the mainstream adoption of cryptocurrency and blockchain technology. In the end, over eleven thousand people shared our advocacy and backed us through our token sale.

Ferraz: Initial coin offerings [ICOs] are becoming an increasingly popular way for tech companies to fundraise. What advice do you have for other people in Asia who might be interested in organizing their own public token sale?

Cheah: What I would tell others who will launch their own ICOs is to distinguish themselves from other companies and to become early identifiers. This is how we went in. And from there, we basically really tried to build and expose ourselves not just in blockchain but even in the banking world. After that, we went to build this really raw product. That product was just an exploratory start of what we wanted to do. Secondly, blockchain companies must be very clear about the use cases of their token. It's easy to get caught up in the innovations that blockchain brings to the table. If there isn't any real use case, the price of your token won't be justified for a long time.

They also have to focus and to build the best product. The rest of the things that are extremely important, like outreach and marketing, which is the mainstay, will follow suit.

Speaking from a personal perspective, I have this habit of figuring out how to create an idea that can be brought from zero to number one. Just the hope that it will explode gives me a strong nudge. But what strikes me very strongly is that doing one thing exceptionally well is so much harder than doing three things okay. And to do one thing extremely well is really the key challenge for any entrepreneur, since most, if not all, have multiple skills and projects they work on.

Ferraz: What do you think is the one thing you did really well that allowed you to take Pundi X to where it is today?

Cheah: One thing that you need to know as an entrepreneur—as a voice for your platform—is how to communicate, especially to different government sectors around the world. Be active and constantly seek feedback so you can open up doors to collaboration.

Ferraz: Are you also working with the government in terms of regulations and compliance in building a framework for blockchain security?

Cheah: Yes, we are. We are the founding members of the blockchain association in Indonesia, which has a direct connection with the regulators. We are also a part of the fintech associations in Switzerland, Singapore, and Hong Kong. But as with anything else, education is key. This is how we get people to support cryptocurrency and blockchain. I think the education industry would be quite helpful with this since we are addressing an industry-wide need. We want to address not only the specific industries that will be covered but also the wide array of issues they face.

Ferraz: In terms of educating the industry-wide issues, how do you make the market more wary of the tokens, currencies, or coins that are perhaps scams or aren't as useful as the more mainstream ones?

Cheah: The very first thing that we take into consideration is that we cannot really do the proper education alone. That is why we have partnered with governments to add more insight and regulations on the whole blockchain and cryptocurrency industry. We hope to see that soon.

Since our government is not much into cryptocurrency, there are some government sectors that are thankfully eager to learn and use this technology. So, now we are working with a separate government entity to see how it can be a part of the project moving forward, especially since we are scaling up.

Ferraz: When I saw the XPOS in the Philippines, I heard that you had to overcome a lot of technical challenges to make such an innovative product. Can you share some of the technical challenges you had to overcome to make this device possible?

Cheah: Yeah, sure. I think one is actually the nature of the device itself. It wants to answer a very real-life question. An example is when I buy a coffee with my Bitcoin. If my coffee costs one dollar, do I want to pay two dollars or one dollar? Of course I'd choose the one-dollar option. So, we focused on the delivery of the XPOS to make sure that it would optimize the process while still keeping costs low.

For this XPOS, by 2021, we plan on getting at least one hundred thousand devices into the market. Now we are taking orders from three groups. One is in the retail group. They have people who are coming to buy from our website. The second is actually from large corporations, so we are also supplying large companies. These big corporations will roll out XPOS through their own networks. And the last one is distribution to large-district companies.

We did it this way to lay out a solid foundation for the development of the business in the future. That's why the contributor sees the value in this project. We wait until it fully spreads, and then we adapt to what the market needs. We listen.

Ferraz: How did you market the XPOS to potential clients? What made them choose the XPOS over other alternative POS systems?

Cheah: A lot of people and businesses are promising the future. They are talking about what will happen in six months or even twelve months, but we do not do that. What we chose to do instead is to already have the product done. This is also apparent when we say we are doing adjustments. We showed the product to the people first.

I think this made the product more compelling, compared to others who might have created a conjuncture. We stayed away from overpromising and instead made it clear what it is our device can provide for them.

Ferraz: What kind of response did you get from the people when you showed them the product? How did they react when you spoke with them in person and when you shared your market education?

Cheah: Mainly, we saw appreciation from veteran crypto people. Those groups gave us the most interesting feedback. There are a lot of opinions about the token industry, and they were interested in finding out the use cases of our token.

Ferraz: Once you're able to establish what your use case is, how do you share this? How did you actually market Pundi X's use case to the people who bought into your public token sale in ninety minutes?

Cheah: We talked to everyone. This involved a lot of countries. We met with people in person so we could show them the product.

Since most of those who buy in have to have experience, we were basically testing out new waters. In this case, a lot of people are first-time public token sale buyers, which means they never had experience buying or selling ETH [Ethereum]. But I guess with the recent advances, they wanted to get into this really huge market where some people are even holding Ethereum for long periods. That's why they wanted to participate. We have a huge community here, and now we also have various interests branching out from Asian countries like Japan, Korea, and Singapore. They make up a huge percentage of our token contributor group. These countries own the largest market share, too.

Ferraz: What are you doing now as you try to scale in the Southeast region and eventually the world? How are you reaching this 99.9 percent of people who don't have any tokens or cryptocurrency yet?

Cheah: I think we are really lucky. The thing for us is that the market has blessed us with token holders who are very talented, knowledgeable, and capable. In the sense that they know which tokens are actually useful. So, we try to educate with as much exposure as we can with these talented market leaders. It is therefore reaching not just the ninety-nine percent but the whole cryptocurrency industry, as well.

Besides, the whole industry is new, so we get to learn and grow together. The great thing is that Indonesians now are one step ahead to buy and use cryptocurrency. We are now regarded as being among the top one percent who are trying to bring this technology to everyone in a more direct, more human way.

Ferraz: Do you have any main issues in your global goal to scale?

Cheah: To scale, we must first face the challenge of how we can make this a truly global movement. We are really working hard on that. That is why we are focusing on mobile delivery first.

We also made an effort to first obtain the necessary certifications for the XPOS before deploying them to our partner merchants. In the past year, we've received different certifications to operate XPOS worldwide, such as the CE certification for Europe; the TRA certification for the UAE, the Middle East, and North Africa; the FCC certification for the United States; and the KC for South Korea. Also, we are working with traditional point-of-sale solution leaders to integrate our XPOS platform.

Ferraz: Going back to the advantage of being based in Indonesia, how do you think this helped you in creating and building your own product?

Cheah: As I mentioned earlier, only thirty percent of the entire Indonesian population has bank accounts. And people really don't think of Indonesia when it comes to any fintech advancements, so we decided to hit two birds with one stone. We wanted everyone to know that we are good and capable, and that we are able to create an innovative fintech product that is set to disrupt our own market—like Alipay, Coins.ph, and other great innovations in Asia.

This actually meant that Indonesia gains a huge advantage as it goes out to a bigger market, including the huge Philippines and Chinese markets. So, with that, we launched XWallet, our version of a cashless wallet, since we want to support every single payment gateway and platform for all to use.

To that effect, we also have an e-money license that allows bank cards to be used in mobile wallet transactions.

Ferraz: Most startups in Asia usually build only one product, but you guys are trying to build a whole entire ecosystem. What are the challenges of establishing an ecosystem with many moving parts and many moving products?

Cheah: The main challenge is what people think. Most people in Southeast Asia will always wonder about the claims of a smart payment app, which is a currency wallet, too. We want to support all the payment methods that are available in the United States right now, and that includes cryptocurrency. We want to bring all types of the payment gateway to Asia.

In our mission to support every type of payment, Pundi X has created a mobile app and a card.

Ferraz: You mentioned that you don't have a comparable device yet. How does XPOS compete with any other legacy POS devices out there?

Cheah: We are actually not trying to replace the current POS, but if we are to do a comparison, we have the capability of the current POS. We are actually competitive already, and we try to be more competitive, if not the most competitive.

We want to become a one-stop payment gateway for all the current payment options, including cryptocurrency. In a sense, we might be replacing the old technology, but it is really adjusting itself into a more mature and developed market whereby we can use cryptocurrency as a payment option.

Still, I think that we are not offering a unique spectrum altogether, but rather a unique service that adds to an existing spectrum.

Ferraz: Where are you now in terms of rolling out the one hundred thousand XPOS devices?

Cheah: Right now, we are focusing on establishing key partnerships around the world that will help us distribute the XPOS. These are not only the partner merchants who will use the XPOS, but also partner distributors that will help us reach these merchants in their respective countries.

We are also adding onto the features of the XPOS by allowing it to accept more cryptocurrencies.

We are doing so through Open Platform, our token listing program where token developers can sign up and have their tokens integrated into our ecosystem.

Ferraz: Do you think you're at an advantage with regards to distributing your device, especially coming from one of the biggest ICOs in Asia?

Cheah: Indonesia is a large market, and since we have a huge advantage from being among the first ones to set up an ICO type of business, we wanted to seize the opportunity of getting into that large market.

Since there was no offering yet in the market at the time, we took the demand and conscientiously decided as a team to focus and develop it here first, and then we could expand further. And who would have thought that we would achieve these initial goals by 2017?

Even though it is very competitive with the presence of Apple Pay and Samsung Pay, we wanted to prioritize the ability to be a working unit as a whole that covers all of these existing types of payment gateways with the addition of cryptocurrency. We do not want to distribute it sparsely.

Essentially, we are all about building and promoting the whole ecosystem. We are not into selling and distributing just the hardware. That is our long-standing motto.

Ferraz: In your business model, I know that you incentivize store owners by giving them a percentage of the transaction fees. How did you arrive at this setup? How do you make it sustainable?

Cheah: We want to be competitive. That is why we let them keep some fees. To really be very competitive is one of our goals. Now, why did we have this motto?

It is actually based on some personal experiences in the tech industry. A number of famous and successful people say that you need to take the market and be the elephant in the room—in a good way, of course. So, we did. We needed to take the market and increase our market share. That is another reason why we do not want to make money by selling hardware alone. We want to have a real, working ecosystem everywhere.

Ferraz: Any major technological challenges or issues during the entire development? I remember that you had more than eight prototypes.

Cheah: On the hardware side, we actually had major issues with security. So, we created a system wherein if you try to tamper with it, then it will self-destruct on its own. Not a literal destruction, of course. This technology is proprietary, and from what we know, we are the first in the world to create and distribute this type of device. We have achieved a real, secure, hack-free system for POS.

Another is the way that we want to confirm small transactions, like purchasing a cup of coffee, so that it is confirmed in real time without incurring large fees to pay for a small-value transaction.

Ferraz: What is your vision for Pundi X in the coming years? Looking beyond the one hundred thousand devices, how do you see Pundi X in relation to changing the financial landscape in Indonesia, Southeast Asia, and the world?

Cheah: I think that eventually blockchain will play a very important role, perhaps as important as what the Internet is today. It took such a long time to be where it is today with so many regulations and innovations that continue to change the game. I believe that blockchain will have as many developments soon, and in order for progress to happen, we need the government and international agencies to regulate everything—from exchanges to currencies to tokens, to hardware, and everything else in between where security is implied. I think that this is the most important thing. It might even be the key to this whole system moving forward. Who knows, it might replace the Internet as more people look for security and privacy.

17

Chih-Han Yu

CEO Co-founder, Appier

*In 2012, **Chih-Han Yu** co-founded Appier with Joe Su and Winnie Lee in Taiwan. Prior to Appier, Yu spent most of his career studying computer science in academe, earning a bachelor's degree in the field from National Taiwan University, followed by a master's degree at Stanford University, and finally, a PhD from Harvard University.*

Yu started Appier as an artificial intelligence (AI) company, before the term was even in vogue. Each of its four products help enterprises make better decisions: CrossX Advertising for retention and engagement across platforms, Aixon for predicting customer behavior, and Aiqua for increasing conversions on company assets.

Now a team of almost 400 employees, Appier serves more than 1,000 brands and agencies from 14 offices across Asia Pacific. Appier has raised more than US$162 million, including from Sequioa, Line, Softbank, and Naver.

Ezra Ferraz: What inspired you and your CTO to pursue mobile games as your first venture together?

Chih-Han Yu: My background is in multi-agent artificial intelligence, and so we wanted an AI that could stimulate and a multi-entity that is actually smart. For example, making multi-robots smart or multi-server interactions smart. Our dream was to build a large-scale system that uses AI and that could potentially change the world.

© Ezra Ferraz, Gracy Fernandez 2020
E. Ferraz and G. Fernandez, *Asian Founders at Work*,
https://doi.org/10.1007/978-1-4842-5162-1_17

We had the idea of building AI engines for games that could simulate multi-player interaction. In particular, we wanted the AI players to be able to mimic the real player's behaviors. We thought it was a cool idea that when you are away, your player can continue interacting with your friends. We've basically built a non-stop gaming community. We tried to sell to game companies, but because we didn't have a background in the gaming industry, that didn't work out. Instead, we built our own games and properties. Unfortunately, we did not get any experts on board. We are still not very good at that, so our game didn't work out. That's why we initially started to build mobile games.

Ferraz: How did your clients let you know they were more interested in your AI capabilities than your game development capabilities?

Yu: Actually, there were a few game publishers that we reached out to after we built our game. They were very nice and gave us feedback on what to change. We worked very hard to improve our engines as well as our games in order to make them work.

In the end, the son of a long-time partner just talked frankly to us. "I didn't know you guys actually knew AI, because every time you try to deal with AI engines, it's very difficult. Not a lot of people know how to do it. Why don't you just take some data from our company and try to see if you can build better gaming engines than our current system?"

What's interesting is that we used a very simple algorithm that worked twice as well as the solutions they were using at the time. They were very impressed, and we got our first contract to sell. We got a game publishing contract, and we got a data consulting contract. We started to realize the value of our skills and capabilities in this industry.

Ferraz: So, after helping that first client and getting the data consultancy, you decided to abandon your gaming startup?

Yu: Gaming startup, or AI engine for games startup. We didn't abandon them totally. We just thought maybe we should get more contracts in order to feed our AI engine. After two or three of these kinds of data consulting contracts, we felt that it wasn't really scalable. People didn't appreciate our capabilities. Then we decided to pivot to a different type of company that used data and also AI capabilities to solve business problems. We started as a digital gaming company that provided a solution to a software problem. We pivoted heavily to start Appier.

Ferraz: When did you decide to abandon your gaming startup?

Yu: This was back in 2012. That was when a lot of our PCs dominated and disrupted the industry. We have a lot of services that are basically mobile versions of those PC nowadays. It became really popular because people started using mobile phones and spending more time on mobile phones. People became more engaged during this time.

We contacted a group of companies that not only did Internet services, but were also in the customer brands, automobile, and financing industries. They didn't know how to reach their digital users through these new devices. What was even more interesting is that even when they were trying to figure out the mobile phone, they would say something like, "How do I win the next device?"

Basically, there's a continuous device disruption. We were thinking that there must be some way to bridge people's data from one device to another. We were thinking, "How can we solve this problem?" We thought we could use AI to solve cross-device bridging problems. We were amazed and were very excited about it, and we were very good at it, so we solved it quickly and massively and became a very popular solution in the industry.

Ferraz: As more categories of devices came onto the market—say, voice-enabled devices like Amazon's Echo—did you also add them to your mandate of optimizing advertising cross-device?

Yu: Currently, we remain focused on cross-device as it relates to desktops, smartphones, and tablets. However, it is interesting to track the adoption of such devices and to see how marketers can leverage the data that comes from them.

Ferraz: Can you share how you built your first product? I know one of your concerns was that purely consulting wasn't scalable, so can you describe your actual first product and how you built it?

Yu: They were two or three data companies, who contacted us if we could do an internal recommendation engine. It would be the best thing for the users, but at the same time, it would cannibalize my current game revenue. The idea was that there were more games, but we don't want my users to spend too much time on the new games. That was the sort of problem we tried to solve. Then, we built a game engine. It was basically a recommendation engine that could take into account multiple contracts that people wanted to optimize. They could actually optimize the right time value and at the same time, not cannibalize the solo products where we really made money.

We built that first product, and it didn't work out that well. Only a few companies adopted that solution, and it didn't become a widely adopted solution. We found that it didn't have a strong, memorable effect. We decided to pivot away and try to build another product that I think was still a very bad, mechanical product back then.

Ferraz: So what were you doing at this point? Were you leading the development as the chief product development officer? What were you doing as CEO?

Yu: Well, the CEO does everything. [Laughs] Because back then, we were only a team of eight to ten people, who were mostly engineers. I was in charge of product, as you mentioned, and I was also in charge of the big business departments. Some of my co-founders also did this. If the lights didn't work, I needed to go fix it. I did everything. I can cook, too.

Ferraz: In terms of product development, did you leverage upon your studies at Harvard and Stanford?

Yu: Yes. Basically, a lot of the products we developed in the early days of Appier were all around AI solutions. Even now, a lot of the algorithm background that I've developed over the years plays a key role in our product design and our algorithm design.

Ferraz: What did you learn in theory in your graduate studies that you eventually applied in practice through Appier?

Yu: There are a lot of algorithms and concepts we apply at Appier now that source from or are otherwise related to my research studies.

Ferraz: Once you moved past your initial clients, the internal game recommendation engine, how did you sign your additional clients? Did you also participate in business development?

Yu: The game recommendation engine idea didn't work, and we repeated it a few times. So, we hadn't really crossed the barriers of bridging technology, which was really getting a lot of traction because a lot of companies wanted to learn how to. I think back then, there was a demand to also start hiring one or two get users through their devices. That helped us grow our business.

Ferraz: What was the target profile of your client companies? Who were you targeting?

Yu: Around 2013, when we were trying out the service officially, we were looking for companies that were PC-based, but wanted to reach into mobile. That was the typical ideal, but it grew into pretty much all kinds of companies that wanted to bridge across devices and channels and gain a cross-device advantage.

Ferraz: In terms of business development, did you have to offer exclusivity? For example, if you had a client in ride-hailing, say Grab, you couldn't work with Uber? Is it sort of like that, or no?

Yu: It wasn't like that. They just wanted to see whether it worked. The first batch of clients were just curious. "Can you guys really do that?" We made it work. There was no exclusivity around it.

Ferraz: What was the most common KPI for your clients? Was it downloads or additional purchases?

Yu: Initially, it was only about big capabilities—being able to do stuff. Bridging all of those clients across the barrier was the main KPI. Of course, when our service became full-fledged and was not only all kinds of marketing, but also consumer insight predictions, even consumer purchase and management behaviors, it got more complicated. Each product had very different KPIs. Initially, the KPI was very simple, and then we brought it to that, and people were very happy about it.

Ferraz: Were all of your clients primarily based in Asia and Southeast Asia, or did you also service clients from, like say, Silicon Valley?

Yu: Back then, it started in Taiwan, and then Singapore. Only two countries.

Ferraz: Why did you settle on your home country, and why Singapore?

Yu: When we were trying to do some research around Asia. We bootstrapped ourselves, and that was actually interesting. Basically, the company didn't make any revenue for two to three years, and then suddenly, three months after launching the service, we were able to make a profit. Not only revenue, but profit. We were very excited about it.

We were counting our profit, and we thought, "We can hire one or two international salespeople." We started thinking about where to put these people. In Japan, China, or in Singapore? We started going around these countries and also talking to salespeople with industry background who wanted to join us. It turned out that the first person who committed to join us was from Singapore, so we decided to start there.

At the same time, the media was releasing reports that China and Japan were the two biggest economies in Asia. The reason we chose to explore Singapore was because it was in the top four in Southeast Asia. We didn't think we'd grow really fast in those few years, so that's why we chose these three places to start exploring.

Ferraz: Out of those initial markets that you had, can you share maybe one of your success stories on how you helped one of your clients?

Yu: There was one really big department store in Taipei. It had some Internet traffic and people, in the past, always went to their website to check their discounts, but people started spending more time on mobile so the store sharpened its approach to those digital customers to show them discount messages when they were around their department store areas. It still sounds impressive now, but it was super impressive back then because people wanted to bridge devices, but we also did location-based intelligence. That was a type of cool technology to get to. They were super excited about it.

Ferraz: What was the positive outcome for that client?

Yu: The outcome was that we were able to get people to carry their mobile phones when they walked through the store. They used to be interested in their service and then the department stores. Because of our solution, we were able to bring them to actually visit the department store.

Ferraz: What inspired you to pursue your second product, Aixon? How did you see this complimenting your original solution?

Yu: That was very natural. Originally, our motivation was in large-scale data and our AI capability to solve business problems. That has always been our vision and also our motivation. Our product across the marketing area allowed companies … once we established long-time partnerships, to say to us, "Can we give you our data for you to build our in-house capability? Because you can help us predict what kind of customers are interested in my product and what kind of people would actually be looking for our services."

We internalized show them in-house capabilities. It started two years ago. We had a goal. We hoped that we would be able to empower our customers to build their automotive data science team in-house without the hassle of build-ing the whole team there. We started to build a data science team on top of the empowering capability of being able to predict consumer behavior. That was sort of the motivation behind building our second product, Aixon.

Ferraz: Can you give a few examples of what type of consumer behavior Aixon can predict? I understand it gets better over time, so can you also share about that?

Yu: Actually, it's super powerful. You can predict and define your own goals. For example, if you want to predict who would be interested in certain products, who is exposed to certain products, or you can define these and predict what-ever goal you want. That's the first capability.

The second capability is that it can let you understand your own gains, not only on your web store, but what kinds of topics customers are interested in on your website—down to an individual basis. We also provide data and pre-diction capabilities for outside your website.

So you can imagine, someone opens the door and you can not only observe anyone inside your store, but you can actually know what happened outside of the store. Pretty much, before the customer even comes in, we already know what to sell to them. That's how we empower or allow our customers to have super capabilities like these. It's really driving the difference. They can define their own goals and are able to know their territory. They get insights on behavior from outside and inside. It's the most powerful capability that Aixon has.

The third one is being able to segment users. Every user and every customer who visits you or becomes a customer is different. How do we smartly segment them and have very personalized media conversations? That sets apart Aixon's capability.

Ferraz: Can you share a story of how Aixon has helped a company over the past two years?

Yu: We not only helped a company with better recommendations for their customers, but also generated more revenue. One top media group in Taiwan has digital media that's on the Internet. It's a bit related. They also do a lot of activities and try to re-engage with the people who are interested in the business. They have a lot of different offerings outside, like magazines and online media. They also have regular courses for executive training. One of their biggest problems is that they don't know how to correlate their current database users with their more personalized, in-depth offerings.

Those in-depth offerings may be executive trainings, or maybe they are financial products we help them with the user's topic of interest on the website and also onsite behavior—we can collect a very holistic view of their audience's interests in financial products and financial topics.

They can segment the audience into very fine commonalities and very personal conversations with promotional messages that can be sent to them. They are very grateful for the service provided by this tool.

Secondly, because they have very tremendous data, we've also helped them segment those data and promote to people with all kinds of financial needs. To reuse the data, monetize their audience, and debunk group companies that sell competing products.

Ferraz: I mean for Aixon, and just for Appier in general, you have to have a lot of technical talent. You mentioned having a data science team, and I know you've been really successful at recruiting top talent not just in Asia, but from around the world, including Silicon Valley. As a founder, why do you think you've been so successful at recruiting top technical talent?

Yu: Top technical talent, loves to work with other top technical talents. We really want to build a community and atmosphere where people really appreciate each other. That's the most important thing. We have been fortunate because my co-founder is very connected. He was part of a national team for programming in Taiwan.

When we started, we only had a few people, but my two co-founders national programming team members. They represented the country. Taiwan actually is probably one of the top-five or top-ten most competitive programming national teams those were very interested in the topics they are pursuing. They created a very positive recruiting look. That's how we started from a few talents to a group of great talents.

Ferraz: I see. So, other than trying to bring the best talent—because great talents like to work with other top people—in terms of culture or benefits, how do you make it very developer-friendly to help attract these talents?

Yu: I think programmers usually want to work in challenging departments. We're always trying to challenge ourselves to do what's next. We have one solution to a problem, but we immediately jumped into developing our next generation solution and finding a problem to disrupt. Taking on challenges and being able to address these problems excites people. We also ensure that they have their freedom and that they have some autonomy to choose the way they solve problems.

We also encourage them to use new tools and technologies. We don't use a very conservative approach when developing a new product. Whenever they hear there's a great tool or hear about someone publishing a powerful algorithm, we always encourage them to try. That kind of culture and mentality really is appreciated by a lot of the great talent at Appier.

Ferraz: Are you still very actively involved in the recruiting side of your top-level talent?

Yu: After we're done here, I have to finish a whole series of recruiting interviews. [Laughs]

Ferraz: My next question is more related to the business development and sales side. You generally service businesses in three categories: consumer brands, e-commerce companies, and mobile commerce or game developers. Each of these has its own unique sale cycles and idiosyncrasies. What are the challenges of selling Appier's solution to each of these three categories, and how do you deal with it?

Yu: Each category has different needs, and what we do is to really understand the customer's needs and provide the appropriate solution. Basically, when should we present X model or Y model to match the customer's needs? That's something we need to provide in our internal training. We have been actively dedicated to training our people to be able to match the problems that the customers face with the solutions that we are able to provide. We still think that one of the best things about us is our customers. To match the solution that can solve their most urgent needs is the most important thing.

Ferraz: You mentioned just a few moments ago that what attracts developers is solving big problems. What are the next big problems that you're looking to solve?

Yu: I said from the get-go that AI was going to change a lot of things that we do nowadays. There's one saying recently that I think really matches the current situation. "There's no standalone AI industry, but every industry is transformed by AI." Basically, we will continue. We have seen a lot of opportunity in each industry. For a specific push that we can solve problems, or there are processes we can automate or make more optimized—those are the opportunities for AI. We think that there is a lot that can be foreseen—some of them are relatively dead already, some are bigger markets.

Ferraz: You now have a well-funded war chest of venture capital and serve more than 1,000 clients worldwide. Of course, Appier is successful, but how do you define Appier's 2,000? What is your ultimate goal for the company?

Yu: I think our success doesn't rely on whether we can deliver on the very best solution and on how we drive change for the customers or the industries they are working in. Our success is not defined by the amount of funding we've raised. It's also not defined by the number of people we have. It's rather defined by the success of our customers, by how much we have changed the way businesses connect and interact with audiences.

Ferraz: I understand you have customers all over the world, including some of the top tech companies in Silicon Valley. What are the challenges of being an Asian company servicing Silicon Valley companies?

Yu: If you really have a good solution, there are no particular challenges. Maybe sometimes there are some differences, such as we cannot have real-time communication. That's pretty much the only one. But we think that now, society really has no boundaries. There's no specific challenge.

Ferraz: How do you see AI changing the lives of consumers in ten to fifteen years? Just the everyday person, not a brand.

Yu: I think you can imagine everything will become intelligent from the most complicated things to the most interesting things. I remember when I was doing my PhD thesis, there were these body chairs that can ultimately save people's postures and provide the best support for the lower hip. I think someday, that day will come. Starting from the most immediate technologies to passive devices and furniture and the Internet of Things—all will become intelligent. We will be surrounded by intelligent devices and be making decisions in a much more abstract way. That's what I perceive in the next ten to twenty years.

Ferraz: Even today, looking toward that future, how can even small businesses leverage or get into artificial intelligence if they're not the size of Gojek or Grab?

Yu: The first step is to start collecting the data. Organizing your data well is very important. Data, in the future, will become a very important asset for any business. Not only for big businesses, but also for small businesses. Small businesses will also grow bigger. In the process, an organized way of collecting data and records. Media across time, across different customers, or across different services and products that will actually inform you to make much more intelligent decisions in the future.

Ferraz: Entrepreneurs in Asia get all sorts of advice from the media or from other founders. From your perspective as the CEO of one of Asia's top start-ups, what advice do you give to people who want to build a company as successful as Appier?

Yu: I wouldn't call us already successful, because we're still in the process of building a successful company. I think it makes no difference building a great company anywhere in the world. You need great talent, great ideas, and great execution. It's all about that.

In Asia, I think there's a great opportunity, because the economy is evolving at a really fast pace. How do we localize a lot of our great ideas into each market to capture that opportunity? That has become a very important subject.

In Asia, it's probably that the community of entrepreneurs isn't as active as in Silicon Valley. Here, you be more independent. It's unlike in San Francisco, in Silicon Valley, where if you're working on something, you can ask people for advice, and they're sitting right next to you. Here, having a much stronger mentality is very important.

Ferraz: Because things are different here in Asia as compared to in Silicon Valley, how should founders be more proactive at finding great talent, learning how to execute really well, or learning how to find the best ideas? What advice do you have given our cultural context?

Yu: I think there is no fundamental difference because our community is more spread out. Being able to sort of excite yourself and always pursue a better way to work is important. What other people do may not be what you should also do. You need to have your own determination and your own mentality.

Amongst all my friends, they have been doing very well in Asia. They are probably the first companies of their category in their countries. A lot of the time, you can learn from experience from other categories, other countries, but sometimes you still need to make your own decisions based on what's best for the company and what it's going to attract. If there's no one to guide you, how do you find your way around that? Those things become really important.

Ferraz: You mentioned that a lot of your friends are the first companies in that category. What advice do you have for founders who want to start a business, but don't know yet what problem to solve or product to build? How do they find their great idea?

Yu: I think great ideas need to be validated by markets. It's very hard to hit the nail on the head, so basically, you have to find the problem that people currently have that you believe you can solve, but at the same time, you also need to consider multiple constraints, such as time, money, and regional differences all together—whether those can be solved with your current capabilities. If not, then how can you bootstrap and eventually build toward success to achieve your goal? That's the sort of mentality you need to be putting into place.

Winston Damarillo

CEO and Founder, GlueCode

Winston Damarillo *was the CEO and founder of GlueCode. A self-taught programmer, Damarillo graduated with a bachelor's degree in industrial and mechanical engineering from De La Salle University in Manila, Philippines.*

Upon moving to Silicon Valley, he worked his way up at Intel Corp. and horizontally across engineering, marketing, sales, and finally, venture capital. At Intel, he was exposed to venture capital as an ecosystem builder of the company-backed software or gaming companies that would increase the use cases of their chips.

After Intel, Damarillo founded GlueCode, building the startup in both Silicon Valley and the Philippines. After just one round of fundraising, Damarillo was able to sell GlueCode to IBM, the first in a string of three exits that leveraged talent from both Silicon Valley and the Philippines.

Ezra Ferraz: You were a self-taught programmer before there were online resources like CodeAcademy. Can you share the story of how you taught yourself how to code?

© Ezra Ferraz, Gracy Fernandez 2020
E. Ferraz and G. Fernandez, *Asian Founders at Work*,
https://doi.org/10.1007/978-1-4842-5162-1_18

Winston Damarillo: I've always been an engineer. I finished with an industrial engineering degree from De La Salle University. But when I went to the US, I had this crazy goal to work for the biggest names in Silicon Valley—Microsoft, Intel, or IBM.

I knew I had to learn how to work with computers, so I started with systems operations and networking. At the time, networking was the domain of the Novell Corporation. My first exposure to software development evolved from there as computing, telecommunications, the Internet, voice, and video conferencing were converging. I learned software development through reading SDKs and API documentation, and from the open source community. It was really a combination of wanting to learn and finding things to learn.

Eventually, I built software that enabled businesses to integrate voice and video conferencing into their operations. And this was a decade before Skype. I consider myself lucky having picked a tech innovation that is interesting and important to the way people do business.

Ferraz: How has your stint at Intel Corporation helped you build GlueCode?

Damarillo: I was doing well as an engineer, initially. But as Intel noticed, I enjoy finding new solutions for cool technology, so they transferred me to the marketing and sales departments, and eventually venture capital. It was a progression that was fortuitous.

As an investment executive, I was exposed to a much broader world of technology. I made investments in games, e-commerce, B2B platforms, and open source enterprise software. I believe, at that time, we invested as much as $1 billion a year to new companies. It was the early days of venture capital, way before it became what we know it to be today. Venture capital then was just geeks helping other geeks to turn their new innovations into reality. It was exciting to become part of that process.

Intel's main reason for investing was to grow their ecosystem. We realized one way to convince businesses to buy more computers was to show them how they can innovate with tech.

The financially motivated VC came much later.

As I became more immersed in the world of investments, I realized the Internet was transforming from a static directory of pages to a global enabler of platforms. Websites no longer merely enabled communication between two parties. They were providing channels for transactions, too. Then I saw how these startups were making lots of money, and I knew I could develop the tech they were making, too. By then, I knew I wanted to become part of the new phase of the Internet. So I left, and built GlueCode.

Ferraz: What problem did you want to solve with GlueCode?

Damarillo: I've always championed inclusivity in technology. As the Internet was becoming a platform for conducting business, the ability to participate was limited to the few corporations that could afford expensive proprietary solutions offered by IBM, Oracle, and Sun. We wanted to build an alternative that was collaboratively built and accessible to all. The goal was to make sure that people could transact over the Internet, and that the ability to transact was broadly enabled to as many people as possible. That is the essence of open source technology—it is free to use by everyone, a total disruption to how things were done by the big guys. Somehow, GlueCode democratized innovation.

I built it in a way that could compete against IBM and Oracle—but at a lower cost. It was a battle of David versus Goliath, and I made sure to win.

Ferraz: Isn't open source always known as a not-for-profit platform? How did you create a viable business model within the open source world?

Damarillo: I've always likened it to an auto business. GlueCode was selling cars for twenty percent of the cost of a brand-new one, since the main unit was offered for free. Customers were merely paying for the extra accessories.

Back then, there were three revenue models at play in the industry. First were services offered over free software. Second was dual licensing with enterprise support, like what Red Hat is doing with Linux. And third, and what GlueCode embodied, was open core—wherein paid add-ons were offered to create a better experience for users.

The entire model was disruptive because we weren't only offering a more affordable product, we were also doing so at a much lower cost, operations-wise.

I didn't need hundreds of employees to run the house. We were a fifty-person company competing against a tech giant, and we won. IBM kind of gave up and just bought us.

Ferraz: Several tech companies in the book are bipolar rather than unipolar in that they revolved around two headquarters, such as Razer with its presence in Singapore and San Francisco. In what way was GlueCode both a Silicon Valley and an Asian-driven organization?

Damarillo: Well, most of the GlueCode architecture marketing teams were based in Silicon Valley, since that's where the market is. We wanted to make sure that we were close to the demand and close to the competition. This ensures that we are always on our toes. Manila and Cebu were the machinery to execute software development. A nice side effect is around-the-clock engineering. We were cranking code twenty-four hours a day. The local operations were pioneering in that sense, since at that time, most foreign companies operating in the Philippines were providing services to company headquarters based elsewhere in the world. They were not building products.

Most of the innovation and market demand was driven in the US and therefore the Philippines followed the Silicon Valley model. The ecosystem followed the US model as well. There was no RISE or Echelon or Slingshot then.

The popular option back then was to outsource software development from China and India, but I knew Filipino engineers had it in them to develop world-class products.

That culture of innovation was refreshing to Filipinos, especially since they were so used to building products based on specifications. We had to introduce the culture among local programmers. They had the freedom to create products on their own. We gave them the right tools and a collaborative environment, and they were excited to do their jobs.

It was a complete departure from the frenzy and energy in Silicon Valley, where retaining talent was a constant challenge.

In the US, everyone is recruiting everybody almost every other month. There is a "What's in it for me?" feeling. There is a high sense of entitlement. But in the Philippines, Filipino engineers are just happy to create complex and innovative products.

Building a team culture in a short time is honestly very difficult. It is compounded by time differences, distance, or dual-site operations. What made it easier for us was the open source community. I focused on recruiting people that were already of a "like mind" being involved in open source development. That became the core of our culture and mindset.

The local operations also kept the product cost competitive. The duality was there, so I could build the best product possible—attuned to my customers' needs for a better cost.

Ferraz: Can you go deeper into explaining your business model? What were the paid add-ons that you sold to your clients?

Damarillo: The business model delivers an enterprise model of software from open source. They pay an annual subscription for support and bug fixing for a specific open source version, tools and utilities that make the platform easy to use and maintain, and training and development assistance.

These are all on an annual subscription basis.

Ferraz: What were the challenges of converting your clients toward your paid add-ons, and how did you address it?

Damarillo: Mostly making sure that they realize the value of supported open source. Their biggest concern that to make sure that the software is free from infringement. We addressed it by working with reputable organizations like the Apache Software Foundation.

Ferraz: Did you develop any strategies to expedite the time it took a client to avail of your paid add-ons? What did you do?

Damarillo: It was a very cost-effective alternative to paid software. The biggest benefit of open source is that people can try it for free.

Ferraz: At Intel, you had done many different things, from sales and marketing to business development and investing. At GlueCode, which aspect of the business, did you find yourself focusing on the most, and why?

Damarillo: Sales [laughs]. I was the geek who could sell. So it was a unique capability to help the team.

Ferraz: Communities can be unnecessary gatekeepers. Did you get any backlash from the open source community about your business model? How did you respond to these naysayers?

Damarillo: There was generally no backlash, but there was a lot of hesitation in taking it seriously. Having big brothers like IBM and Oracle support open source was key to acceptance.

Ferraz: You seemed to nail both your revenue model in Silicon Valley and your service delivery and product creation model in the Philippines. Did you keep this model for your other businesses?

Damarillo: Yes, and we are now extending it to ideas in fintech, insurance tech, and regtech, where we inject key innovations to existing mainstream businesses.

As an entrepreneur, I've always been more fascinated by innovating and building teams that can compete against a large player. I wasn't really interested in winning new markets and customers. I enjoyed being the game master, while the rest were scrambling to compete in the markets.

For GlueCode, it was honestly opportunistic. There was so much demand for enterprise open source M&A, we were acquired even before we could spend our VC money. LogicBlaze and Webtide were natural ingredients of large company portfolios, so once the market and technology risks were addressed, M&A followed. We did not have to build the customer base.

After one investment, I sold the company. I enjoyed it since I still maintained control until we exited.

Ferraz: How so?

Damarillo: It was a silly thing to do, but I felt at that time, who knows if this will happen again? So I signed the deal about twenty-four to thirty hours later than intended. GlueCode exited on five-five-five—May 5, 2005. When it's your first, you want it to be memorable. I wouldn't advise it to anyone, but it was fun to do. I used to commemorate the exit and do something special on every fifth of May, but it came to a point that it was time for new milestones.

Ferraz: In what ways do you think GlueCode was a predecessor to the boom of open source and platforms like GitHub?

Damarillo: GlueCode was a pioneer in bringing open source to enterprise customers. The business model innovation we brought to the table was hybrid licensing, community-tested and verified software, and enterprise-quality service and support.

Ferraz: What did you do in the first one hundred days after your exit?

Damarillo: Work on the next one? That sounds cocky, but I didn't feel I was tired. It was addicting for me to create new companies. I thought the first exit was fun, so I wanted to do it again.

After my first exit, I had a rule: keep a third for savings, another third to enjoy, and another third to invest for the next venture.

After selling GlueCode, I wrote my next business plan. Right below our first office, I set up another firm called ActiveMQ, which eventually became LogicBlaze. It was later acquired by Iona and is now part of Red Hat.

Ferraz: After three exits, didn't you think about an early retirement?

Damarillo: I was thinking of creating impact after a while. I thought I could do that serving as chief strategy officer at PLDT, knowing there were so many problems I could help solve in terms of Internet infrastructure. While I thought that was rewarding, I realized that I could have an even better impact on the Philippines and the region as an entrepreneur. So I went back to doing what I do best: building startups.

Ferraz: Can you share more about your present ventures?

Damarillo: I created Amihan Global Strategies first, which is sort of my laboratory. I realized that I am a creature of habit, so I did what I've always done, which was building the factory before the product.

I'm always reminded of a mantra popularized by Andy Grove at Intel: "Intel is the great microprocessor company because it's a great manufacturing company."

I fine-tuned Amihan by working with the biggest conglomerate in the Philippines—SM Investments Corporation's Banco de Oro. Once I was confident, I built Talino Venture Labs, which has become the main hub for all the other startups I've launched in 2019.

Unlike my previous ventures, though, I am now more fascinated in reaching new markets and helping millions of customers.

What is new and exciting is that Southeast Asia now generates its own market demand and innovation requirement, similar to Silicon Valley ten years ago. This is an exciting opportunity, as I can now disrupt regionally while maintaining a global benchmark for quality execution. The region is no longer creating products for the West, but creating products for itself. We are our own markets now. It's an opportunity for technology to bridge a lot of inclusion gap.

One of my startups, Saphron, is providing digital microinsurance for the base of the pyramid. The advance tech we've employed for it is revolutionary in its simplicity. We have learned to redefine the user experience by understanding the workflows of the mom micro-entrepreneurs, or *nanays*. We've helped them onboard new clients in a matter of minutes, which took hours before.

Knowing that your innovation can create that much impact to the base of the pyramid is ten times more rewarding.

Ferraz: But it sounds more challenging considering you're working with mass markets now, unlike your previous ventures.

Damarillo: That's true, which is why it's important to be "smart lazy". When you're lazy, you think of ways not to waste energy. I wouldn't write my own software, so I'll tap what is available in open source. I won't spend time building data centers, so I'll use cloud computing instead. I won't chase customers, so I'll partner with conglomerates instead.

Smart lazy is being smart enough to leverage available innovation, infrastructure, and strategies. I'd rather use my brainpower to build commodity, or improve the customer experience. There's a lot of people doing something that has long been commoditized, which I tend not to do.

That's why for Saphron, I worked with the largest microinsurance provider in the Philippines, Pioneer. I'm not going to spend time buying customers. That isn't only time taxing, it's costly and quite dangerous.

There are companies that have gone four, five, six rounds of funding, yet never really lived up to their potential. They spend much of their money buying new customers so that they create an artificial momentum, but when it busts, they fail to maintain it.

It has worked for Google, Amazon, and Facebook for sure. But that strategy is a big gamble. It's the reason why there are more honestbees than Google.

I'd rather stick to what I know best and stay in my lane. I'm good at coming up with cool new technologies and product design. I'd rather piggyback on conglomerates' customers.

Ferraz: Can you elaborate on your theory about how startups and corporations can innovate together?

Damarillo: The ASEAN market is still developing, which makes it hard for a startup to hit escape velocity to success. At this point, partnering with the big guys is a critical strategy.

Conglomerates have started to embrace the startups that have long tried to disrupt them. I think we're at a time when the two parties have seen each other's value to their long-term success.

Min-Liang Tan

CEO and Co-founder, Razer

*In 2005, **Min-Liang Tan** co-founded Razer with Robert Krakoff in California. One of Razer's earliest initiatives was sponsoring esports players. The company also supported popular gamers on livestream platforms like YouTube and Twitch. For gamers around the world, Razer and its triple-headed snake logo became synonymous with quality gaming hardware and esports.*

Razer's growth has mirrored the rise of gaming and esports. The shared ascent is no coincidence. One of Razer's biggest marketing coups was sponsoring esports players, and later, popular gamers on livestream platforms like Twitch. For gamers around the world, Razer has become synonymous with quality gaming hardware.

This brand reputation proved crucial as Razer expanded into other gaming-related products, such as keyboards, monitors, laptops, and phones. As an avid gamer himself, Tan contributed to product development for all of Razer's hardware.

In November 2017, Razer went public on the Hong Kong Stock Exchange, cementing the company as one of the largest brands in gaming.

Gracy Fernandez: Coming from law, you have a very uncommon background for a tech founder. How did your legal background give you advantages as a founder?

© Ezra Ferraz, Gracy Fernandez 2020
E. Ferraz and G. Fernandez, *Asian Founders at Work*,
https://doi.org/10.1007/978-1-4842-5162-1_19

Min-Liang Tan: It was not so much my legal background, but what my parents taught me—if you do anything, do it to the best of your ability and with maximum attention to detail. I apply this mindset to everything that I do. Being a lawyer reinforced a greater attention to detail and the importance of intellectual property in innovation.

Fernandez: Why did you choose to pivot from the legal profession into becoming a tech founder?

Tan: I have always been passionate about gaming since my student days, and I was aware that there was an unmet demand for high-quality gaming equipment. At that time, no one in the industry saw the need for it. But I believed that gamers were being ignored, and they needed a dedicated gaming mouse.

Ferraz: Can you explain high-speed tracking technology? What were the challenges of integrating this technology into a gaming mouse?

Tan: Before the gaming mouse was invented, mice were all developed with office use in mind. We wanted to change that by developing a mouse with superior technology specifically for gaming, which demanded high precision and accuracy.

Fernandez: What was the most difficult part about building the company around the gaming mouse?

Tan: There were many doubts from others about whether such a product category could take off. Investors saw this as untested waters, and a lot of people laughed at the idea.

Fernandez: Can you take us through the highs and lows of your first year in operation?

Tan: We started Razer on a hunch without proper market reports or studies and faced many challenges. The only thing we knew was that we gamers wanted a gaming mouse for ourselves. But we firmly believed that setbacks and obstacles are what keeps the company going. If we are not facing any challenges, then we are not growing. If you are looking at it from a gaming perspective, whenever you face a tough level and lose, you simply pick yourself up, respawn, and start all over again. Sometimes you read a guide/walkthrough. Other times, you call a friend. But you don't give up.

Fernandez: If speed, accuracy, and precision were the primary goals for a high-end gaming mouse, what was the goal for your first high-end keyboard? What specs were you trying to provide gamers and enthusiasts?

Tan: We launched the Razer Tarantula keyboard back in 2006. It was a natural step forward since our company had become the market leader for gaming mice.

The aim was to ensure that gamers have full control over their movement and speed. So our first step to creating the best gaming keyboard was macro programmability. We created the ten-key, anti-ghosting keyboard to cater to gaming-specific, multi-key input and extensive customization capabilities.

Subsequently, clear actuation, reliability, and durability grew in importance. To tackle that, we launched a mechanical gaming keyboard. The Razer BlackWidow was the first of its kind back in 2010.

Fernandez: Even as Razer grew rapidly as a company, to what extent did you try to remain active as a gamer in order to give first-hand advice on product design?

Tan: I've never stopped gaming. Whether it's a few rounds of PUBG Mobile, or playing Witcher III on a long-haul flight. I think it is important to not just think that you know your audience, but actually be part of the community and embrace yourself in the culture. We have always lived by our motto, "For Gamers. By Gamers." It informs every choice we make.

Fernandez: Do you vet candidates in the hiring process to ensure that they are truly gamers?

Tan: First, we ask if the person about his favorite game. Remember, "For Gamers. By Gamers." At Razer, it is incredibly important that our employees have an appreciation for what gamers really want.

Fernandez: As you built the company, did you feel it was important to maintain a gaming-centric culture, even among your non-product employees?

Tan: Absolutely, I don't think it is possible to identify with your community if you don't know what they want. Whether they are casual or hardcore gamers, it is a mentality that applies to all Razer employees worldwide. Everyone even has their own gaming handle in their email signature and on their business cards. Ever seen a bunch of colleagues playing a round of DOTA 2 during lunch breaks? That's us. Every Razer employee also receives an annual gaming allowance to buy their favorite games.

Fernandez: As your product portfolio becomes increasingly diversified, how do you continue to ensure that they all meet the high standards required by gamers?

Tan: We do all product development in-house and set up rigorous quality-testing processes to ensure that each component used in our products is top of the line. A good example of this is the Razer optical keyboard switch that can last up to 100 million keystrokes.

We also work together with some of the best esports athletes in the world to test product prototypes at all development stages to make sure it meets their demanding standards.

Fernandez: Can you share a story in which you made a product or feature change based on feedback by one of your partner esports athletes?

Tan: To build a mouse for esports athletes, we needed to take their needs into consideration, and that included shape and feel. It needed to be comfortable and functional. With our latest Razer Viper gaming mouse, we provided a prototype to TACO, one of the top players in SK Gaming. He gave us key insights on the balance and ergonomics of the Razer Viper.

With his feedback, as well as other athletes', every design feature and component of the Razer Viper underwent multiple iterations. From the feel and performance of optical switches, texture of the side grips, flexibility of the cable, to even the positioning of the buttons, every aspect of the product was relentlessly revised to perfection.

Fernandez: Can you go into the process of working with esports athletes? How do you identify which esports athletes to sponsor or partner with, and what exactly do these deals typically consist of?

Tan: We select teams and athletes based on their performance and passion, how well they engage with their fans, and the level of collaboration with Razer. This could come as product feedback or joint content creation to elevate esports through our partnership.

Fernandez: Now that Razer is the standard par excellence in the gaming world, what do you have left that you want to accomplish?

Tan: We've just gotten started. With the explosive rise in popularity of esports, the future for Razer is blindingly bright.

Fernandez: What unconventional advice do you have for founders who want to be as iconic and as successful as Razer?

Tan: I believe in drawing experience from everything you do and using it to better yourself in other areas. Never be afraid to learn something new, even though it might not have a direct link to your end goal. Most times, you will realize that you are actually gaining knowledge and experience that will be applicable to get you to where you want to go. Most importantly though, be passionate about what you do. Good results can come from hard work alone, but to be truly great, you need to be passionate and believe in what you are doing. This will allow you to not only keep yourself motivated, but to also motivate others who share the same approach.

Maria Ressa

Co-founder and CEO, Rappler

In 2012, Princeton graduate **Maria Ressa** *co-founded Rappler in the Philippines with Glenda Gloria, Chay Hofileña, and Lilibeth Frondoso. Rappler was a social news network that disrupted traditional media in the Philippines with its emphasis on social media engagement, smartphone-based reporting, and other proprietary digital tools, such as the Mood Meter.*

Ressa was able to disrupt traditional media because she was well familiar with its inner workings. She worked for CNN for 18 years—first as the Manila bureau chief and then as the Jakarta bureau chief. She then went on to manage the newsroom of local media giant ABS-CBN as vice-president of its multi-media operations.

Under her leadership, Rappler become one of the most visited news sites in the Philippines, and has expanded with a media bureau in Jakarta. In 2018, TIME magazine named Maria Ressa Person of the Year, alongside Jamal Khashoggi, Wa Lone, Kyaw Soe Oo, and the Capital Gazette under the thematic banner, "the Guardians."

Of all the top tech founders in the Asia Pacific, Ressa may have the most contentious relationship with the government. She has sparred with the Duterte administration over their war on drugs, and she has been jailed several times. Now represented by a legal team led by Amal Clooney, Ressa is stewarding Rappler into the future as a key change-agent in the battle for truth in an era dominated by fake news.

© Ezra Ferraz, Gracy Fernandez 2020
E. Ferraz and G. Fernandez, *Asian Founders at Work*,
https://doi.org/10.1007/978-1-4842-5162-1_20

Ezra Ferraz: Most people don't think of journalists as founders. What skills did you pick up at ABS-CBN or CNN that would lead toward you being a founder?

Maria Ressa: Learning how to manage an old-world system, which is a large newsgroup of a thousand people at ABS-CBN, meant understanding how to be efficient and how to create efficient workflows. But that also meant legacy systems that don't move well in the real world.

Being a news reporter teaches you to go with the flow. You have to have a deadline. You are filing a story—the latest fact is coming in for your story, or the latest element could come in, right before you go live. And, you've got to take it in, ingest, and then move. Those are the two things.

It is a combination of being in numerous breaking news situations and dangerous breaking news situations, planning your way in and out of war zones, understanding threats that could be a life-or-death situation. At the same time, you have a mission and you are learning how to take your people through that and then managing the situation.

For twenty years, I had a team in Jakarta—first in Manila, then in Jakarta—with four to six people. But then we could expand up to thirty to sixty people, depending on the breaking news situation. So I was used to something like that. ABS-CBN, being the largest news group in the Philippines and being multiplatform, taught me how to deal with a P&L that brought revenues of two billion pesos by the time I left. It made me realize that the real power is in who decides where the money is spent.

Part of the reason we created Rappler is that we wanted to be independent and to be able to experiment. That was really what it was. When we decided to set Rappler up, there were four or five of us above forty, and we recruited the rest. It was extremely humbling to throw away everything you thought you knew. You keep the values and the mission, and then you improvise. When it works, you keep it. When it doesn't, you eject and improvise again. I think what made Rappler work was we had old-style management skills, which is systematizing the information as it comes in so you could create a workflow. But then being able to throw away the workflow, I think that's the challenge because it just moves too fast in this day and age.

Ferraz: Stepping back a little, can you share the story of how you left ABS-CBN and how you founded Rappler?

Ressa: I was with CNN for almost twenty years. During that time period, I lived on adrenalin. I really loved it. It was like the front seat to history, in Southeast Asia and South Asia. Yet I felt like after that long period of time, I was telling everyone else's story but I wasn't building anything.

At a certain point, running after another breaking news story didn't really get me anymore. I needed to build something. What is that? And then that coincided with "Where's my home?" I gave myself until forty to actually decide, "Where am I going to make my home?" And then at that point, ABS-CBN—Gabby Lopez and his family who own it—tried to recruit me several times in the past. And I thought, "I'm young enough to still want to make a difference but old enough to have real-world experience." My ego was out of the way, and I wanted to build something.

The first year was incredible. I wrote a standards and ethics manual, doing training for every single post. One of the first things I did was to have industrial engineering students follow every single major post inside the newsroom so we could see the entire workflow. And then I looked through all of them, and we found efficiencies. After the first few months, I cut twenty percent of the newsroom. And that is huge. We did it in the best way possible. We gave three months for every year that the person had been there. So it was giving them also a nest egg so they could move on, and then allowing me to prune the organization so that we could talk privately about better things.

At that point, we pivoted the reporters to become a one-man band. But it's really hard. The first three years was creation again: understanding the way the organization works, then creating an organization that becomes more efficient but it's still workflow. At that point, I couldn't put my best people on digital, which was where everything was happening. In every major newsgroup around the world in 2007, you'd see that digital had the youngest people or people who weren't quite at the top of their trade at that point in time. I really wanted to play with it, but I couldn't because I had to put my best people in my main revenue earners. After three years in, I was just looking at P&L. By the fourth year, I was starting to get bored because money doesn't get me. [Chuckles] It's not what makes me excited. What made me excited was the technology.

I was reading *The Starfish and the Spider*. Do you know that book? When you cut off the head of a spider, it dies. When you cut off an arm of a starfish, it grows another one. You don't want a spider organization. You want a starfish organization, which leads you to the network effect. At some point in 2010, I felt like I was already done. It kind of was just a P&L job, and there was a change in administration. I thought, "Ah, I really want to write a book." And so I did. *From Bin Laden to Facebook*, the book I wrote from Singapore was really the caldera of the ideas behind Rappler, which are network effects.

It is information cascades. If terrorists can convince the people that they need to kill themselves, why can't we use these networks for good? And again, social networks are your family and friends. Social media are your family and friends on steroids without boundaries of time and space. So I was hoping to find ways—this is before ISIS—that we could use social media as a way to build communities from the bottom up, especially since our institutions are so weak.

This was the idea behind Rappler. Why don't we try? And I said, "Why don't we take a year? Why don't we all take a year? If it doesn't work, we can all go back to whatever we were doing." I didn't realize how well it would work. We all loved it! When you're in your forties or nearing your fifties, you're going to feel like you're the master of the universe, especially if you've been doing the same career. Fifties is about reinvention. "Oh my God! We fell into something!" I felt like this was a way to build something that hadn't existed yet.

We had huge ambitions, because when you have something on the Internet today, it's not local. It's global. The elevator pitch for Rappler was never just about investigative journalism or journalism in general. Journalism is just the food that we feed the communities to inspire action. In a country where institutions are weak, this idea is incredibly empowering for us.

I will never be a politician, but I do believe in nation building. I felt like media, in general, was looking for a raison d'être. We were looking for our mission, and we found it in technology. We raised the money amongst ourselves, and all of us, the founders of Rappler, had at some point been involved in multinationals outside. We came back and we said, "This is going to be it. We're going to take what we've learned and put in." And I thought, "I have a fantastic board. I have great people. The best I could find."

The series A was the first time we looked outside. The round was about getting a global imprimatur and getting strategic help that we couldn't find in the Philippines. In the Philippines, you have to use Philippine depositary receipts. I went after North Base Media who are journalists my age. We were cohorts. We were reporters together in Jakarta. Marcus Brauchli, who founded North Base Media, headed the Wall Street Journal, and then he headed the Washington Post. So, this is the evolution like us, but Western.

And then I went after Omidyar Network because it was both technology and civic engagement. Those are the two things that Rappler had. One of the first things we rolled out was a community of action for disaster resilience. How do we build these volunteers? Because the Philippines gets an average of twelve to twenty typhoons every year. We built a platform that we essentially handed to the government. We created volunteers during every major typhoon. We created a system of hashtags. And if you needed rescuing, all you had to do was tweet #RescuePH and post where you are on the map. Then, someone from the Office of Civil Defense, or Red Cross, or another citizen near you will respond. So that was really the idea at the beginning.

Because really, it's about communities. Without them, we really don't have anything, right? That's something I knew from CNN because I was tired of doing stories and throwing them into a black hole. That's why we love Rappler. Our first few years, we were growing one hundred to three hundred percent year after year in both reach and revenue. We were going around schools and telling people to open their Twitter account, their Facebook accounts, so it's partly our fault. We saw the best of what social media can do with our rally and cry for the social good.

We were able to find that sweet spot, where journalism's function is critical in the evolution of society because it is building institutions bottom up. That is the end goal. And given that our target were really young people—our median age in the Philippines is twenty-three years old, out of a hundred million people, I was hoping that entertainment and sports would somehow act as a sugar, but that your generation, the kids today, would go toward the vegetables. That's actually what's happened, because now, your generation is going to be forced to fight for free speech. Forced to fight for human rights. Forced to fight for a world that they want their children to grow up in. And that's got to be a good thing.

Ferraz: How was choosing your co-founders different from a typical founder who's making a hardware or a software for a social news network like Rappler?

Ressa: I think journalists and reporters make really good startup founders because reporters take bits and pieces, and create their story. And we're forced to do this very quickly. You have to be agile. But the best part about it was the core managers all had come from what we call "startups" today. I came from Probe, which was a startup in 1986. Some of my co-founders had formed Newsbreak. They wanted independence. And then Beth had come from traditional television—eleven years running all of the newscasts on ABS-CBN. So she knew the pulse of the mass base.

I'm really a big corporate person. That's the weird thing. But what made us different was this fusion of agility, a little bit of wisdom and experience, and youthful idealism. We're idealistic enough to think that we can help build institutions from the bottom up, that the mission of journalism is really important. We had put in our ten thousand hours. We're good reporters, and I think I have the best news managers in the Philippines managing Rappler. I don't really do any management. I don't manage the editorial, but I look at the big picture. Where is technology taking us? How do we deal with disinformation because it will create a dystopian future for us if it's not stopped? And this has put us to the forefront of these problems, that every democracy around the world has had to face and we actually have a leg up. Because not only do we have a database that can chart the kind of death by a thousand cuts of democracy in the Philippines, but we also can compare it to other countries around the world and we work directly with the social media tech platforms. So it's an incredible time. It's creative destruction.

I think the other thing that makes a difference for me is total brutal honesty. We are old enough that there are no egos. Number one, we know each other really well because we used to run the largest network. We've done the old style management and are confident enough to try a new style. We've gouged out mid-level managers. There are none here. The top managers also do transcripts.

When I was in ABS-CBN, I had four assistants and an entire management committee that did different things. Here I am, my own assistant. [Laughs] I'm kind of lucky sometimes, but we all share Cecille. She's an administrative assistant because she goes through all of the receipts. She is also a makeup artist. This is Rappler! One of the things I love about it is that in a normal organization, people use their job descriptions to let the ball drop. In Rappler, we all decide this is where we want to go and we leap. When we see something falling, five or six people will come in and save it. That's the thing.

I hate to say, "All for one, one for all." It's not the Three Musketeers. It's a spirit of creativity. I think in a normal organization, once you have a workflow, you look away, and you're not present tense. My gosh, I can say I've never been able to do that with Rappler. And when we do look away, I understand the stagnation that happens.

Innovation is this word that everyone talks about, but it is all about being present tense, looking at the context of the world you live in, the technology that is driving our world today, and being able to pull that together and create magic. That's how we were able to find a sustainable business model—not just deal with the weaponization of social media, the weaponization of the law.

Ferraz: Earlier you mentioned how you try to teach journalists to be a one-man band. Can you talk a bit more about your early journalism, and how you pioneered agile tactics?

Ressa: I saw it when I was still with CNN. Our team in Jakarta was the experiment team. It wasn't a one-man band but a shift away from a large team. In the old days at CNN, we would have a minimum of four people reporting because we would have the reporter, producer, audio, and camera. I've watched that shrink to one.

And then beyond that, the satellite engineer became a "toko." The first time I was there, when the "toko" was brought to Afghanistan. I was coming out of India, and the plane was hijacked from India and went to Afghanistan. And we carried the "toko" in Jakarta—this is like using satellite, but it's not satellite. Then after that, it became DNG. CNN pioneered digital news gathering, which leads first news ISDN lines to be able to broadcast video. We transmit it. Now it's so much easier, with Facebook Live and YouTube.

I knew that that equipment was changing so fast. But look at how fast. When we formed Rappler in 2012, we decided that we were going to use cellphones as the primary camera. But at that point in time, there were no cases for cell phones yet. So we actually had to build metal casing. We built the tripod. We kind of gerrymandered it out of what existed. We built them their own lights, and then added our own mics. This was coupled together.

In addition to that, because we came from television, we even built our own OB van. But it was an IP satellite van, and it really worked! At least this is how it worked for two years. By 2014, you could already transmit with Facebook Live. So everything changes so fast. We still have that satellite IP van, which was instrumental in getting things out of Tacloban during Typhoon Haiyan.

Number one, everyone was a one-man band. Everyone, including the editors. Number two, it would be real time. You wouldn't wait until the end, until your report is ready. You would be sharing, so you're atomizing your story before it becomes a story. Number three, you're opening the kimono to your community. That is how you build community—varying levels of success because it is hard to get rid of old habits.

Television is the most unnatural way of being natural. And even that way of being, it shaped the way I am. I can get rid of it now, but it took me a bit. Otherwise, you talk TV talk. You can see the difference: when somebody who's anchoring on TV versus somebody who's just randomly talking. And the new world is somewhere in between. What is authenticity? Because frankly, that's also for show. So that's not really real because it's very made up. People now live their lives publicly, and we caught that on-stream. Part of what we do is to keep track of the digital equipment that was able to automatically give us the reach of a television network, but since our outlook was always through digital—at a fraction of the cost.

I'll give you an example. I bought cameras for ABS-CBN. Ikegamis are $35,000 each. iPhones, guess how cheap they are? They have the same quality video—depends on your transmission. So we learned a ton.

What about people? I think what made Rappler different is that when I was introducing Macs and cameras, editing their videos, we had seventy-five reporters in the session in ABS-CBN. Forty-something reporters look at it as added work. There is less time to talk to people.

We started Rappler with twelve people. When the Macs came, it was like Christmas Day because everyone was so thrilled to have their Macs. Digital natives are different. And that is the other part. I really realized that digital natives look at the world differently, and we need to have this combination of both. The morale has moved far beyond those early lessons for us. Now we are in a whole other place. But I think this ability to improvise, experiment, measure, and execute those things is important.

Ferraz: Looking more inwardly toward Rappler, when did you start to productize it and have these proprietary features like the Mood Meter? What was the thinking in the evolution of Rappler as a product?

Ressa: I am not so sure I've even gone that far. Although I guess I have because we are now building a new platform. It is the fifth evolution of it. But at the beginning, I was a TV journalist, and in our first year, I treated it like a

TV journalist except the tech was different. I read as much as I could. I was really open to learning. But it took us a while. You were here during part of that.

In the first part, it's hard not to just look up what you write. It's hard for a TV person not to just look at how and what I say and fuse these, and then find a new method. Look at how we're recording this now. So I think it evolved as re-evolved. The funny thing is, at the beginning, I was treating it like I would treat a three-year plan or a five-year plan. At the end of this three-year plan, we would have everything. Then, you realize, holy cow! The tech changes every six months, and we have to keep evolving with it. It never stops. It never ends. It's just a whole different world. I think every year I keep looking for the stability of the old world, and we've never had it—even before President Duterte attacked us.

It's just not that kind of world anymore. I think startup founders know this more than anyone. You want stability, and you look for an exit. I think the difference with a normal startup is that the exit was not as important to me as the journey and the impact. Impact in our world was incredibly important, which is I guess why we're more of a social good company, because that's what journalists protect. We protect the public sphere. I've seen these dynamics play out in our board—the social mission versus the need to have a sustainable business model. How do you give back to your investors? How do you retain control? One of the things that was very clear to me is the economic control had to be with the journalists. And that is embedded in our shareholders' agreement. I think we're the only news group that has that. Not just editorial control but the ability to actually disperse our resources.

Ferraz: I think you mentioned this earlier, but you pitched Rappler differently to investors. What did you pitch as the endgame if it's not an exit? Like a traditional startup?

Ressa: Understand that the difference was that our investors were betting on us. We had dreams of exits, I guess. But I never took the money that seriously because I gave up a lot of money to start Rappler. I was probably one of the most highly paid journalists in the Philippines, but that wasn't what was important to me.

When the government started attacking us, we had to cut the budget. The founders were the first ones to say, "Let's cut." We volunteered twenty percent of our pay. I had a five-year plan. We would break even in five years. By the sixth year, we would have a new platform and we would then evolve more on a global stage. By 2014, in our third year, I had opened a bureau in Jakarta.

For me, it was never about the Philippines. The Philippines was our base. The reason why we set up in the Philippines is not only because were Filipinos, but because this is the petri dish for social media. For three years running now, the people who spend the most time on the internet, even though it is crappy at times, are Filipinos. People who spend the most time on social media, globally, are the Filipinos. I think we were the test case for Cambridge Analytica. The United States is the country that had the most compromised Facebook accounts in the Cambridge Analytica scandal. The Philippines is the second country with the most number of compromised accounts.

In 2016, the dystopian future social media happened. In May, the election of Duterte, a month later, Brexit. By August, after the drug war began, we could see the data. I went to Facebook, and I said, "Guys, this is really alarming!" This is so insidious. They are using hate to pound people into silence. It's not censorship. It is a whole different thing. Free speech is being used to stifle free speech.

Then, I went to Facebook in Singapore, and I said, "You know if you don't do something about this, Trump could win." And we all laughed because in August of 2016, it didn't look like Trump could win. And then when he won in November, they came back and asked me for the data.

I feel like we've had a front seat to the biggest battle of our generation. Let me rephrase. There are two battles of our generation. Climate is the first one, because if we can't breathe, we can't live. Truth is the second one. Rappler is at the forefront of the battle for the truth. We have data on how the democracy transforms because of information operations linked to geopolitical power. The link to the IRA [Internet Research Agency] and Russian disinformation. It's here. I just came from London, The Global Media Freedom Conference, where we saw pro-Assad, pro-Assange, alt-right from Canada, alt-right United States, Brexiteers, along with the Duterte groups. And they each have different links back to this geopolitical power play.

The biggest battle that journalists would fight is the battle for truth. And this we stumbled into because we were doing investigative reporting and data analytics. So we saw that the way democracies are crumbling is by attacking and by making a lie a fact. You do that by pounding it. You say it a million times, and then it becomes a fact because no one has had a chance to actually dispute it. The old world is dead. So if a lie spreads faster than the fact, democracies are weaker. If you don't have facts and if you don't have truth, you can't have trust. If you can't have trust, you can't have democracy.

The research reports started coming out as early as November 2017. We saw it in August 2016. We came out with our first reports by the end of September 2016. We were among the first to do this globally. You are seeing it globally. Authoritarian populous leaders are rising through elections, and they are enabled by technology. The accelerant is technology.

Social media needs to step up. They took over the distribution of news globally but they left behind the gatekeeping power that goes hand in hand with the distribution of news. Lies cannot spread faster than facts. That's the basic problem. You tech people have to fix it!

Ferraz: Certainly, most founders don't experience the level of strife with government that you have, but a lot of startups do deal with regulatory issues. What advice would you have for founders about conducting government relations?

Ressa: You can see Facebook, right? The startup that it is. Google, YouTube, Twitter—they are all grappling with the same things because they didn't grapple with it earlier. Facebook, who has a move-fast-and-break-things mentality, broke democracy. And now it has to deal with that stuff.

So let's start from smaller versions. We were all so enamored with the empowering ways that social media could deal with it. But news people could see the dangers of personalization. If we each have our own different versions of reality, where is the public sphere? We need to have a public sphere to be able to have discussions that impact governments.

Anyway, so let me get off the journalism thing. I think first, it is truly a brave new world, and it is being changed by everything. I think the biggest problem is that many of the people who are conversant in the language of the new world, which is technology, have no links to reality or governance. This new power has no idea of how old power had created this order in the world so that we could prevent the excesses of humanity, the evils of humanity. And old power didn't understand new power enough. And the world has turned upside-down because of that.

And I really saw this because I spent the weekend in Berlin with Madeleine Albright, with former government officials, with Facebook, with Microsoft. There were two journalists in this. There were less than fifteen of us around the table. I think you need to look at the world today. You need to look at the past. Tech people have to have some sense of history. Everything you build has an impact on the society you live in. Dealing with government is a conflict of interest. Dealing with government is for your own business.

But there was little care on the tech part, and Silicon Valley was this. They thought the decisions they made were very liberal that infused the algorithms that now run our lives. Yet the countries that are most violently affected are in the global south. We didn't have a seat at the table. Now, the world is realizing that every day that Facebook didn't change means someone dies in the global south. That finally came together 2018 when Mark Zuckerberg was testifying in congress, when Mark and I finally came up as an issue, and Sri Lanka had to shut down. When Indonesia, India, Pakistan, and the Philippines were talking about a drug war that the United Nations claimed killed at least 27,000 people from July 2016 to today. So, that's a lot to say for advice.

I guess the first thing is, when you're creating something, most startup founders will think about what they want, what they can do, and the money they're going to make. There are a lot more now who are aware of social impact because the technology has the ability to do that. And I think even Silicon Valley is starting to pivot slightly to this because they've really unleashed a dystopian reality right now. So, I'm still not going to your advice. Move beyond making money. You need to do that because ninety percent of startups fail. Sure, you need to do that but, I'm sorry I can't get beyond being a journalist. While I think the public sphere is really what we're after. That is really important to me.

So, let me think as a startup founder. Ah! Here is my advice. Know who you are. Know your values, because those values will really be tested. Sit those values first before you begin to think about them. If you decide you're all about money, then okay fine, go make money. But what's changing now is that social impact becomes more important because we now have to save our democracies. Look at Uber. Look at Airbnb. These are all transformative. Yet in the end, if you don't solve those two biggest problems that I've outlined— climate and truth, our societies will suffer. You can't have any of the businesses. My lenses are so colored by the battles we're fighting.

Ferraz: What is your day-to-day like? How much time do you divide between Maria Ressa, the journalist versus Maria Ressa, the founder?

Ressa: I just don't sleep that much. [Laughs] Like the last two nights, I had three hours of sleep each. I travel a lot because the only defense that we have against the weaponization of the law is to shine the light. That takes up as much time. I don't think you can separate it. You live. You breathe. You do a startup. And you have a mission. Be prepared to throw 150 percent of yourself in. I think I'm very lucky because I'm not alone. Our founders work doubly hard. When you're looking at Rappler, these are four women who work insane hours.

After the government attacked us, one of our young journalists said, "Now I know what it feels like to be a real journalist." Because sometimes when you're fooling around with your tripod or lights, it feels like it's muscle memory, but you don't realize the mission is there. Rappler journalists know how important that is now.

Ferraz: So many people, I'm sure want a sliver of your time, how do you, as a founder, prioritize what will benefit, have an actual impact from your organization?

Ressa: You spend ninety percent of your time with your most important managers. And then you make sure they're aligned with the strategic vision that you have. And then they will be the ones to grow the organization. That hasn't changed for me. That's been the way I managed CNN, ABS, and now, Rappler. And they're right here, right next to me.

I think that beyond that, it's how to prioritize tech. It's critical. I look at that all the time. I look at how the algorithms are changing. Obviously, Facebook is a critical part of that. The news is to going to need to look for new ways of distribution.

Ferraz: What composes the other ten percent?

Ressa: Maybe sleep. I travel a lot but I'm also online all the time, this is the nice part. And the stuff when I'm traveling, I am also making sure that, I rarely now look at the content as our team does that themselves. They're really much more up to. But I look at how we connect to the global landscape. And that's how we found Russian disinformation in the Philippines because our team found it looking bottom up. They were looking at experts and quotes. These new experts that came in, and then when they surface the name that I knew from Russian disinformation, I thought, "Holy cow! Let's look at this data that was just released by the United States." So it's that. I don't know why I've always done news. The adrenaline is incredible. Because you know, it's real, it drives you. But what's more interesting and fun about Rappler is it's not just about the adrenaline of news. It's the adrenaline of building something. It's a team that is tested, that knows we need to have a great idea today, execute it, and have a great idea again a month from now. The lifespan is radical. You need a great team.

Ferraz: You mentioned that your growth at Rappler was so incredible at the beginning. What has been the biggest impediment toward scaling a social news network like Rappler versus the experiences of other tech founders?

Ressa: We care about journalism.

Ferraz: So you've had to sacrifice growth to stay true to your values at some times. Can you share an example?

Ressa: There are so many big ones, but I think tech in general has pushed for atomization of content and atomization of meaning. We care about good journalism, which means I'm not going to do a factory line. That is the way a lot of different groups have spurred growth at the beginning. They just factory lined it. I don't want to be a BuzzFeed. I'm sorry, Jon Steinberg. He is a Princetonian. But BuzzFeed tried to figure out how to make something go viral. They started with cats, and slowly they moved toward journalism. But journalism was never their reason for that. The mission was always a driver for us. We would try cats, but we would never do that forever because it would bore me, and it wouldn't fulfill the social mission of journalism. So that's the first impediment.

We said no to a lot of things. We said no to corruption. And then the third thing is, when the government is killing people, when we fought impunity on two fronts. And I knew that that would have a business impact. And I brought that to the board when we did our first propaganda series. Before we released it, I brought it to the board because I knew we would become a target. And our board said, yes go ahead. I don't think anyone knew how badly it would go.

We've been doing an impunity series from the beginning of the drug war. The last one is a seven-part series. No other newsgroup in the Philippines would touch it. Vigilantes who were given a list by the police and paid by the police to kill. That won an award in May, but no one else touched it. Why? This is what we're living for. That's not good business.

President Duterte singled out Rappler. We were not the first. We were the third. But we were the only one to act and we fight back. Would a businessman, a CEO and president, would they have done that? Most likely not. But I had enough confidence in my team. I knew that we had to be true to who we are, so that's the other part. Who are you? What are your values? If you know who you are, then your product—whatever it is that you were creating for the world—will have the integrity of who you are.

In the end, I think we're driven by values, and I'm going to bring you to where I think the solution is. How do we fix this kind of dystopian, dystopic universe that we're living in right now? Where democracy is really under siege or broken. I think after the Holocaust in World War II, the world realized that we need to put in place to prevent the worst of humanity from killing people. The kind of killing that happened during the Holocaust. And so what happened, we had Bretton Woods, we had the universal declaration of human rights.

We don't have an equivalent of any of these agreements for the Internet, and there's been impunity on the Internet. And these Jewish political power players have been taking advantage of it. That has to stop. So who will do that? I just really hope that in the short term, it's only the social media technology platforms. Are they going to wait for laws? For legislation to do that for them? I hope not.

We're at the dawning of the new age, and technology did it. But the people who were at the forefront kind of broke it. They were irresponsible. So that's what we're pushing for. My ambition is not to be a unicorn. My ambition is to have real change, to have impact in our world. And I would sacrifice revenues to have that impact.

Ferraz: You've touched upon your battle with the current administration. You've been arrested a few times now?

Ressa: Twice in five weeks. Detained once.

Ferraz: How do you stay sane during this? This is like the most extreme example of what can happen to a founder.

Ressa: I had to post bail eight times in three months. And eleven cases in fourteen months. It's like being in a war zone. Keep your presence of mind. Have clarity of thought. Know your mission.

I know what's right. I know my values. And I said this before the government really filed the cases. The standards & ethics—we wrote it for ABS-CBN. We wrote the standards of ethics, man.

So, this is not something that is like a layer on top of who I am. It's part of my identity. And so in a way, this is what Rappler is. This is why I'm not alone. It's incredible. That's why I'm really thankful. I just want a little more sleep—that's the only thing.

Advice to founders of how you can deal with it—a good team, clarity of thought, and a vision for what you want for your company. For us, it really is impact that's more important than anything.

Ferraz: On a very serious note, do you fear for your safety, for your life?

Ressa: That's always been part of being the kind of journalists we are. I'm not the only one who's gotten death threats before Rappler even happened. I had to have guards. We'd have terrorists come after me. Glenda had to deal with funeral wreaths being sent to her. I mean, this is part of who we are. I wish the government did a little bit more research. We don't intimidate easily. And if anything, when somebody runs after you the way they have, it shows me they're afraid of something, or they're hiding something. And now they've given me firsthand experience of the kind of abuse of power that goes on. We will shine the light on that. In a strange way, by arresting me, they unshackled me, because I'm no longer just a journalist. Now I am a Filipino citizen whose rights have been violated. Makes it very easy for me, so thank you.

Ferraz: Another recent milestone, of course, is TIME's Person of the Year. Where were you when you heard the news, and what does it mean for Rappler as an organization?

Ressa: You know what? TIME didn't tell me. I found out when the tweet came out. And it wasn't even TIME that tweeted it. So there was a tweet, "TIME Person of the Year." I thought it wasn't real, so I sent it to social media to fact check that CNN called. And that's when I thought, "Oh my God. It's real." It was 6:30 where we were. A few of us were having dinner, and when CNN called, my stomach sank, because that meant all of a sudden, I'm more of a target.

In the beginning, you try to negotiate. That particular day, I had posted bail four times in the morning. And then that afternoon, I was thinking through if I needed security. You have to have clarity of thought about these things. And then, in the evening, I was TIME's Person of the Year. So, I wish they had told me so. CNN put me on the air almost immediately, and I kinda stumbled because I wasn't sure if it was good or bad. You know, it could make me more of a target.

And then I realized, it was good, because the only weapon you have as a journalist is to shine the light. And this was the biggest shield that I could find. The biggest light. Oh well, now I'm with Amal Clooney. I have a little flashlight. She's got a lighthouse. So it's been good, and I think that we'll continue fighting our cases in court. We'll continue doing our jobs. Our business is moving, and we've hit positive net income. So, what doesn't kill you will make you stronger. It works.

Ferraz: What's next for Rappler? What is your vision at this point in 2019, and the next five to ten years?

Ressa: Our sustainable new business model actually leverages off of the investigative reporting—the digital forensics that we did to find how this information works. We were able to find a model. Obviously, advertisers were scared the minute we were attacked by the government. And we found something that stems out of our journalism. And so, this is something that we'll continue exploring.

On the bigger global stage, I sit on the Information and Democracy Commission. It is something that was put together largely in France by Nobel peace laureate Shirin Ebadi and RSF—Reporters Sans Frontieres—secretary-general Christophe Deloire. It includes twenty-five people from eighteen different countries. And that's tech and academics. Really smart people trying to figure out how to pivot the world. How do we pivot information? Information is power.

I think the future of the information ecosystem is all intertwined. And that's really exciting. In London last week, at the Global Conference for Media Freedom, Britain and Canada stood up to say they're going to defend media freedom. They were going to call out these acts of against human rights. That's huge. Because silence is complicity, and so far, the world has been so stunned by what tech has unleashed that it's been silent. This is the first time governments are actually coming together to say they're no longer going to be silent. The next step is how tech is going to be involved in this. Anyway, other groups did that, and they've come up with a fund to help support independent media.

So when you ask me what's the future going to look like, when I see Rappler, I can see a future. It is connected to technology. It is connected to finding and stopping the lies. We need to restore facts. We need to restore the credibility of the institutions. That won't happen if you don't have facts.

Ferraz: You have such a unique perspective compared to the other founders of more traditional tech companies. What unconventional advice do you have for people who want to build tech-enabled, socially-oriented businesses in Asia? Perhaps like Rappler.

Ressa: The technology manipulates people. It is the new spy network. It is Shoshana Zuboff's surveillance capitalism. The tech can know us better than we know ourselves when it moves into artificial intelligence, right? This is very transformative, and we need to really think ethically. We need to think about the unintended consequences. Facebook always talks about unintended consequences. It doesn't matter if it was unintended if it destroys the world today. It is a powerful tool that could transform us for the better but that could also throw us back to the dark ages. This is an existential moment, and it's not just for journalism. It's an existential moment for democracy. And tech is the first actor that can fix it. If it takes much longer, it's going to transform our world. It would be irreversible. Even in the Western nations where institutions are stronger. They need to jump start it. Or democracy as we know it is dead.

Mark Sears

CEO and Founder, CloudFactory

Founded by **Mark Sears** *in 2008, CloudFactory addresses two problems at once. First, the shortage of jobs in emerging markets like Nepal, and second, the structural gaps in traditional outsourcing models. Inspired by Henry Ford's assembly line framework, the platform splits up work into smaller tasks and delegates these simpler, more manageable workloads to the CloudWorkers on CloudFactory. This streamlines how individuals accomplish whatever has been outsourced to them, allowing them to do more, and hence, earn more without sacrificing quality. Client businesses are then able to focus their efforts on higher-value work.*

CloudFactory is Nepal's flagship tech company and has more than 100 clients, spanning from big enterprises like Microsoft to companies like Expensify and Ibotta, which are scaling fast, to early-stage startups like Drive.ai, Ripjar, and Zola, which are disrupting industries across the spectrum.

Ezra Ferraz: What experience motivated you to create CloudFactory?

Mark Sears: In 2008, I traveled with my wife, Laurel, to Kathmandu. During our visit, we met young Nepali people with remarkable tech-savvy and digital expertise. They told us stories about how many people struggled because work was scarce in Nepal. We saw that talent is equally distributed but opportunity is not. That fundamental truth inspired us to create meaningful work for people, and the CloudFactory journey began.

© Ezra Ferraz, Gracy Fernandez 2020
E. Ferraz and G. Fernandez, *Asian Founders at Work*,
https://doi.org/10.1007/978-1-4842-5162-1_21

Nepal is a striking example of the lack of opportunity that exists in many areas in the developing world. Tribhuvan University in Kathmandu is among the largest universities in the world, with a half-million students in Kathmandu and across the country. Yet one in four Nepali households have someone working abroad, due to lack of work.

It's important to find ways to connect these skilled people to meaningful work that allows them to stay in Nepal with their families, grow as contributors to the global economy, and become leaders who can help raise their own communities out of poverty.

Ferraz: Nepal is neither a hotbed for BPOs [Business Process Outsourcing] like India or the Philippines, nor a hub for tech entrepreneurship, like Silicon Valley or Israel. Can you give us an overview of what the BPO and the tech ecosystem was like when you began CloudFactory and how that landscape shaped the way you built the company?

Sears: We identify places rich with talent but lacking in infrastructure and work opportunities. This is where our innovative workforce model and technology approach really thrive. What we found in Nepal was a very tech-savvy population with limited opportunity to tap into the global economy. With our model, we gain access to untapped talent pools and get to make a meaningful impact in emerging locations where it's needed most.

The lack of infrastructure years ago when we started in Nepal greatly shaped our model by pushing things to be more distributed. Instead of one point of failure—one massive delivery center with one electricity and Internet supply, we got a lot of redundancy by having things more distributed. As the infrastructure has improved, it's allowed us to bring most of our workers in-house, which brings our teams closer and allows us to provide a more agile solution for our customers who are scaling vital data processes.

Ferraz: All of these ideas finally became something tangible in 2010, when you founded the company, but it wasn't until 2011 that you launched its beta at TechCrunch Disrupt in San Francisco. What were the challenges of preparing for your launch?

Sears: Version 1.0 of the CloudFactory platform took time to develop, along with managing the proverbial "chicken and egg" challenge of every two-sided marketplace. We were able to get enough capacity and clients to get things off the ground and launch at TC Disrupt near the end of 2011. The original CloudFactory platform was generally viewed as a big value add, but we had a lot of work to do to educate the market on the potential of its many different applications. It was a perfect solution for businesses that needed to scale massive data workflows. What we found over time is that our customers needed a more agile approach that enabled them to iterate on processes before achieving massive scale. That need is what our current WorkStreams offering is built to address.

Ferraz: While there are many companies that try to tackle this problem, CloudFactory is unique in its application of technology and the use of WorkStreams to divide large goals into small tasks. How did you come up with this approach?

Sears: We have always believed that technology and innovation are key to creating meaningful work at scale. At our core, we are techies who love people. Good intentions and hard work are not enough to create the scale of impact we are aiming for at CloudFactory. We continue to iterate on our workforce model, technology platform, and how we price and package cloud labor to the world. WorkStreams enabled us to provide our customers access to cloud labor in an hourly model, while at the same time, provided our workers more predictable and reliable work schedules.

Ferraz: Even with the novel approach of WorkStreams, many companies may have been reluctant to outsource. Offshoring has always been met with some level of aversion, especially for key business functions. What do you think are the reasons for this?

Sears: Unfortunately, many BPOs lack innovation in work delivery, which has resulted in persistent customer experience problems for BPOs over the years—high costs, lack of process control, poor communication, and problems with quality. We're changing that by leveraging technology to scale our delivery model while investing a lot of resources into communications, analytics, and incorporating AI.

Knowing about these problems inspired us to use technology to speed change and lower costs, which gives our workforce the agility to act quickly on changes and share best practices with one another. For the client, this gives our workforce the same feel as an in-house team.

Ferraz: CloudFactory raised $700,000 in its seed funding round in 2012. How were you running CloudFactory prior to your fundraise?

Sears: We bootstrapped CloudFactory in 2010 to 2012 through software consulting income from a previous business. Like many companies transitioning from a services company to a product company, it was a challenge, but it allowed us to get things to a place where we could attract international investment. We had a lot of talented people eager to get to work, but we needed to attract the right clients to make it all work and start making an impact in Nepal.

Ferraz: To ensure this product and technology excellence, CloudFactory has a screening process for people who want to become CloudWorkers. What is it that you look for in applicants?

Sears: As part of our focus on our people, we screen workers for character, skill, tech-savviness, and cultural awareness. We train them on quality work, tasks, and business rules, and place them in small teams where their skills and strengths are known and valued by their team managers.

We train workers on our core CloudFactory principles and what we call the "five Cs"—composition, character, competence, community, and calling. The combination of our small-team approach, training, and infusion of our principles results in workers having greater passion for and engagement in their work. All of these things contribute to quality work for our clients.

Ferraz: CloudFactory also promises to extensively train CloudWorkers to expand their skill sets. Can you share more about process?

Sears: CloudFactory invests heavily in creating a unique work culture to support and nurture our teams. Our goal is to empower our team members as leaders in their families and communities while we connect them to the global digital economy.

We provide regular opportunities for professional training, personal enrichment, and participation in community service projects. These experiences grow each worker's confidence, work ethic, knowledge, and upward mobility. Everyone celebrates with workers as they move up within CloudFactory, or move on to other companies for new opportunities.

Ferraz: You're in Kenya, which is dubbed to be Africa's own "Silicon Valley." What made you decide to scale there, and how different is the context there as compared to in Nepal? What were the country-specific difficulties that you ran into as you expanded into Kenya?

Sears: Indeed, Nairobi is one of the most important tech hubs in Africa, with nearly universal mobile access and ever-expanding Internet access. We chose Kenya to expand our services across multiple time zones for the convenience of our clients.

We also chose Kenya for its highly skilled workforce with strong English skills, its growing youthful population, and the nation's commitment to developing its information communications technology [ICT] infrastructure.

Our work in Nairobi aims to address poverty, inequality, and the skills gap that exists between market requirements and Kenya's educational system. Kenya's recent improvements in the country's infrastructure, its growing and dynamic private sector, and the new constitution bode well.

Ferraz: As CloudFactory has grown, how have you changed your product to suit your clients?

Sears: One significant change was the ability to offer cloud labor to work on any tool or platform, not just CloudFactory's platform. We work in our customer's platforms and have developed expertise across a variety of tools. The flexibility of being platform and tool agnostic has been really helpful for clients who already have tools but are looking to scale up their data work.

Ferraz: As CloudFactory is both a tech company and a socially-oriented organization, what metrics do you use to measure success? How have you done so far according to these metrics?

Sears: As an impact sourcing service provider [ISSP], CloudFactory creates economic and leadership opportunities for talented people in developing nations. We connect people to meaningful work to help raise them out of poverty and give them the skills to be leaders in their own communities. Workers get ongoing training opportunities to grow in their professional and personal lives. All of this is a virtuous cycle that grows our business.

Internally, we measure both the quantity and quality of work through different metrics. Some of those important metrics for success are based on our annual worker survey. Here are the highlights from our latest social impact report. One, a six hundred percent average increase in wages for workers who join CloudFactory. Two, ninety-three percent improved their English and computer skills. And three, ninety-one percent say they are happier since working at CloudFactory.

In February 2015, The Rockefeller Foundation awarded CloudFactory a $2 million program–related investment under its Digital Jobs Africa initiative. We have invested those funds into expanding our workforce in Nairobi, providing more opportunity to talented people in Kenya.

Ferraz: Outside of your social impact metrics, when did you really begin to feel that you were making a difference?

Sears: Just a few weeks in with our first twenty-five CloudWorkers, we knew we were on to something. Those first five teams of five CloudWorkers were meeting weekly and going through leadership and character lessons, where they set goals and held each other accountable. The stories from workers, and even their families, about small but tangible positive change alongside of them earning and learning, really signaled that we were heading in a great direction for engaging and investing into the next generation of leaders in Nepal.

Ferraz: Can you also share how these CloudWorkers have helped one of your clients succeed?

Sears: Our latest client success story is Ibotta, a cash-back rewards app. Its operations team partnered with CloudFactory to improve accuracy and processing time on important data-verification work. Retail consumers use Ibotta to submit photos of receipts for cash-back rewards from brands. With nearly twenty-two million downloads, it is one of the most frequently used shopping apps in the United States.

We combined CloudFactory's technology and people with Ibotta's tools to achieve fifteen percent higher accuracy and a fifty percent decrease in processing time. We also established elasticity in the process, making it possible for Ibotta to manage seasonal volume spikes, including the winter holiday season, its busiest season of the year. While we cannot share any new client success stories, we can say CloudFactory is trusted by more than one hundred companies to process millions of tasks a day for companies, including Microsoft, Drive.ai, Expensify, Ibotta, and GM Cruise Automation.

Ferraz: CloudFactory helps companies scale and become more efficient by outsourcing simple tasks that others can do for them, which allows them to focus their efforts on higher-level and more technical work. What advice would you give to founders so that they can decide on which functions they should do on their own versus delegate or outsource?

Sears: Start by asking, "What is one thing we do better than anyone else in the world?". Figure out what your core business and core capabilities are. Once there is clarity in these areas, you can begin to look at everything else as potential places to delegate or outsource.

Ferraz: How do you see CloudFactory growing from here?

Sears: We see it growing a lot and quickly! We plan to expand our investments in workers and double down on Nepal and Kenya to become the best gig in town for smart, talented youth.

Ferraz: What can you tell hopeful entrepreneurs in Asia who want to start businesses as inspiring and successful as CloudFactory?

Sears: Focus on discovering and cultivating a deep purpose and mission. Figure out the why before the what. There are so many challenges, twists, and turns in a startup. You want to make sure there is a strong foundation and guiding north star beyond just an MVP product.

Teresa Condicion

Chief of Data and Operation, Co-founder, Snapcart

Teresa Condicion *co-founded Snapcart in 2015. Unlike other startups, Snapcart had a regional presence and focus from the beginning because its co-founders hailed from different markets in Southeast Asia. Laith Abu Rakty, Reynazran Royono, and Araya Hutasuwan are from Indonesia, and Condicion is from the Philippines.*

The retail veterans had found a way to upend market intelligence in their space. Most fast-moving consumer goods companies relied on data from providers that was sometimes months out of date and often inaccurate. Condicion allowed them to get data on their stock-keeping units exponentially faster by giving consumers the ability to take photos of their receipts in exchange for a small reward, like a cash rebate or a cell phone load.

The development of this proprietary computer vision technology was led by Condicion, who started as Snapcart's chief of operations and data science. Operating in Philippines and Indonesia, Snapcart counts over 10,000 retail chains in their network and has processed 5 million receipts.

© Ezra Ferraz, Gracy Fernandez 2020
E. Ferraz and G. Fernandez, *Asian Founders at Work*,
https://doi.org/10.1007/978-1-4842-5162-1_22

Ezra Ferraz: Prior to co-founding Snapcart, you were working at Procter & Gamble as a Consumer Insight Associate Director for seventeen years. What specific experiences did you have in the industry that inspired you to start your own company, and how did you get the idea for such a unique product like Snapcart?

Teresa Condicion: Being a consumer of this product myself, I was one of the most frustrated people receiving the data for offline sales and tracking from traditional providers like Nielsen and Kantar. They were three months late, by which time it was really difficult to action. Knowing that you were losing share for the last three months—it's too late to act. Often, the data was not very accurate, so I would spend half of my time just trying to reconcile the information with whatever internal information was available, like shipments, etc. This was very frustrating.

At that time, you saw Google, Facebook, Netflix, and Amazon getting real-time information and making real-time decisions based on it, and being able to market to their users immediately. It was such a massive divide in terms of information availability.

If you really think about it, over ninety percent of sales still happen offline. E-commerce is simply still one percent in the Philippines. Even in the biggest e-commerce markets like China, it's still only twenty-five percent. In the United States and the United Kingdom, it's fifteen percent—even after so many years of Internet development. Why? Because there will always be a part of us that will want to buy across the store. They will never really want to buy everything offline. That means that there's so much opportunity to digitize this information and make it available for us to make decisions in the same way that Google and Facebook are doing essentially.

Ferraz: How did you make the leap from recognizing that problem and realizing that you could take photos of receipts, and build a solution around that?

Condicion: My last project in P&G was about a world without surveys, essentially. All of this information is currently being done through surveys. With the advent of big data, there was so much inspiration that came from how other companies are digitalizing everything, and crowdsourcing was becoming a very big thing. We take a picture of everything—our food, selfies. That's how Google has built a lot of their products—through a lot of the pictures that are uploaded on social media. So, we said, "Why not do this for receipts?"

At the same time, there were so many loyalty programs happening. You could get cashback. It was a good time to launch something like that because people were open to submitting a picture of everything. There was the massive growth and penetration of mobile phones. Just two years before we launched, it was about twenty to thirty percent in Southeast Asia. Now, we're getting closer to seventy to eighty percent. That's been the projection. That's been the projectile growth. Mobile phones have really made it a great time for us to launch this kind of product. So, the timing was right, the consumers were ready for this type of product, and the need was at its largest.

Ferraz: Why did you choose to ask the consumers to take photos rather than try to partner with, for example, the chains?

Condicion: That's a great question. We asked the same thing. We realized it will be much more complex to partner with retailers given the immense fragmentation in the market. It's still a very viable option, but going to the customers straight for receipts is a much easier path for us. A lot of retailers also don't feel the need to share their data.

Ferraz: What were the technical challenges in having customers take photos of their receipts?

Condicion: Absolutely. We spent about a year trying to crack the OCR problem because the phone in Southeast Asia has very low picture quality, and some are as low as 0.2 megapixels. On top of that, the receipts are really very basic or really blurry. We tried off the shelf OCR but it didn't work well for our purpose.

The next challenge we had was even when we could read the receipts, we couldn't find the items written on it, there were thousands of retailers per country, and each of them would have a specific code for a specific SKU. And since they had a hundred thousand SKUs per market, it was almost impossible to identify the products manually.

So we had to build our own receipt processing platform, and we built over 400 machine learning models to specifically tackle all these issues.

This is a competitive advantage for us, and even during our Google Accelerator days, they said our tech was just a year ahead of some of their Google projects.

Ferraz: You said off the shelf solutions offered ten percent accuracy. What were you able to reach early on?

Condicion: We achieved over ninety percent accuracy, which is much higher than what you can find elsewhere and which met the exacting standards of our clients who needed to have a very high accuracy level.

The human accuracy is around eighty percent at best, so the machines were much accurate than humans. But that's because there are simply some patterns that we can't figure out ourselves but the machines can—such as having the same letters in typical types of categories. Being able to do that, the machines are so much better than what we can do.

Ferraz: It would be like differentiating between a P and a Q if it's blurry, or something like that?

Condicion: Yes, but also identifying which letters are typically part of, say, a shampoo product. So, the machine can figure that out that, typically, a shampoo would have S and H. That's very simple, but then it gets more and more complex as you get into other categories, like fresh foods, or soft drinks and beverages. There are so many types of beverages. Being able to differentiate between an iced tea versus a soft drink—the machine can do it so much better, which is quite cool, really. It's one of the fun things that I do at work.

Ferraz: This is probably different from what traditional retailers were used to. Can you share your experiences with convincing your first clients to come onboard with you?

Condicion: There were a lot of questions upfront. Market research is very standardized. We have a lot of standards for everything. We have to do sampling in this way and that way, so there were a lot of questions like, "Is your panel representative?" Does it really represent the Filipinos or the country that you're trying to report about? Are you getting younger or older people? Are they giving you receipts that are actually not theirs? Is there a lot of fraud, and therefore, can I really trust your data?" There were a lot of questions on the veracity of the data. And so because of these problems, we started building things.

I needed to be able to identify anomalies in the purchases of our users. So, for example, if we find that the typical purchase behavior of a shopper—maybe x number of receipts per month or anything that is outside that or an outlier, we start flagging and looking into that. We've found users who would snap three receipts in succession within thirty minutes, and the receipts had slightly different names but the same cashier name. Then, we realized it was the cashier who was snapping it. We started understanding all of these things, and built our product stronger in the process. So, it was hard to sell at first because of these questions, but because we developed all of these solutions, we were able to convince our first clients.

What a market researcher needs or what a consumer insight professional would need—that was something that I understood because I was one of them, so I knew that they would be looking for something that will represent the country. I knew that they'd be looking for the veracity of the data. Is it true? I knew that they would be looking for insights coming from the data and so, the best way to convince them is to show them. So, we showed them.

We said, "We'll give you a trial for the data." Then, we gave it to a few, very big clients. They said, "Okay, fine. We're willing to try it." And they're some of those really more innovative companies and when they got the data, they came back and said, "It's actually matching with the retail data that we are getting, which are actual data from the POS machines, like the specific retailers." They loved it. It was the first time that they saw anything that was matching as close as that. In the end, what convinced them was the fact that we delivered something that was really consistent with what they wanted to get.

Ferraz: In terms of data veracity, you mentioned that they were concerned about someone just uploading a bunch of receipts. What is the difference between me collecting everyone's receipts and everyone individually submitting it? Why would it be problematic if I do collect receipts and try to turn it into some sort of small, side hustle?

Condicion: Technically, for some, there will be some problems in terms of being able to represent or read the market more appropriately, and therefore, develop marketing plans.

Ferraz: So the receipts are matched to the user's profile?

Condicion: Yes. For example, a particular brand would want to target heavy users, or would want to identify their target audience. You see a lot of behaviors that are actually not consistent with what's happening in reality. It then becomes very difficult to make marketing plans based on this data, so the data needs to represent the actual purchase behaviors of users in order for it to be useful.

Ferraz: When you convinced these early brands to sign up with you, did they share what kind of actionable business steps they were able to take from your data? I imagine that's a big selling point.

Condicion: I think the very first benefit for many of them is just the availability of this data. We were meeting very basic needs. In the Philippines, some of the biggest chains don't share information. It's just being able to understand how their brands are performing for the first time. Pharmaceutical brands, for example, had never read their shares in the past and were surprised. A company thought they were a massive market leader. They realized, actually, that there are hundreds of other brands taking up half of the share of their market. So, that's the first type of learning. But then, it becomes more advanced.

For example, we are able to share with them some information about how effective an advertisement is a few weeks after they launched it by partnering with publishers, matching it with users IDs. We are able to see if those people who saw the advertisement eventually bought the product, or if they did not buy it. Therefore, we are able to see if it really caused an impact, or give you a lift in terms of purchase, which is a massive need in the industry. There's no way to do it unless you do some market mix modeling, which takes three years to do and by which time it is irrelevant information. So, being able to share that allowed them to pull out advertising that was not really impactful and to push spending on advertising that is impacting the performance of their brand.

We do the same thing with promotions. You're able to understand if when you're doing a promotion, you're getting a lift in terms of sales for your brand in the store, or if it's really forward-buying. Meaning, I get immediate lift, but then after three weeks, customers stop buying. It doesn't give me any return on investment, and that's not good for profitability. So, what we've been able to provide are means for companies to have basic tracking of how their brands are performing, but more importantly, really optimize a lot of their spending, which for many of our clients, are billions and billions of dollars globally.

Ferraz: Jumping to the consumer side, I'm sure there was a lot of experimentation in trying to figure out the proper incentive scheme to get people to make this a regular habit. Can you share how you discovered how to properly incentivize this behavior?

Condicion: As with everything we've learned, we test quick, we learn fast. We always experiment. In fact, right now, we're trying to experiment on different types of rewards, like non-monetary rewards or vouchers, for example. Or our expense tracking, which proved to be very popular. We tried varying levels of rewards, one percent, half a percent, up to a point system. The idea is we really need to balance user engagement with cost for it to be a sustainable business. We need to have this optimized. We experimented with phone credits because, again, a lot of people in the Philippines or Indonesia don't have access to banks. So it would be limiting if we kept it to banking.

We are trying different levels of reward. Should we be putting it at one percent, two percent, half a percent? We want them to be engaged. The way we do it is we push it in our app, see how they respond, test it again with a smaller group, see how they respond, and see which one is better. Then, we scale up based on the responses of those tests. We test everything within our app, basically.

Ferraz: So, there's not really a silver bullet. It's really a combination of incentives. Is that right?

Condicion: It's a combination of incentives. We're even experimenting on non-monetary incentives. For example, expense reports. Maybe some people don't really care about cash. Maybe I just want to be able to snap my receipts so that I can track how much my spending is at groceries. Or, maybe I want to be able to donate my cash back to a profitable company. So, there are so many things, and it really depends on the profile of users that we want to attract. But yes, there's no one silver bullet. Different people will want different things. We test them all in our app, learn from them, and then experiment and implement quickly if it worked.

Ferraz: What are the common trends of fraud, and how have you combatted it?

Condicion: This is actually really hard. Basically, we look at patterns of behavior within a population and within the history of a user, and see deviations from norms, which are outliers, essentially. So, we look at the number of receipts or the number of brands that you use. Most people will use two or three brands in the same category, say shampoo, but if you see twenty brands of shampoo or twenty different variants of shampoo within a week, that's typically fraud.

We've seen, for example, somebody snapping twenty brands of medicines, and we realized that that person was working in a pharmacy. Or we will see somebody who will snap, say, one hundred receipts in a month. Now, we've tried combating that by capping three receipts in a day. So, we do that. Of course, no algorithm is perfect. It will still always have somebody who will be caught, but is actually not committing fraud, because let's say you had a birthday party, and you bought ten types of drinks and alcohol for that party. So, we apologize, and we say we're very sorry, but generally, we use a lot of machine learning to be able to see these patterns, just the way banks do in identifying inconsistent or irregular patterns in the system.

Ferraz: Can you share more about the business model? How do you charge your clients? Is it based on the number of SKUs?

Condicion: The traditional way by which the industry works is that you have a subscription, and then you get the data on a monthly basis—specific reports based on what you like. If you want to get market share, basket affinity, switching behaviors, or promotion analytics, we have different modules for that. So, a client may choose which product and modules are most relevant to them subscribes for one year, two years, three months, or a snapshot. Depending on that, we charge them a fee.

The other thing that we do is surveys. We push specific questions to users that allow brands the whys behind the data. Why did a particular user switch from brand A to brand B? Or why did he or she buy another product that was just launched?

Ferraz: In terms of your overall pricing strategy, are you trying to price yourself as a premium service compared to the traditional market research services, or are you trying to undercut them?

Condicion: We're definitely not charging a premium. We want to provide value. We are trying to cut the costs of this whole process by doing away with fieldwork and basically automating the processes. But then, you can't really cut it too much, because we are essentially paying our shoppers for this data. So, instead of paying the retailers, we're essentially asking shoppers, "Would you like to sell your data? You'll still be anonymous. We won't share it at a user level. We'll share at an aggregate." But they get paid for it.

But we do offer a value proposition because not only is our data overall cheaper, it is also faster, and more granular.

We can't really cut costs too much, which is fair because it's actually very valuable, and the kind of decisions that this data is used for are multimillion-dollar investments for the brands. So, it's actually really worth it, but at the same time, we're definitely not premium.

Ferraz: You mentioned that Snapcart almost gives consumers the power to take control of their data. Did you have to educate users about the value of their data? Because we're not used to selling our data, even in the aggregate. Is there a lot of education there?

Condicion: We let them know that we use this data. We aggregate it, we share it, and we sell it. In return, you get cash back. Our users know. It's part of our FAQ.

Ferraz: You mentioned that your data is so powerful that some companies which thought they were a market leader actually ended up not being a market leader. What were some of the most surprising insights that businesses have gained from your data? Can you give a few other examples?

Condicion: There's so many. Some clients will find out, for example, that the promotions that they've been running, which they thought was giving them a lot of volume in the past, were actually not making a lot of money for them. Because in the end, they're the least users. They buy only during promotions, then they get out, and buy again when there's another promotion. The clients didn't know this.

There are clients who've seen advertising that they thought was very popular because it got a lot of likes, but actually, it was not really impacting the brand. Because the sales were not happening in return. There are many examples of those. There are clients that learn a specific view of the data that they didn't have before. For example, they used to only be able to see data at a national level, but now they see it by chain.

Now, they understood that actually, while they're a market leader and all, there are some specific chains where they're actually doing poorly. So why is that? So then, their action plan became much more specific, rather than a national plan. They have a marketing plan for this specific chain, which therefore helped them in the end. Basically, it provides many more insights because of the granularity of the data and the speed by which the data comes. It used to be ten to twelve weeks with traditional providers, but we can deliver it in two weeks. We're working to get it to one week, which is essentially a tenfold improvement in terms of speed. Because we are also five times the size of the competitors in terms of the number of users and the panelists, it means that you're much more able to slice the data into smaller chunks, which gives you much more detail about how your brand is performing.

Ferraz: Brands get powerful insights from your platform, and you're the provider and the messenger. For example, if a brand finds out they're doing very poorly in one area, to what extent does your role extend into making recommendations or helping them strategize on what the likely cause of that is and helping them arrive at a solution?

Condicion: We can do that, but we find that they are much better at doing that than we are. We are more of a technology company, rather than a consulting company, and that's how we want to build ourselves in the future. Getting more things more automated, being able to really help them plug-and-play. If you look at Google Analytics, you plug in, you get the data, you make your own decisions, and then you go. That will allow us to really become much more scalable as a company, and more able to extend not just in market research but beyond. If you look at it from an offline data standpoint, this is not the only place where it will be useful. It can be very useful in advertising spaces, in aiding advertising decisions, or in fintech and so forth. So, the vision for us as a company is to be more technology-driven, more scalable, and less consulting.

Ferraz: But they do sometimes occasionally ask for that, and you provide it as a service?

Condicion: We are very experienced with providing recommendations because that's how we grew as an industry.

Ferraz: Earlier, you mentioned that you're not a Philippines company or an Indonesian company, but a Southeast Asian company. Can you share where your operations were initially located and how you expanded?

Condicion: We started and conceived it as a team of four co-founders: one Thai, one Syrian, me—Filipino, and an Indonesian. Indonesia is the biggest market for us to crack because it's the biggest market in Southeast Asia. Three of us are Southeast Asians. Thailand was very hard to launch because of the script. You cannot read it with the OCR model that we were building. The Philippines was definitely next.

We started with Indonesia. We knew if we could crack Indonesia, it would be a little bit easier in the Philippines. We look at four criteria when we discussed market expansion with our board of directors – 1) How big the market is 2) how easy it is for us to adapt our technology 3) what is the data gap and the right to win and 4) do we have the right lead to run the country. Philippines fit all the criteria as the next market so we launched in 2016.

Ferraz: Does each country serve itself?

Condicion: Right now, we're a group. So, the headquarter team is serving both Indonesia and the Philippines.

Ferraz: When you work with multi-nationals, is the engagement typically region-wide or global?

Condicion: It can be very global because our clients are global. Many times I've been asked to launch our products in Japan, India, in Latin America, but it's always a decision that always be taken carefully because expanding too fast too soon can be very detrimental to the business. And what we learned there are immense opportunities in a country that we can leverage before expanding to the next.

Ferraz: As you grow your market reach, how do your clients traditionally treat you? Do they treat you as a complement to their existing legacy services, or as a replacement?

Condicion: Their current data with our services, but in most cases, where they find value is when we are providing them with Blue Ocean products that aren't available but are very valuable. For example, being able to track pricing is something that seems easy but is actually not easily available in the region because most retailers are not able to provide promotions and pricing data, which is very valuable for a client.

The other thing that we learned is we could be providing data in stores that are not captured by current providers. For example, cosmetic stores are popping up like Sephora, or independent mini-markets that current providers aren't picking up. It becomes really difficult to cover all of them by partnering with retailers. At the same time, you're just less and less inclined to interview shoppers and go house-to-house and say, "What did you buy last week?" You can't even enter condominiums anymore, so the data is becoming poorer and poorer. The future is digitization, and because they see the power of data being digital, they're more open to switching. We've seen that happening in a couple of clients.

Ferraz: To piggyback on that question, you have a very disruptive product and business model in traditional market services. Have you seen any attempts from competitors to duplicate or imitate what you're doing in real time? How are you making sure to stay ahead and be a market leader?

Condicion: Many tried. Not only competitors, but many others. It's hard to be nimble when you're larger and to have the right DNA for innovation because moving to a new product will eat up existing sales. That's always a little bit of a difficult thing and an innovator's dilemma for many big companies. So, that's always a challenge.

From a smaller company standpoint, we're always very careful to innovate and keep ahead. So, you know, "What's the next level of data receipt processing automation?" We never sit still. We're always looking for the next AI solution, the next machine learning solution, how we can make it better and better, and grow it. It's really difficult, and we took a couple of years to do it. That gives us a little bit of comfort, but not so much that we just sit and stop innovating.

The third thing is that, because we're dealing with a limited number of clients at this point, which is in the market research space, being able to get the trust of these clients is very valuable. In fact, we've met a lot of similar companies who said, "I want to partner with you because we have the data, we have the solutions, but we can't sell it." Because they don't have access to the same clients. In the same manner that they stayed with traditional providers for a hundred years, they, therefore, were very hard to move. It's really very hard to penetrate into this industry until you have the credibility that you know what you're doing and you really know how to serve their needs well. In a way, we have the advantage of being that because I had seventeen years of experience. My CEO, my co-founder, has fifteen years of experience. He was also from P&G. It's actually a really small circle, and we understand things very well.

Ferraz: How much of your advantage over any imitators or copycats is in your technology, and how do you protect it through patents?

Condicion: For a long time, we thought about whether we should patent it or not. We realized that if we patented it, it would make it available broadly. So, we had to put it out for everyone to see. We realized that there's no point in a patent. Anyway, it would evolve quickly. As I said, the way we purchase will always change. The receipts will change. It might not be receipts in the future. It might be something else. So, we decided not to patent it. And in the end, it's not just the technology that sets it apart. While it is obviously a very important aspect of it, the networks and understanding the industry, domain expertise, strong leaders who have experience in building companies and building businesses—I think all that is what sets us apart.

Ferraz: That's such an interesting point of view because when I speak to other founders, sometimes their general idea is to make sure to protect themselves through patents. Did you experience something in your background that led you to think that patenting it would give undue exposure to competitors?

Condicion: We researched this a lot, and basically, for you to patent it, you have to publish it. The other thing is that it's really hard to patent anything in IT, because if you change just one line of that code, you can say, "It's mine." So, the truth is that, in the IT industry, the whole patent is questionable. It's open source everywhere. Everything is available to everyone, and there's nothing that is built that was not built by another. The whole history of innovation is such, even computers. Even Google was based on something, and that's why there are so many things that are around. There's so much contention in this space on that topic. So, no, we did not patent at this point.

Ferraz: Snapcart recently raised $15 million in a series A. How are you using these funds to become a global brand?

Condicion: Right now, we focus our funds on automation on beefing up our technology and data science team, and of strengthening our local operations in the Philippines and Indonesia. One example of a future innovation that we're building is being able to launch in a country a plug-and play, meaning the minute you launch it will automatically learn the new receipts structure and products in a very short amount of time using auto training and that will allow us to scale in ten countries at a time. That's really where the majority of the funds are going. The rest of the funds are going into sales.

We're hiring some of the best sales people in the region. We have some very big professionals in market research joining us. One, because they see the future with us. We've spent a lot of our funds in that space as well because we want to be able to reach out to more clients and be able to serve them better.

Ferraz: What is your official title?

Condicion: Chief of Data and Operations.

Ferraz: CEOs have such a hard time recruiting capable data scientists, especially in Southeast Asia. What makes a culture attractive to data scientists, and how do you try to build that at Snapcart?

Condicion: There's a war, a battle for data scientists. Everybody is getting pulled in one direction versus another. I think data scientists are excited about a few things. The first one is learning. Is it a place where there's an opportunity to learn? In our company, we allow them to learn. We let them, for example, get their master's degree and give the flexible time to do so. You say, "I want to work, but I also want to study, which means twice a week, I will have to leave at two p.m." We say, "Yes. Please." If you want to, say, go to conferences, yes, please, go ahead. We encourage learning a lot in our company.

The second thing is that, it's an opportunity to create something amazing that will leave a legacy because we're building something that disrupts an industry, and data is our product. Essentially, we're selling data, and we're selling data scientist solutions. And our products are built by data scientists. It's exciting for them.

Many companies say, "I want a data scientist," but they actually don't have data. They're actually not building something, and it's actually not central to them. It's just more of a trend, where they just want to hire a data scientist because it seems cool, without really understanding what they do, how they are really going to help you. I've heard some companies say, "I just want any data scientist," and actually, what they're looking for is not a data scientist, but a business analyst or a data engineer who will build pipelines and automation, which is a completely different thing. Being able to really understand what they do well is so important.

The third thing is being part of something that is growing. It's very unusual, for example, in the Philippines to serve the globe from the Philippines itself. If you look at data scientists, most of them are based in the United States. If you get hired as a data scientist in the Philippines, you only serve the country. So, for them, being able to see that they're handling Brazil and Singapore is super exciting. It's exciting because it's an opportunity to see a broader world. Again, it's an opportunity to see something that gets bigger and bigger over time, which they helped build.

Those are some things that helped us really build a very strong group. We have some of the best in the world, and I have no doubt about that because they've learned a lot from us. I think they're very engaged and very happy with what they do.

Ferraz: Did you personally recruit all of the data scientists?

Condicion: Yes, every single one. We have about fifteen data scientists and business analysts. At the end of the year, we will have twenty-one, which is probably one of the biggest data science groups in the region. We'll probably double next year. Just for perspective, two years ago, there were only four. So, it's kind of doubling every year.

Ferraz: I'm curious about the profiles of your data scientists. Is it mostly self-taught people like yourself, or do some of them have academic backgrounds or industry backgrounds?

Condicion: It's a mix. There's a myth. The whole data scientist unicorn is a myth. The data scientist unicorn is somebody who understands technology, meaning that they can code well, who understands analysis, meaning that they can think mathematically, and who understands the domain, meaning, in this case, FMCG and retail.

There's no such thing as being able to understand it all. I hire people who are very good at one, and knows a little bit about the others. I encourage everyone to work together and learn from each other. So, one project will always leverage the strength of another and another and another. There's no one project that will only be done by one person. That's how we basically ensure that we get the right skills onboard.

Ferraz: Earlier, you mentioned that a lot of founders or business owners have mistaken assumptions about data science—that they actually want a business analyst even though they're trying to hire a data scientist. What advice do you have for founders and business owners on how they could really incorporate data science into their business, even if they're not necessarily building a data science product like Snapcart?

Condicion: Start with what you want to build, instead of who you want to hire. What you want to build is, say, a data solution that is very simple. In our case, we didn't say we're going to hire data scientists. We had a problem to solve. Who were the best people to solve this problem? It happened to be data scientists. So, you always start with the business solution at hand, and then you always also start with what you want to build. Sometimes, what you want to build perhaps is more of an engineering problem, rather than a data science problem. If you don't have a lot of data, that's typically a key. If you don't have tons and tons of data coming in—even if you do have tons and tons of data, but you're not going to sell it—it's probably not so important. Maybe, you just need very specific solutions.

For example, Netflix has a very big amount of data, but they have a very narrow focus. They want to recommend the right films. They don't do AI. They don't do deep learning. They don't do image recognition. They don't even call it data science. In fact, the person who's leading it is actually a Filipino. She doesn't call herself a data scientist, even though what she does will probably be in the realm of data science. It is machine learning, but it's very focused on that.

So, first, do you have the data? Second, what are you trying to do? What are you trying to automate? Is it going to be solved by AI, or is it going to be solved by a simple, tabulation of data? If you're just going to tabulate data, you probably don't need a data scientist for that. That's what I would suggest—really understand what you're trying to build, which skills are required to build it, do some research on that, and then hire the right person for it, rather than the other way around.

Ferraz: You're one of the most successful Filipino founders in Southeast Asia. What advice do you have for general founders in Asia on how to build a business as successful as Snapcart? I mean, you guys are already global, which is the dream of many companies here.

Condicion: I wish there were more of us. In fact, it's a lot to do with the right timing, and also being able to collaborate very well with people who have complementary skills to you. In my case, I've been very lucky to meet my co-founders because all four of us, for example... We can't do each other's job. My CEO can't do my job. I'm the only person who understands data analytics in this depth. I can't do my CTO's job. I can't do our CFO's job. Even in terms of personality, we're very different, so I've been very lucky to have that, because we became a superpower with the combination of four people who have really different skills and trust each other a lot. For me, having the right partners, having the right co-founders, and working with them, a diverse set of people, is super helpful in being able to achieve this level for the company.

The second thing is, as I said, timing. It's a combination of luck. In fact, you'll hear a lot about companies not succeeding—not so much because it was a bad idea, but it was because it was not launched at the right time. It was just the right time for it, and I think we were listening, obviously, to the trends. I was in the industry, so I knew that in five years, market research would change a lot. I understood what was happening in the whole system, with the mobile penetration, and all the digitization of everything, and the big data strength.

But, I think for founders, being able to understand the right timing for your solution is really important. The third thing is just endless curiosity and grit. We've had so many technological problems. We failed so many times, that we thought, "Okay, we can't solve this." But we just kept on trying, even when people said it was impossible. And we had this crazy amount of confidence that we would be able to build something that helped us. Those are the three things that helped me a lot.

Index

© Ezra Ferraz, Gracy Fernandez 2020
E. Ferraz and G. Fernandez, *Asian Founders at Work*,
https://doi.org/10.1007/978-1-4842-5162-1